MW00616812

ACCLAIM FOR
COLORS OF FRANCE: A PAINTING PILGRIMAGE

"The wonderful text . . . is at once informative, inspiring and funny."

—Barbara Lloyd McMichael, *Northwest Books*

". . . a rare combination of breath-catching paintings and lyrical prose—a full spectrum of the artistic experience."

—Marjorie Reynolds, author of *The Starlite Drive-In* and *The Civil Wars of Jonah Moran*

"[There is] flawless, subtle and cohesive synergy between the lovely watercolor images and the delicately written short essays, which read like pages torn from the author's travel journal—so personal and intimate."

—*Writer's Digest* Self-Publishing Competition

Millions of Americans move every year. Although *Move* describes the life of a military family, the stress and emotions involved apply universally. *Move—And Other Four-Letter Words* demonstrates that, even when completely frustrated by our inability to significantly alter an unpleasant situation, changing our attitude toward it can make it both survivable and meaningful.

—Suzie Schwartz, wife of the Air Force Chief of Staff

MOVE

AND OTHER FOUR-LETTER WORDS

Memoir of a Mobile Marriage

Joan Brown

Joan Brown

Especially for Kendra,
Tom says this may come in handy, even though you two have already been there, done that.
All best wishes,
Joan

HEARTHLAND PUBLISHING
SEATTLE, WASHINGTON

Hearthland Publishing LLC
1425 Broadway #56
Seattle, Washington 98122-3854

ISBN 978-0-9841693-3-7

Library of Congress Control Number: 2009907793

Cover: Ryan Peinhardt
Photography: Bennington Photography
Gorham Printing

For orders, call 1-800-398-7414
or email HearthlandPub@aol.com

For Don, Cathy, Jim and Nancy and the friends who helped me find the way on the journey

Leaving home in a sense involves a kind of second birth in which we give birth to ourselves.

—Robert N. Bellah, *Habits of the Heart*

Contents

Author's Preface:
For Better or Worse—and Heaven Knows Where
ix

Changing Places
xiii

Prologue: Across a Crowded Room
1

Chapter 1: Alice in Yonderland
3

Chapter 2: Through the Looking Glass
10

Chapter 3: The Mouse That Roared
17

Chapter 4: The Best Laid Plans
24

Chapter 5: Pick a Pot of Pickled Peppers
29

Chapter 6: Jesus Loves Me, Yes I Know, But . . .
32

Chapter 7: From Howdy Doody to Mickey Mouse
38

Chapter 8: I Guess I Do Care

43

Chapter 9: Winning the Masters

53

Chapter 10: California, Here We Come

64

Chapter 11: Hafa Adai

77

Chapter 12: Getting to Know You, South Pacific Style

86

Chapter 13: Sayonara

94

Chapter 14: Stuck Between a Clock and a Hard Place

101

Chapter 15: Spiritual Galoshes

112

Chapter 16: How Do You Do and Shake Hands

120

Chapter 17: Gypsy Caravan

127

Chapter 18: The Winter of Our Discontent

138

Chapter 19: Back to Nuts and Bolts

147

Chapter 20: Emptying the Nest

154

Chapter 21: Attitude Adjustments
166

Chapter 22: The Impossible Dream
172

Chapter 23: Our Lady of Perpetual Guilt
182

Chapter 24: Where Comes the Bride
190

Chapter 25: Mary Backstage, Noble Wife
196

Chapter 26: Another Blooming Move
202

Chapter 27: And Miles to Go Before We Sleep
208

Chapter 28: Stop the World, We're Getting Back On
215

Chapter 29: Things That Go Bump in the Night
220

Chapter 30: The Joy of Jumping
225

Acknowledgments
231

Author's Preface

For Better or Worse—and Heaven Knows Where

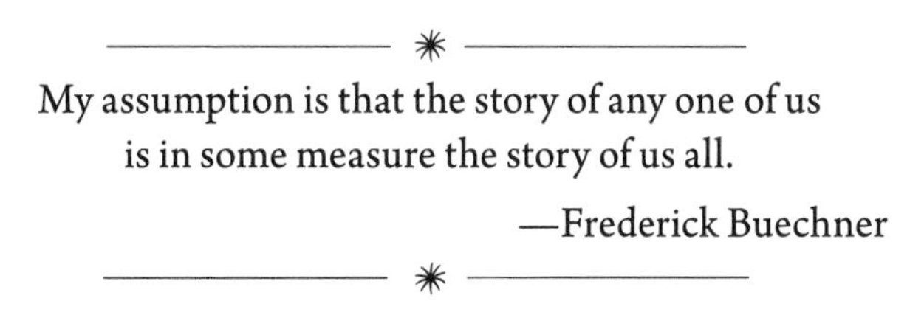

> My assumption is that the story of any one of us
> is in some measure the story of us all.
>
> —Frederick Buechner

Although I was drawn to the man in my life from the very first time our paths crossed as teenagers, I soon found I wanted nothing to do with the itinerant existence he introduced me to as a newlywed. Miserable at first, I trudged along only to be with him.

Twenty-one moves and thirty-three years later, I realized I had come to cherish the richness of the experiences and family of friends I had gained, along with the personal baggage I'd shed in the process. A hate-to-love transformation, it might also be called a growing up.

In this country's mobile society, pulling up stakes is no rarity. Whether singly or as part of a couple, most of us move at least eleven times over a lifetime. And, no matter how you slice it, it's never easy. There's no cosmic button that shuts off all the other demands on our time and energies that stem from earning a living, family obligations or the basics of eating and sleeping. In most cases, it is the woman who bears the brunt of it. Small wonder then that sociologists say we are also the ones who find it most stressful.

When we hear about frequent relocations, most of us think "military," but corporate moves also abound, often without as sturdy a support system as the armed services provide. In addition to job changes, family needs like education or the care of elderly relatives, expanding families, emptied nests and retirement also cause us to move on.

Over the years, each time a new novel about the lives of military families came out, a friend would say, "Someone needs to tell the real story," especially when the author of the book in question clearly had had no such experience. But telling it straight is just one of the reasons to do so. Helping others to see comedy—and hope—in the chaos of everyday problems is another.

"The more things change the more they stay the same" is more truth than cliché. The details of life may differ, but the problems we all face—whether pioneers, World War II or contemporary women—have a way of staying constant.

Certainly military spouses share much common ground with other married women, particularly the single parent. Stir in a mobile life—uncontrolled, often sudden moves around the country and the world, the need to adapt to a new culture, the seemingly trivial but real need to find good medical and dental care, child care, or someone to cut your hair—and you've added another component. Mix with the tempo of the Cold War and you have "the way many of us were" in the mid-fifties through the late eighties.

Men have long told stories of the poignant and absurd in their lives, "battlefield" tales of Normandy Beaches, Wall Street or the "south forty." From *The Odyssey* to *Caine Mutiny,* literature abounds with such sagas. But, as author Carolyn See asks in *Making a Literary Life,* "What about those hundreds and hundreds of years lived *inside* houses, the lives of women...?" These seemingly less than epical days are what mold and send each of us on our way in life. To ignore the distaff threads in the tapestry would be to forfeit half the adventure.

For the Kalahari nomad, "story" is his most sacred possession. Indeed, it is for all of us. Here, then, are one woman's "war stories," set down, to tell you how it was—or, at least, how it seemed to me.

Changing Places

Queens Village, New York (Joan); Astoria, New York (Don)

August 1954–May 1955	West New York, New Jersey
May 1955–September 1955	Hollis, New York (J)
May 1955–July 1955	San Antonio, Texas (D)
July 1955–January 1956	Kinston, North Carolina (D)
September 1955–January 1956	Kinston, North Carolina (J)
January 1956–June 1956	Lubbock, Texas
August 1956–September 1956	West Palm Beach, Florida
September 1956–September 1959	Lumberton, New Jersey
September 1959–September 1960	Mount Holly, New Jersey
September 1960–December 1960	Montgomery, Alabama
December 1960–January 1962	Mount Holly, New Jersey
February 1962–June 1964	Midwest City, Oklahoma
July 1964–July 1965	North Syracuse, New York
August 1965–July 1966	Arlington, California
July 1966–July 1968	Andersen Air Force Base, Guam
September 1968–November 1969	Florida; Vietnam (D)
September 1968–August 1973	Mount Holly, New Jersey (J)

August 1973–September 1975	171-S "B" Street, Scott Air Force Base, Illinois
September 1975–March 1976	186-S "B" Street, Scott Air Force Base, Illinois
March 1976–February 1979	McChord Air Force Base, Washington
February 1979–September 1984	Scott Air Force Base, Illinois
October 1984–February 1987	Travis Air Force Base, California
February 1987–October 1987	Vacaville, California
October 1987–Present	Steilacoom, Washington

Prologue:

Across a Crowded Room

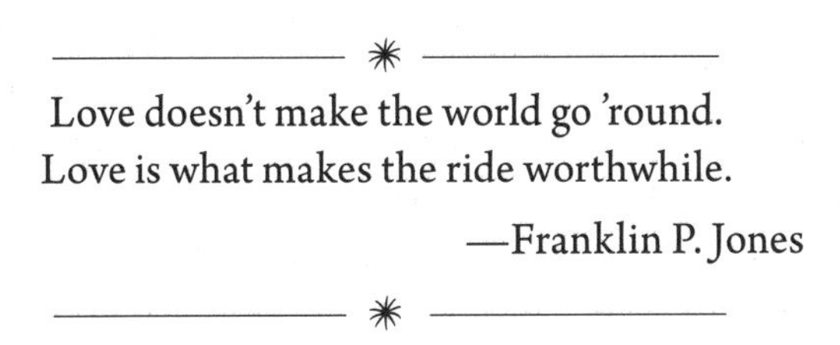

Love doesn't make the world go 'round.
Love is what makes the ride worthwhile.

—Franklin P. Jones

Just a few months before my sixteenth birthday and the beginning of my senior year, our high school writing club had a Christmas party to which we were free to bring a guest. I felt selfish that I hadn't invited the boy I was dating but I was looking for a way to gracefully bow out of the relationship.

Vinnie would've picked me up in his family's car. Instead, I made the long trek to get to the party alone, by bus and train and long hikes at each end in the blustery cold of a December New York City night. Guilt plodded right along with me, a kind of proxy date. In the 1950s that's the way things were, dating-wise.

It wasn't until almost the very end of the evening that I met Don. I found myself smitten, then dumbfounded, when this handsome, funny, intelligent, graduating senior actually asked to take me home. I hadn't yet realized he was also president of the senior class.

Never mind that, unlike Vinnie, Don didn't have a car with

which to do it. He quickly enlisted someone who did to deliver us miles away to where I lived on Long Island. That was the end of Vinnie and, over time, everyone else—and the beginning of our lengthy journey to marriage.

After completing my own senior high school year while Don was a freshman at Columbia University, I also began college in New York. There was no way we could even consider marriage before graduation with Don working nights and weekends to earn every cent of his tuition and neither of our families willing or able to support us. Where we were coming from, it just wasn't done.

Another norm of the day, at least in my family, was that a gal absolutely did not call a guy. So, when I went away for a few days one summer, Don became very upset with me when he learned I'd been back home quite a while but hadn't called to let him know that.

For my part, I couldn't understand why he hadn't called me for so long after I returned. I was sure I'd told him before I left just how long I'd be gone. When he finally did, he just couldn't buy my side of the story and we each hung up angry—end of the call and the end of "us" for the rest of that long August.

In September when I returned to college I was both shocked and delighted to receive a postcard from him, mailed from his annual end of summer family visit to Montreal.

I showed it to my best friend, Norma, explaining, "Of course, I won't answer him after all that nonsense about my not calling him."

Her reply took me aback. "Why? Are you so proud you can't just forget about it? Answer the guy."

If it weren't for Norma, I'd be telling you a different story.

CHAPTER 1:

Alice in Yonderland

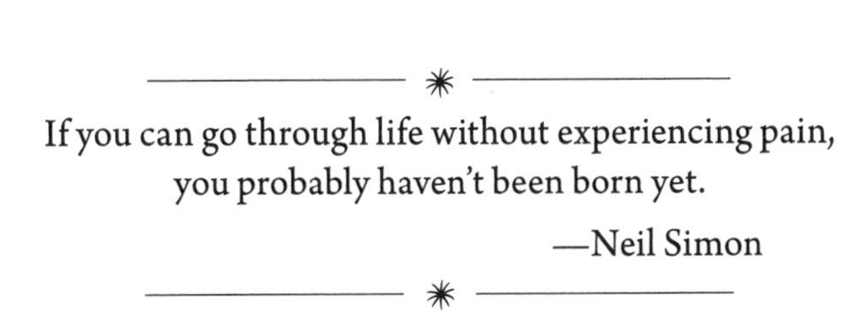

If you can go through life without experiencing pain,
you probably haven't been born yet.

—Neil Simon

After going together for five-and-a-half years, Don and I were finally tying the knot. But as soon as I walked in the door at the end of the school year from teaching in upstate New York, finally back home on Long Island to get ready for our August wedding, my parents greeted me with an announcement.

"We've sold the house, Joan."

"When do you have to be out?"

"In August, one week after the wedding."

Their moving so quickly out of the place I'd called home for the past twenty-one years seemed like terrible scheduling on their part, but it didn't really matter to me—or so it seemed. Perhaps it was an omen of things to come. I wouldn't have another settled abode for the next thirty-three years.

Although Don and I had gone through the motions of looking at places to live in New York, we carefully chose an apartment in

West New York, New Jersey for our first home together, guarding our privacy by avoiding any that were too near either of our families on Long Island.

We knew that, in about a year, Don would be assigned an Air Force pilot training slot. The Korean War was going full bore while we were still in college and Don could easily have been drafted. As a result, his love of airplanes and determination to finish school made him jump at the chance to join the AFROTC when the program came to Columbia. I wasn't too concerned because it meant only a three-year stint in the military, and then back to New York.

By the time the Air Force notified him to report for duty nine months later in May 1955, I was almost seven months pregnant and certainly not expecting to hear the doctor veto my going with Don to Texas for basic training. I was also too naïve to realize even doctors can be mistaken.

Despite our determination to maintain our independence, we couldn't afford for me to stay in our apartment by myself. There was nothing for it but to pack up all our things to store them in my folks' basement and drag myself back across the Hudson River to Long Island. There I took up residence on a sofa bed in the living room of the tiny apartment over their electrical business, where they were now living.

For the next two-and-a-half months I kept myself sane by sewing enough baby clothes for quintuplets. And every day I took lengthy walks to try to ensure an on-time delivery that would speed up my being able to leave with our firstborn and join Don, who'd now moved on to North Carolina for pilot training.

I'd already been forced to stop teaching before my pregnancy "showed." Unlike today, when an actress can pose nude, proudly displaying a swelling abdomen on a magazine cover, in 1955 I could no longer teach lest the results of my having had sex with my husband become obvious to the students.

But I'd never expected to have to give up having that husband with me for the delivery as well. Unlike the message that I had finally gone into labor, which got right to Don in Kinston and prompted an excited call from him, it took a full day for him to receive word that our first child was born.

I cried myself to sleep in the hospital, waiting for another phone call that didn't come until the next day. Where was the boyfriend who'd spent hours getting to and from my house by bus and subway to pick me up and bring me home from a date? Where was the fiancé who'd waited up all night at a New York City terminal the day my bus had been caught in a snowstorm coming home from teaching upstate?

Cell phones and email were not even on the horizon yet. Instead, we were dependent on message takers. The phoned "birth announcement" had been left by mistake in another flying student's mailbox and it wasn't until the following day that Don learned he had a daughter. As soon as he finally received the message, he managed to wangle a three-day pass home for the weekend right after we'd talked. I was ecstatic at the thought of being held in his arms again, along with our first child.

That Thursday night he was whizzing north through the Virginia countryside when a twirling red beacon in the rearview mirror signaled him to pull over. Driving without headlights, a Virginia sheriff had tailed our car, with a judge right alongside him in the patrol car to issue speeding tickets. It seemed illegal, but who argues on a dark, isolated road?

They demanded payment of the fine—big bucks for us—right on the spot, a major problem for Don just days before his once-a-month payday, with a wallet all but emptied from having just filled up the gas tank. Only an AAA bail bond card kept him from spending the night in jail.

Undaunted, he pressed on, only to run out of gas as he was entering New York's Lincoln Tunnel in the early Friday morning rush hour. When the gas station he hiked to wouldn't trust him to return their container, it took almost all the dwindling cash he had left to buy a can and the gallon he needed to get the car out of there. With no other choice, he stopped at his parents' house to borrow money for gas. He called me from there as I was getting ready to check out of the hospital.

"You're where?" I asked, unable to grasp why he was calling to say he was on his way from his mother's. It meant, even with my husband so close, it would be my parents that drove me and our new daughter "home" from the hospital. What was worse, I'd learned it would be another six weeks before the doctor would approve the baby's traveling south to what would truly be our new home.

The doctor, a family friend in general practice who'd acted as both obstetrician and pediatrician, was also quick to insist on supplemental bottle feedings when Cathy developed colic. More likely, it seems to me now, it was not lack of milk but the solid foods he had me introducing almost immediately, one after the other, that were causing her problems. But he believed a woman had to be of pioneer stock to nurse a baby and soon decreed, "You have no choice but to take pills to dry up your milk and wean her completely to the bottle."

Even reading Dr. Spock like a second Bible didn't clue me in to refuse. Despite a smothering New York August heat wave, our first anniversary was cold with the reality that it would not only be weeks before Cathy and I could fly to Carolina, but moving her to the bottle had not solved one bit of her digestive problems.

And there was more. When we finally got off the plane in Raleigh-Durham on Labor Day weekend, Don waited to break the news until we were well on our way to Kinston and I'd finished struggling with a bottle warmer that plugged into the cigarette lighter to heat a bottle for Cathy.

"The student pilot who's been living in the garage apartment I rented for us just flunked his final check ride. Now he has to wait for a non-flying assignment, which means he and his wife aren't going to vacate for at least another week."

"So what do we do?"

"I'm sorry, Jo, but I did manage to get us a room in a boarding house for now. At least it's not one of the red-light district ones where, every hour or so, new customers come and go."

I soon discovered we'd lack more than a red light. There was also no place other than the landlady's kitchen to make the formula Cathy now needed every day. At Don's urging, we visited a local pediatrician who promptly switched her to goat's milk and admonished, "What you should've done was nurse this baby!"

Dumping out all the formula I'd just bottled and making new became a recurring nightmare as we moved speedily from that of goats to soybeans and, finally, cows. With no cooking or laundry facilities where we were staying, there were also regular cloth-diaper-laden trips to the Laundromat as well as nightly excursions to restaurants, at least for dinner, all worked in around a baby's pained crying. Most nights I spent walking Cathy to try to soothe her and keep the un-air-conditioned room quiet, staggering into bed about four o'clock in the morning—just as Don was getting up to go fly. This was togetherness?

When the steamy September day finally came for us to move into our apartment, Don had to fly. And, because of a scheduling mix-up, the movers for the couple leaving were picking up their things the same day ours were being delivered. The prospect of each of us ending up with one another's "stuff" was daunting, but once Don deposited me in their living room, I had no alternative but to squat there with a colicky baby until the other couple finally agreed to the whole bizarre procedure.

The chants of an auctioneer hawking tobacco from a warehouse down the lane from our garage-apartment sounded like quaint foreign music to my northern ears. And we proved no less a wonderment to the Carolinians who told me they'd never before seen a child napping outside anyone's door in a "baby buggy"—then the custom in New York—to say nothing of my pushing Cathy down to the Piggly Wiggly in that carriage to buy groceries.

The two-story pine-paneled converted garage-apartment we were living in, though cooled by nothing but the tenant's fans in summer, was warmed in cold weather by a kerosene stove in the first-floor living room. The staircase funneled all of its output upstairs, stifling the tiny bedroom and leaving the kitchen on the other side of the wall frigid.

Every morning a rude awakening awaited as we sat down to breakfast, only to rebound from the icy shock of metal kitchen chairs. We could either roast or freeze. There was little middle ground.

The kitchen was also the only place I dared feed Cathy. It seemed like almost everything I fed her came back at me. I pretty much spent my days on those snow-white enamel chairs at that table, despite Dr. Spock's mealtime advice to relax with baby in a comfortable living room chair. Instead, I kept Shirley Jackson's *Life among the Savages* in hand to devour as I held the bottle. Somehow the realities of a mother's heir-raising experiences carried more comfort and weight than the theories of a pediatrician untested in the trenches.

We were also learning, firsthand, about Southern hospitality. Don's flight instructor, Homer Cook, and his wife regularly gathered his students and their families for cookouts at their home. The students, some married but most single, and very few with children, hailed from all over the country. In between suppers at the Cooks', we got together for potlucks of our own. By the time we moved west to the next flight school a few months later, I was surprised to discover I'd already put down enough roots that it hurt to yank them up again so soon. At least this time Don and I would be moving on together.

Driving across the Texas panhandle that January in the mid-fifties felt like riding through the movie sets I'd seen in westerns as I was growing up in New York. We'd have looked more at home, I thought, coming through on horseback or covered wagon.

Finding a place to live in Lubbock was tough, but not as hard as we later discovered it could get. As we were looking at a rental house, the outgoing tenant confided, "The only problem here is we've had cockroaches galore."

That was just what I needed to make me obsess on my New York doctor's warnings that these critters were so plentiful in the South the natives called them by name. The landlord assured us he would spray until they were gone, but I moved in with as much trepidation as if Godzilla were sharing the premises.

A more valid concern was preventing the brown mottling of Cathy's newly-forming teeth from the overabundance of fluoride in the local water supply. Giving her bottled water easily took care of that though, so I wiped one of my worries off the list.

I soon found another to take its place. Living in the dustbowl we'd only read about in books or heard talk of locally meant keeping an eye turned heavenward to keep tabs on incoming storms. Cathy was out on the porch, napping in the carriage, on what had begun as a glorious spring afternoon when I first sighted the clouds barreling across the horizon like an overloaded dump truck of dirt. I wondered if I was looking at a gathering dust storm, and I didn't have to wonder long.

From that day till we left a few months later, a swirling dervish of soil from the plains of Oklahoma and New Mexico periodically arrived on our doorstep. Not even taped doors and windows, a particular joy on stifling hot days, would keep it there. Inside, nostrils and teeth filled with the grit that applied itself to every horizontal surface in the house.

Don was gritting his teeth in basic flight training, too, as his instructor pilot threatened to wash him out. Ironically, that guy was later caught buzzing—flying too low—and court-martialed. Instead of washing out, Don got a new instructor and graduated at the top of his class. That gave him the chance to pick his next assignment and we rejoiced at the chance to head back east to New Jersey, just a three-hour drive from our families.

It was in the buffet line the night of his graduation dinner that we got the news that one of the C-118s he would be flying (a military version of the DC-6) had just crashed on takeoff from the base to which we were headed, killing almost everyone aboard. That was a kind of separation I didn't even want to think about.

Chapter 2:

Through the Looking Glass

It was déjà vu all over again.

—Yogi Berra

In between Texas and our arrival in New Jersey in the fall of '56, we spent a sweltering August and September in a West Palm Beach motel while Don learned to fly the 118. Just before we'd left Lubbock, it appeared I was pregnant with our second child. The doctors had since managed to stop the spotting I'd been having and the morning sickness that began in Florida was not as acute as it had been the first time around.

I found it a bit unsettling though when one wife whose husband was in Don's class told me that *she* certainly wouldn't get pregnant—even once, let alone twice—until she had a dishwasher, washing machine and dryer. I'd been feeling lucky to now have a small, wringer-style portable washer the size of a kitchen stool that saved my going out to Laundromats.

Now that we were in New Jersey and had finally stopped moving every few months, we'd even ordered an automatic washer. No matter whose values you applied, things definitely seemed to be looking up.

Wagon wheels, painted school bus yellow, flanked the driveway of the tract house we'd finally rented here. On the West Texas plains we'd called home six of the past eight months, they'd have fit in just fine. But here in South Jersey, an hour out of Philly, in fields more accustomed to sprouting corn and tomatoes than ranch houses, they looked as displaced as I felt. Only the isolation of this new suburbia reminded me of the New York neighborhood in which I'd lived almost all my life. Nothing else about this treeless sprawl of postwar development bore much resemblance to the northeast I'd grown up in, a settled block of English Tudor style brick bungalows in the Borough of Queens.

Not that anyplace else we'd already been had either. It was hard enough to adjust to the solitude of being a housewife in mid-fifties suburbia without also finding yourself adrift in a whole series of them, each miles away from family, friends and everything familiar. I already knew I was no June Cleaver, probably more akin to *The Egg and I's* Betty MacDonald, struggling to stay afloat in a sea of impossible expectations.

We'd wanted this new assignment so much—a chance at stability after moving every few months. But, as Don's first flight trip out of New Jersey went on and on, over twice as long as scheduled, I began to suspect we'd been granted only half a wish: I stayed put while Don flew all over creation, hauling people and cargo.

The thunk of a car door slamming shut in our driveway as Don hopped out—finally—should have produced only joy. For the first time in weeks, someone had gotten it right when they'd said he was on his way home.

Quick steps bounded up the front stoop, followed by my husband's knock. And there he stood at last, beaming like a poster boy in Air Force uniform, reaching out to scoop me up in a bear hug.

"Am I ever glad to be back!"

If I said anything else first—something loving—neither of us remembers it. All we know is that I erupted. "We're getting out! Out of this house, out of this neighborhood—out of the Air Force."

"Hey, maybe I should go back out and come in again. Are you OK?"

"God, Don, it's been just awful. Mice popping out of the toaster, nosediving down the kitchen stove. Your being stuck out. Just everything."

"I'm sorry it was so bad," he said, trying again to wrap me in his arms. But the pent-up frustration kept spewing out and, much as I feared waking up our fifteen-month-old from her nap, I couldn't seem to stop.

The past few weeks I'd been reliving the negative experiences of my youth. All the emotions of being a child rushed over me again, carrying me back to the Queens Village street I'd grown up on during World War II—a latchkey kid before the term was invented—with no siblings and two parents always away at work. A couple of years of marriage, a child of my own and another on the way, I was now the parent, but I was not only still home alone, but a transient as well.

Despite the fact that I'd graduated from college with honors at age twenty and taught junior and senior high school English for a couple of years, I seemed to be flunking real life. Home had always been the same Queens Village house for me and I considered New York the center of the universe. In contrast, when Don was only seven, he'd come to the States from Montreal with his parents and toddler brother and had at least six moves under his belt before we were married in 1954.

Newly arrived in South Jersey, we'd barely found a place to live and had the movers deliver our household goods that had been in storage before Don had to take off on what was scheduled to be a short trip to Saudi Arabia and back.

Instead, he was gone much longer, incommunicado, and the shipment with the baby's crib and all the other things we'd had for our two months in Florida had also gone missing en route. If it were not his very first trip, I might have been better prepared for what to expect. I longed to just once pick up a phone and hear him tell me what was going on.

As it was, one of the few adults I got to talk to was the command post duty officer. Even that was only when the flight was already due back.

"They're AOCP, still headed east," he said, sounding impatient to get on with the more important things he had to do.

"What's that?" I asked, annoying him further.

"Aircraft out of commission for parts."

When I couldn't understand what that meant either, he explained that the crew hadn't even gotten where they were going yet. The first day out, the plane had sprung a fuel leak, putting the crew on hold for days in the Azores while they waited for the parts to come in to fix it.

Every day I got the same story, "They're still waiting for parts."

Now Don was filling in the details.

When they finally did get out, he'd had to stay behind in Libya because he didn't yet have a passport, while the rest flew on to Cairo and Saudi Arabia.

As Murphy's Law would have it, Cairo weather delayed their getting back to pick him up for the return flight—not that anyone could tell me all this while he was gone.

When the crew was finally rested and on their way home, a storm on the East Coast diverted them to Bermuda. Again out of crew duty time, that meant still another day's mandated rest.

"If you could've just picked up a phone!"

"You know we can't afford it. That's why you call the squadron."

"But what you're telling me proves they never knew what was really happening."

"This time was different. That's not the way it's going to be."

I wasn't buying it. For months, I'd sensed I wasn't cut out for this kind of life. Now I was sure of it. Rereading parts of the *The Air*

Force Wife, the 1951 distaff "bible" while Don was away did not make its advice seem any less absurd:

> The average Air Force wife of even ten years' service has truly lived . . . Perhaps she has lived through the horror of knowing her own husband is lost in a Panamanian jungle or has been forced to land in the shark-infested waters off Guam . . .
>
> You are just like every Air Force wife if you have spent a sleepless night now and then while your husband is on a cross-country . . . Dawn usually brings relief from these unjustified worries, and, of course, no true Air Force wife would ever think of admitting them even to herself, let alone her husband. It just isn't done.

But we were doing it. The rest was as far from my idea of "living" as one could get. And, if discussing it when my husband finally got home "just wasn't done," I surely didn't qualify—and never would.

If there was one thing Don and I agreed on, it was that we would tell each other what was on our minds. We'd already talked our way through five-and-a-half years of dating and two years of marriage. When I was still living at home, even my father, who worked two jobs and was rarely there, had noticed. One day, just before our wedding, he had kidded us, "What do you two talk about for hours out there on the front porch together? Physiology?"

As much as Don shared my dislike of separation, being part of a crew meant teamwork and camaraderie for him. More important, he could already tell he loved the kind of flying he was going to be doing. Considered a choice assignment, the smartly uniformed transport crews—no baggy flight suits in these cockpits—were still ministered to by flight attendants. But I wanted no part of any of the new things I'd learned.

I was now well-versed in "Air Force as a Second Language," at least the acronyms relating to broken airplanes that were still heading one way when they should have been going the other. Translated, they all came down to the same thing: It would be days before Don got home. And a "stage," in this brave new world, meant not the Broadway kind we both loved, but crewmembers awaiting their turns for a plane to fly.

After spending almost all my life in the suburbs of New York City, I'd now discovered how not to set a mousetrap for the rodent swat team that was trying to commandeer our kitchen and set up headquarters there while Don was away.

And, in spite of all the scruples of a strict Irish Catholic upbringing, I found myself ready to break the law to get the movers to deliver our fifteen-month-old's crib so our daughter could sleep safely. Without batting an eye, I'd altered the expiration date on my outdated power of attorney, boldly signing the papers authorizing the mover to deliver the shipment we'd been doing without for over a month. Legally, I would have had to wait for Don to get home, request delivery and sign for it.

Now we both knew that a "short" trip, positioning people and equipment, could turn into a much longer haul. And we'd soon learn that a crisis anywhere in the world, like an earthquake or flood, meant evacuating refugees and moving patients, supplies and medical teams on the Air Force transport planes Don flew, often transformed into airborne ambulances. In my heart I knew there would be ever more trips like this one. There was no doubt in either of our minds that I, for one, wanted no part of any of it after Don's three-year commitment was up.

Right before I went to sleep that first night Don and I were together again, when I could reach out and touch him for the first time in weeks, I remembered something else I'd heard during the time he'd been away. "The good ones," they said, "always got out." Even the head of the ROTC at Columbia University had told me at Don's swearing-in to the Air Force that very few Northeasterners stayed in.

Don was both a New Yorker and one of the best. But I could already feel the seductive power that flying had over him, like that of some "other woman" whose siren call would keep luring him away. Clearly, although I wanted out, Don did not. His civilian flight instructor in primary pilot training in Kinston, North Carolina, had cautioned him, "That l'il blue-eyed blonde of yours isn't going to wait around forever while you're off flying the world."

Three years earlier, when we were engaged and friends had forewarned me of TDY (temporary duty), PCSs (permanent changes of station) and "isolated tours" away from families, I had gone to the chaplain at the College of New Rochelle where I was a senior. I asked him what he thought of the military life the Cold War was propelling us into, at least as far as family was concerned.

"Well," he said, stroking his chin as he carefully considered his words, "I certainly think you'll learn the meaning of pilgrimage."

The journey had begun and, already, I had a boulder in my shoe.

CHAPTER 3:

The Mouse That Roared

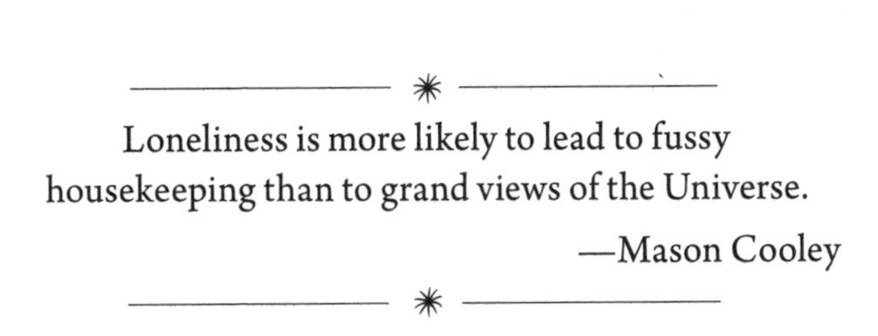

Loneliness is more likely to lead to fussy housekeeping than to grand views of the Universe.

—Mason Cooley

When we'd first arrived in South Jersey, we knew finding a place to rent would not be easy. McGuire Air Force Base, an old World War II base, had just been reborn and was already growing by leaps and bounds. But the surrounding farming communities included no crop of homes or apartments to house the influx of people that needed shelter. We'd already heard the stories. Renovated chicken coops, they said, were all there was to offer many of those who'd come in just before we had. There was no way we could settle for that. We'd just have to hunker down for a lengthy search.

First, we dropped off our fifteen-month-old with my parents on Long Island. Three hours' drive later we were back to begin the search. Because it was cheap, we got a room at the base "transient hotel." To me, the name summed up our new status. And a chicken-coop could not have looked much less homey than the converted barracks building that housed us.

With bathroom and shower a trek down the hall, and the knocking hot water pipes that heated the place visibly scaling thin wooden walls not much changed since first hurriedly nailed together, I took what little comfort I could in the fact we at least had our own sink. Even the scratchy GI-khaki blankets on the hard twin beds removed all doubt that I too was an inductee, however unwilling, into the forces now governing our lives.

That made the next decision easier. We could move into row housing on Fort Dix, the Army post next door to McGuire, or we could start looking for a place to rent in the rural civilian countryside. We had learned that families were scattered all over an area that stretched from Philadelphia and the New Jersey shore to New York City. There was no family housing on McGuire.

Although living on the Army post at Fort Dix would have been cheaper, it too was vintage housing, much like the place we were temporarily staying in. Since we both yearned for green acres, we decided to cut corners some other way and begin the search for an apartment or house in one of the many tiny surrounding towns.

For the next ten days we spent every waking moment scouting, starting from off-base housing listings, even pulling into strangers' driveways for leads and knocking on the doors of nineteenth-century stone homes for road directions from rocking chair residents.

An offer of help came from an unexpected source when we were trying to turn around one dark night on a narrow country lane and ended up instead in a drainage ditch off the side of the road.

Among those who pulled over to see what they could do, a woman hopped out of her truck, stopping only long enough to hoist out a mass of sturdy rope before she took command of our rescue. When the car was finally back on the road and ready to go, she paused to inquire, "Anything else we can do for you?"

Don laughed and said, "Well, now that you mention it, we're new here, looking for a place to live. Do you know of anything available to rent?"

"Depends what you're after. I know a place has everything—

unless, of course, you're fussy and want indoor plumbing."

What it finally came down to was the rancher we were now in, a half hour's drive from the base. "Out in the sticks," as my dad put it. But the bathroom was definitely inside. So, it seemed, were all the neighbors that late in the fall. No one was out mowing lawns or watching children, and, even if they had been, the drifts of ground fog that wrapped themselves around the houses day after day that autumn would have screened them from our view.

When we'd rejected the communal living of the Army post's matchbox apartments we hadn't considered the fact that we were moving into the cold and foggy Delaware Valley in late October. In effect, we'd marooned ourselves on a tiny island of postwar-building-boom boxes, adrift in what still looked much like the agrarian countryside of the American Revolution.

The morning after Don left on his first trip out of McGuire, I was delighted to awaken to a river valley that had shrugged off its misty autumn shroud. Five months pregnant and impatient to settle and brighten up our new home after two years of being a gypsy, I planned to get busy on the sewing machine, making curtains for the baby's room. Maybe I'd even start drapes for the living room while Don was away. Rejoicing that our daughter was still asleep, I headed for the kitchen to enjoy a leisurely breakfast by myself before I had to feed and run after a busy toddler.

But I stopped dead in my tracks when I rounded the corner to see a mouse streak across the counters and plunge down one of the stove burners.

Had I lost control of everything—even our own home? On counters I'd left pristine only the night before, droppings now trailed. The kitchen had been the one room I'd managed to practically sterilize, as I did each move in an effort to ensure any dirt and germs from then on were ours, not leftovers. In fact, it was the only place in the house that I'd succeeded in getting fairly settled. I'd been so happy to be done washing out all the cabinets and cleaning and putting away dishes from the shipment we'd received so far.

In college, I had always been the spider killer in our dorm room. It seemed silly to me that my roommate could be afraid to "take care of" something so much smaller than she was. I'd just met my own match.

Heart pounding, I managed to dial the phone number of a family across the street, the only one who had come over to say hello when we moved in. If there had been a 911 system, I probably would have tried that.

"Oh, those are just little field mice. Coming in out of the cold. These houses are so new. Built right over the fields where they have their nests," the friendly voice of the Marine wife across the way reassured me. "The pipes all have huge spaces 'round 'em where they can get in."

"How do I stop them?"

"They won't hurt you. We watch 'em run back and forth across the living room at night."

"But what can I *do* about them?"

"Just make a lot of noise. They won't come out to bother you. Be sure to get the crumbs out of your toaster though or they'll go in there to feed on 'em. We'll bring a trap over and set it for you tonight."

I was relieved to hear we were at least safe during the day. Early that evening, when I did the ironing, I made sure I had both radio and TV blaring and every available light blazing as I stomped around, slamming hangers down on the counter between pressing shirts. Then the toaster popped.

I'd left it plugged in and the intruder foraging inside it now had not bargained for burnt fur. Out he flew across the kitchen counter and, like the last, down the stove. All my illusions about noise and light protection scurried away on little mouse feet.

It was definitely time for the Marines. Fortunately, our neighbor and her husband were not far behind, with baited trap, ready to position it on top of the stove for me. We adjourned to the next room, sitting to chat as if the world had not just come tumbling down around me. When no mouse succumbed immediately to the lure of the cheese, they finally left, leaving me to face my paranoia alone in the now quiet house.

I knew at least one creature was stirring when the trap snapped closed loudly in the middle of the night. Thoughts of disposing of the body in the morning filled my fitful sleep. I prayed we'd be able to stop this nightmare when Don got back. In my dream, he was home, closing up the holes around all the plumbing, just as the neighbors had outlined the battle plan.

The next morning it seemed simplest to just throw the trap away, mouse and all. That done, I called friends from our college dating days, who lived in an adjoining town and were, I knew, already veterans of the field mice wars. They came over that afternoon with a slew of new traps and tried to show me how to set them. But my panic had erected such enormous barriers to the lesson that not much got through.

There was to be no respite. That night, enemy reinforcements arrived, and I could clearly make out at least one gray form on the kitchen counter behind the canisters. Shaking, I went to the refrigerator to get out the cheese and carefully cut a generous piece to set the trap the way I thought I'd been shown.

Terrified of being touched by the mouse in the process, I slung the trap toward the canisters on the counter, only to watch it spring.

Again I tried the same technique, trying to glide it into place. Knowing a mouse was right there, I was sure I'd end up with my own finger in the trap if he ran out as I set the trap down. No matter how gently I tried to slide or pitch it, it would inevitably pop on landing.

The situation grew so tense that even the mouse could no longer stand it and began to squeak at me. Not sure what to do and unable to endure being in the same room listening to him, I finally put the trap down somewhere else in the kitchen and went to bed for another night of anxiety.

The next morning the cheese was almost all eaten, but the trap remained unsprung. With saintly patience, my friends explained it was all because of the mammoth treat I had used for bait and, in the mouseless daylight, we all laughed together over my folly.

Each night it was another story.

At first sighting, I would get on the phone to neighbors.

Another day, another mouse—and another call to a nearby friend. "Nothing to worry about," a 4-H honors homemaker from Broken Arrow, Oklahoma, chuckled. "I'd rather empty a mousetrap than change a baby's diaper any day."

By next night's intruder, I knew I had to stop bothering friends or I wouldn't have any left. There wasn't much of my rationality remaining either. I called my mom and dad, long distance. I had to talk to someone.

Don's parents, also on Long Island, had next dibs on the panic roster. They were patient, trying hard to mask their amusement, but listening and refraining from laughing out loud were about the only ways they could help from such a distance.

Clearly, we were going to have to close up the holes under the house before I could stem the gray tide.

When Don came home, he took charge, armed with steel wool and tin strips, climbed down into the crawl space and closed every opening he could find.

"No more mice now, hon," he assured me over and over again as time went on, even as I continued to conjure up ways they might still get in and he countered with diagrams of siding, foundation and other construction details to convince me. Certainly, there were more important things for me to concern myself with, what with a toddler running around and the premature birth of our son just a few months after we'd moved in.

Still, as if by some fiendish plot, almost without fail, whenever Don was about to go out the door on a trip, or the night before, we would hear or see new evidence "they" had indeed found one more entry point. Broom in hand I would stand, barring my husband's passage through the door, until he went after the latest blockade runner with my chosen bristled weapon. I had no desire to pound mice to death. I just wanted them swept out of the house—and our lives—forever.

If we won individual skirmishes, we never succeeded in winning the war. In a purse I'd hung on a high hall closet hook months before, I found brand new lollipops the kids had been given when I'd taken them for shots—all gnawed by mice teeth. A taunting reminder. We were still being stalked.

By almost the end of our lease we had three children, but the mice—and virtual single parenthood—persisted. Early one morning we heard scurrying in the kitchen between the subflooring and the base cabinets as Don was getting ready to leave on a trip. It was four in the morning. I had some sort of virus and longed to get back to bed. Besides there wasn't much anyone could do to reach this intruder anyway.

I told Don not to worry. I'd finally grown up about mice: "This one is clearly underneath the kitchen cabinets and isn't going to bother me or the kids back in our rooms at the other end of the house."

With that I headed for bed, snuggled back under the covers and was just about asleep when I heard our oldest scream out. She never did that. And was I really hearing funny little scratching noises under my bed?

"OK," I said to myself. "You know it's all in your mind. You can prove it's only your imagination. Put the light on and you'll see."

When I did, a mouse ran out from under our bed. He seemed to embody everything in my life I was unable to accept. After three years of fighting them, the mice were still in our house and, most of the time, Don wasn't. I felt defeated, by mice and men.

CHAPTER 4:

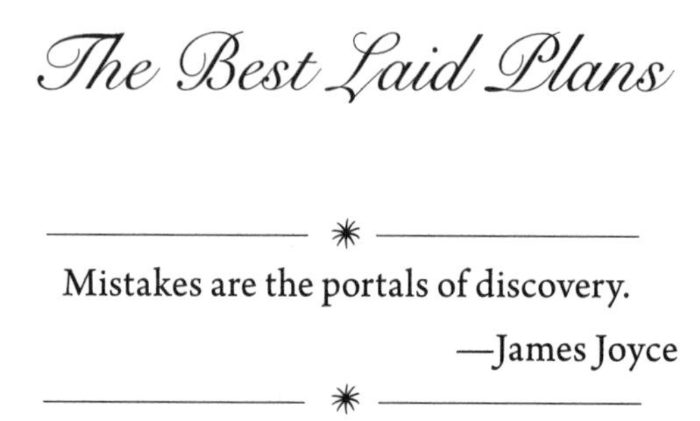

The Best Laid Plans

> Mistakes are the portals of discovery.
>
> —James Joyce

Over the years we'd known each other, Don and I had adopted a pattern of looking ahead, shaping a course. It took a little while for us to realize our new way of life meant being flexible. Plans, even for visits with friends and family or for vacations, were in a constant state of revision. Eventually, the only way to simulate control was to assume things were going to be perpetually on the verge of spinning out of hand and do what we had always done—talk to each other about them.

People who've lived in an area all their lives can be slow to warm to newcomers, especially the "here today–gone tomorrow" military, no matter that some of us wished we were still "civilians." Our main chance to make friends was to meet people in the same boat, either at the squadron's monthly cocktail party or, for me, at the wives' coffee. But no matter how hard he tried to plan, Don would be home only every three months or so for the nighttime get-togethers. With everyone showing up in this same sporadic way, it would take almost a year to meet most of the people in our group.

As we did each time we moved, we tried to anchor ourselves by registering right away at the local parish. Exchanging Sunday babysitting with another family down the block brought us two new friends our own age. Then a slightly older Air Force couple around the corner took us in hand. Never mind that a snowstorm wiped out power for a week. We gathered around their Coleman lanterns for supper as Cathy sang "Happy Birthday" with toddler logic. These were the first of many lights lit in our lives by the Carters. Helen shared recipes and common sense. Two years later, Jim rolled up his sleeves to tackle the dishes at our third baby's summer christening, not only because he and Helen were the godparents, but because he recognized parental exhaustion when he saw it.

But there was nothing either one of them could do to stop the relentless trips—even though I childishly thought at first that complaining to such good "older heads" would get the word to some squadron scheduler that Don was doing more than his fair share and see if the trip schedule could be eased up.

We were only a few hours away from our Long Island roots, but newfound friends, rather than family, soon became our main support system. Since everyone was in the same boat, you tried not to ask for help too often.

Everything took on fresh complications with our new way of life, even the little matter of family planning. It was pre-Vatican II, and, for the Catholic in the pew, the use of any form of birth control device, commonplace for everyone else, was a serious sin. Rhythm—which meant no sex around a wife's fertile times and hope for the best—was the only sanctioned birth control to avoid unplanned pregnancies. In the squadron, Ron and Tommie, Don and I were among the practicing Catholics. Likely as not, husbands were home for their wives' fertile times and gone for the "safe." With the men spending two-thirds of their time flying, away from home, our only alternatives to what people jokingly referred to as Vatican roulette were total abstinence, mortal sin or instant pregnancy.

At one cocktail party Tommie confided, "Can you believe Ron's mother tried to put us up in separate beds in different rooms when we'd purposely planned our vacation trip home during our 'good time'?"

I could. Unless you'd been there, who could picture sex teetering on a wing and a calendar page?

It wasn't something you talked about to many people. And it was all tied up with another unplanned part of our lives: the calls from the base when the men *were* home. I hated the phone. Even when Don had just gotten back from a trip, answering its ring meant responding to the summons to fly away to Iceland, France, Greenland or Germany for the better part of the week. And breaking down in Goose Bay, Labrador, for sure, either coming or going. Although Don refused to believe it, I knew from other wives there were those who didn't answer when their men were still on crew rest.

The phone broke into our lives with other intrusions as well. One night, when Don was on a trip, a captain they'd nicknamed "the deacon" called to invite me to a revival meeting at his church. Before he hung up, disappointed I'm sure that I'd declined, he confided, "You know, most of the people in the squadron are going straight to hell." I certainly hoped not and told him so.

Perhaps because he couldn't afford a telephone of his own, a young sergeant and his wife, who'd moved in just around the corner, used ours as the contact number for the squadron to call at any hour of the day or night to alert him to trips or other notices. With Don gone so much of the time, snow on the ground by now and my own advanced state of pregnancy, I didn't feel joyous at the need to get up at one or two in the morning, dress, race around the corner and pound on their door to deliver the message.

Wives talked a lot—and often I wished they didn't. One neighbor who stopped by to visit while Don was on a trip shared the story of the sheets a wife refused to wash because the scent of his body on them was all she had left of the husband she had just lost in a crash.

Another wife became so depressed she'd desperately slashed her wrists to try to stop her husband from going on a trip. Like the birth control others took for granted, that was plainly out of the question—but not beyond imagining. Instead, I stayed frenetically busy, overdosing on work and sleep deprivation instead of pills.

Don and I had little more control over what we could do to make our house a home than he had over his flight schedule. Our landlords, a young Army couple, had just redecorated before the husband got orders to move on. Since they planned to return there to live, we were forbidden to repaint anything or change any of the color scheme. That left us stuck with a front door painted school bus yellow (to match the wagon wheels framing the driveway) that opened directly against hot fuchsia living room walls.

By the time I was seven to eight months' pregnant with our second child, nesting instincts had me clucking about, trying to reconcile color clashes and put every last twig and feather in place. But it took at least an hour's drive to get to what we thought of as real shopping.

Just before Christmas we'd gone into Philadelphia to buy a hide-a-bed for the living room so that our families could come down from New York to visit. We'd chosen the most muted charcoal gray upholstery we could find. That still left two hand-me-down chairs at war with purplish-red walls. We opted to redo them later during the midwinter upholstery sales.

"Why don't you schedule some people to come talk to us about it on Saturday?" Don suggested. "I have altitude chamber here next week so I should be home."

My fingers did the walking as I set up appointments with upholsterers to bring their samples to us. This way, we could see which fabrics jangled least in the raucous room, look at all the possibilities and still get the best price. I dialed every single upholsterer listed in the Yellow Pages.

That February Saturday morning glowed with optimism because Don was indeed home. Although the first appointment failed to show at ten o'clock—he was coming all the way from Philadelphia—the doorbell soon rang as #2 stood smiling on our doorstep, his arms loaded with swatch books.

We couldn't find anything we liked that we could afford in his volumes of fabric, but as he packed and stacked up all his samples, #1 finally showed up. He had just spread out all his wares on the living room floor when #3 arrived early from Camden.

Unfortunately, #1 took longer than we thought possible and #3 was still waiting in his car at the curb when #4 appeared promptly, hat and samples in hand. A weathered Jewish upholsterer dressed in blue serge, he was more like a New York tailor than someone from the little town of Mount Holly, just a few miles down the road.

Gimbels, in pinstripe, #5, came just a bit late, but by then it didn't matter because the sample-laden cars lined up in front of our house with upholsterers waiting their turns all the way down the block.

Hopping mad, Gimbels slammed his books together and didn't even bother joining the lineup. He was followed down the block by at least one other—I've forgotten which number—and finally #4, his heavily starched white shirt and patience undaunted, was the only one left.

He looked old enough to retire, but as Mr. Stanley took down our chairs' dimensions, it was obvious he knew from limited budgets and fabrics that would stand up to kids. He didn't even mind that we were military.

When he finally left, he took with him a debt of gratitude—as well as the contract to redo two old chairs to coexist in peace with a jaundiced front door and all that fuchsia. From start to finish we figure what Mr. Stanley had already delivered was something even more special, measured by what some call a Golden Rule.

CHAPTER 5:

Pick a Pot of Pickled Peppers

Just when you think you've graduated the school of experience, someone thinks up a new course.

—Mary H. Waldrip

"Do the things that you do best and hire someone to do the rest" is great advice if you have what it takes to pay for it. With money scarce, the length of time we'd stay put iffy, and making do embroidered on our hearts as a kind of heraldic motto, we figured (like most Americans) that "do it yourself" balanced the budget.

For my part, I sewed curtains, kids' clothes and drapes. I also started our balky car on cold days by pushing it backwards down the slight incline of our driveway as I ran after it, jumped in and engaged the engine. But, even though I was an electrician's daughter, I left the wiring—and the pipes—to Don. I was pretty useless mechanically, especially if you counted setting mousetraps.

By the time we had two children it seemed like someone was always sick with an upper respiratory infection. "Dry air," the doctors diagnosed. "What you need is a humidifier in your forced air heating system."

Sears filled the prescription with a fairly cheap model and when he was home one weekend, Don descended into the crawl space beneath the house (to me, the mice-ridden depths) to put it in. Cutting off the water, he followed the step-by-step instructions for "simple installation." By then we had learned, of course, that there was no such thing. When the water began to spout out of what should have been an empty pipe, he knew we had a really "unsimple" problem. He had drilled into the wrong side of the supply valve. A geyser was spewing beneath our home.

Don bounded out of the crawlspace to call the water company to find out how to turn off the supply to the whole house from the street, only to be told, "You can't do that yourself. It's Saturday, so we only have crews for emergencies."

"This *is* an emergency. Send one, please—and fast."

We had a small sub rosa swimming pool by the time help arrived—and God knows what our water bill was that quarter, but Don was able to patch the pipe, and get everything back to normal again. We were soon well moistened and I conjured up visions of healthy children above while drowned mice floated away on the ebbing floodwaters beneath us.

With a lot less fanfare, Don built a sandbox for the kids to play in out back and a toy kitchen for inside. He also fashioned an ingenious room divider between the kitchen and dining room to hold the plants that now flourished in our newly humidified home. Doing-it-ourselves had begun to pay dividends.

Next door, new neighbors moved in with, joy of joys, children the ages of our own, and we began to exchange babysitting for several hours each morning to give one another a break, a kind of early co-op preschool effort.

It was during one of those breathers that I was rushing to clean out the expired leftovers from the refrigerator. Lacking a disposal, my mother had always pitched these treasures into the toilet and flushed. And I was busily doing just that when I realized the jar I'd just emptied had contained, not a vegetable green with mold, but one humongous dill pickle. A pickle which was at that very moment on its way down the bowl.

I knew I was in deep trouble when the rising waters crested over the top and the plunger wouldn't budge the displaced dill. There it was, firmly lodged in the trap of our one and only john. Already visibly pregnant with our third child, I definitely needed a functioning bathroom. I tried to calm myself enough to tell Don what I'd done when he came racing in the door to pack a bag for another out-of-the-Air-Force-blue trip. Instead of a broom, I waved a plunger in his face.

"Please, you have to try to clear the john before you leave," I explained, as I ran to find the auger.

We plunged and snaked in vain until I reluctantly agreed we had no choice but for me to call a plumber when I got back from driving Don out to the base. Although we knew no repair people in town because of our frugal efforts to do all our own work, I was lucky to find one willing and able to come out right away.

I prayed as he repeated our efforts with more professional equipment, and protested as he told me there was nothing for it but to take the fixture completely off to try to unclog it.

Thank God that the kids were napping as he worked or they might have wanted to "play" too. Red-faced, I watched as the plumber heaved the snowy bowl upside down out on the back lawn. Wrestling the ceramic behemoth, he bounced and jiggled it up and down all over the yard. I hoped against hope that none of the neighbors were home to witness this seemingly endless contest. The billable time ticked away until, abruptly, the plumber "pinned" the opponent and the pickle in the pot popped out.

"Never saw anything like that before," he allowed, scratching his head. I hoped we never would again.

We were learning a lot of new things, Don and I, and humility topped the list. But if personal growth could be measured by our willingness to do it ourselves and risk mistakes, we were well on our way to sainthood—if only we didn't screw that up too.

Chapter 6:

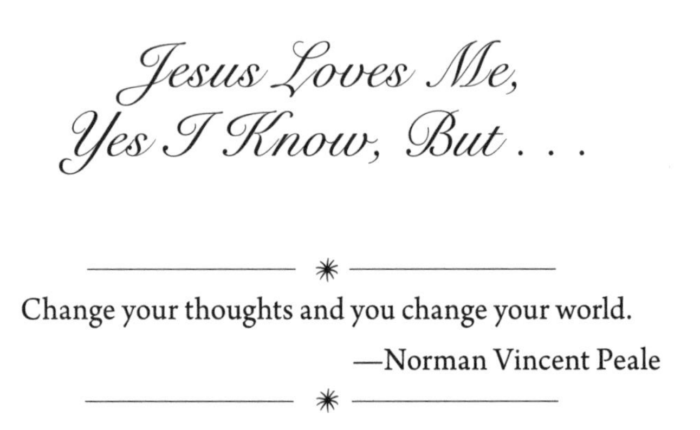

Jesus Loves Me, Yes I Know, But . . .

Change your thoughts and you change your world.

—Norman Vincent Peale

By the time our third child arrived in 1959, we were still in southern New Jersey and realized we needed a bigger house than the one we were renting. I started to scour real estate listings for something we could afford to buy. The people at the base had told Don we were sure to be at McGuire a few more years so it seemed the wise thing to do.

When I spotted a well-built split-level, located on a short, quiet block, I began drive-by reconnoitering to check out the kid population. If we could swing it financially, Cathy, Jim, and newly arrived Nancy would have playmates and a safe, fenced-in yard in which to play. As long as we didn't get caught in an unexpected transfer.

On Cathy's July birthday—surely a good omen—we signed the offer to buy 10 Mitchell Terrace, Mount Holly, New Jersey. But it took until mid-October before we could close, rent a van and move ourselves in. Along with the house came a big lesson in nomadic living: Our teachers were a blockful of neighbors, most of whom were—or had been—in the same boat as us. We were accepted as if we'd known them for years. No cautious waiting period to check out what we were really like. There might not be time. No hesitance to make the effort to get to know someone who they knew would eventually have to move away. Just friendship.

Three years earlier when we'd first moved into the rental house a few miles south of where we now were, both the separation from most neighbors and that recently hatched development had made me feel I'd been plunked down on some new frontier. Now that we'd moved again, our new situation made me sure of it—but for altogether different reasons. Instead of feeling stranded, we found not only a more settled landscape but older heads, among whom there was always someone eager to help, whether it be "building the barn," watching the kids or giving advice, sometimes more freely than we liked to receive it.

Don and my dad would talk out the plans for most of our home improvement projects ahead of time, but when we began to execute them there were always neighborhood consultants around too. If one family solved a heating problem by insulating the wall between the garage and the family room and adding a heat duct, every other split-level on the block soon followed suit. Keeping up with the Joneses here took on a refreshing new dimension.

When the neighborhood kids battled one another with someone's green tomatoes, everyone within a two-block radius knew about it. And we soon found out our children's loving offering of Red Emperor tulips were freshly culled from a nearby neighbor's new blooms.

Despite the fact that each of us hailed from hometowns ranging from Atlantic City to Iowa and California, we became a family with at least as many quirks and as much love as any blood relations. Almost as old as our parents, Jule and Harry Steinberg were straight out of Broadway's *Abie's Irish Rose*, but as unmixed up a couple as a "mixed" marriage gets. A devout Catholic, Jule had finally married her Jewish love, Harry, and followed him around the world for a time as an Army wife. Now they were each there for everyone who needed them.

"Close the fridge door. You'll run up your electric bill," Jule scolded, as I rushed to put away perishables from the grocery store before the kids came in from playing. For a minute I thought I was back home with my mother. As much as the nagging grated, the love comforted.

We even had teenage babysitters right in our own neighborhood for a change. And often, for daytime sitting when Don was away, Ada, our Polish American next-door neighbor, would run in when the kids were napping so I could go pick up an older woman who lived fifteen minutes away.

Of course, things and people continued to break down when Don was on a trip. But I can't remember a foggy winter there, or if there was one I could always see through it to the lights of the next neighbor's house.

As if to test our mettle, just ten months after we'd moved in Don came home with the news he'd been picked to go to Alabama for a four-month school, returning after that to resume his assignment in New Jersey. Much as I hated the idea of packing up and moving again so soon, I knew Don felt as strongly as I did that we needed to figure out a way to stay together, even if it was in Alabama. The only real question for either one of us was how we were going to swing it financially for all of us to go with him. We'd had enough separations we could do nothing about. We decided then and there to always opt for togetherness if we had any part in the decision, whatever it took—even if it involved that dreaded four-letter word *move,* that we'd already had too much of, or the other one, *cash,* of which there was never enough.

From Labor Day to Christmas 1960, the Montgomery apartment we could afford (the New Jersey mortgage and utility bills still had to be paid) left everything to be desired except roaches and earwigs. But at least we were together.

As the cold weather set in, so did illness. Don even ended up hospitalized with pneumonia. Military medical care for the family seemed to be as hard to come by in Alabama as it had been in New Jersey. I spent my life dialing and redialing the appointment line but usually ended up with whomever was sick (and everyone else, who would soon get that way), waiting for hours to see a doctor at a kind of walk-in sick-call.

Now that our oldest had just turned five, we had new concerns. New Jersey offered kindergarten in the public schools and made it a prerequisite for first grade. Since Alabama did not, we enrolled Cathy in Miss Rook's, a private, supposedly nonsectarian school in Montgomery, so she'd be right in step when we got back home. Many of the Protestant churches in the area also had private kindergartens to which other families were sending their children.

We'd been concerned about whisking the kids around the country, away from friends and extended family, to strange homes and places. Now we began to realize the huge differences in school systems they'd be facing as well. Educational requirements and standards, even term lengths, varied from state to state as well as from private to public schools. For now our problems were elementary compared to those faced by people with children in high school. We just did our best to clear each hurdle as we came to it.

To begin with, we were night people. Getting up with the roosters for an Air Force that started work at seven in the morning—and sometimes four-thirty or five—had been one of the harder adjustments for Don and me to make. Now our oldest had to cope not only with the move but with getting up early for school.

On Sundays we were still hearing the Mass in Latin while weekdays Cathy came home from Miss Rook's singing "Jesus Loves Me" and adding a Baptist grace to our stock Catholic "Bless us, O Lord, and these Thy gifts . . . " at meals. To complicate life further, Cathy was immediately moved forward into first grade.

My teacher training in college had warned against "skipping," and, despite the fact that the very same thing had happened to me twice, years before in New York, I hastened to consult the school psychologist to make sure testing justified the move. I was concerned we might be allowing her to be pushed too far too fast. Reassured, I came home to report to Don the only thing we had to worry about, they said, was that she not be put back into kindergarten when we returned to New Jersey.

In fact, once we got her out of bed and on her way in the morning, Cathy flourished at Miss Rook's. By the time we headed back north, the Christmas school holidays had already begun and I hoped my way through visits to our families that there would be no glitch in transferring Cathy into first grade in New Jersey.

I was on the doorstep of Sister Principal's office as soon as Sacred Heart School in Mount Holly reopened after the New Year, and to my delight the enrollment was soon all but accomplished. Until the good Sister noted Cathy's youth on her transfer papers. "Oh, my dear," she explained, "there's no way we can put such a young child into the first grade. It's just out of the question."

Nor was there any way we could put Cathy back into kindergarten, I knew, both on the gut level and from the advice we'd been given in Alabama. But Sister wasn't about to budge.

I went to the public school and found they would take her instantly as a transfer student. But then I bristled. Why should we have to put our daughter into a public school instead of a Catholic one if we didn't choose to? I decided to call a parish priest, who referred me to the diocesan offices.

There the monsignor assured me he would take care of the whole matter with Sister and he did. But, for the rest of that year, our five-year-old seemed to pay the price for my going over local heads.

If Jesus loved her, Sister kept her after school for putting rosary beads on her head during devotions. When she was sick with all the germs we seemed to have carried back from Alabama and missed school, her return was greeted with tons of makeup homework that only tired her so much she became sick all over again. In early June, when she had her tonsils and adenoids removed, there were no little drawings or get-well greetings from her classmates to accompany the assigned work I was given to take to her in the hospital.

I was relieved when the school year finally ended and grateful that religious, like the military, get transferred. It had been a painful way to begin learning how not to deal with schools. As a teacher myself, I found it ironic I still had so many lessons to master.

The following September I was working in the yard when Cathy came in the house from her first day in second grade. She was bubbling over with excitement over her newly arrived teacher and called out to me from her bedroom window.

"Her name is Sister Mary Corn Ears, Mom, and she's from Raspberry Park." And so it was that we soon found out Jesus still loved us, second grade was a whole new ballgame, and Sister Mary Cornelius, from Asbury Park, was, like so many people who'd touched our lives since we'd moved to Mitchell Terrace, in fact, heaven-sent.

Chapter 7:

From Howdy Doody to Mickey Mouse

Love does not just sit there, like a stone; it has to be made, like bread, remade all the time, made new.

—Ursula K. LeGuin

Although I'd worried needlessly about bringing roaches or earwigs back with us from Alabama, it was the other bugs that tagged along for an extended stay that caused us trouble. There seemed no end to the kids getting sick, seemingly bouncing germs back and forth. One doctor even suggested we separate the children, sending each to a different relative and keeping just one at home.

Within the next eight months, our son Jim went through six bouts of pneumonia. The last episode was the most frightening because this time it involved both lungs. Since we were back at McGuire, Don was again on the flying circuit and away on a trip when it happened.

Dr. Ziegler, the jazz musician turned civilian pediatrician who now cared for our kids because of all the problems we'd had with the clinic at McGuire, advised putting Jim into the hospital at Fort Dix—

probably because of the expense involved if we went elsewhere.

Our next-door neighbor, Marty, was also due to leave the following day on a trip that would take him away for several weeks. He and Fran planned to celebrate their anniversary early by going out for a quiet dinner together. But as soon as they heard about Jim, they canceled everything so Marty could drive us out to the hospital to run interference in the system, as only a military man seemed to be able to do.

The doctors at Walson Army Hospital agreed Jim should be admitted. He looked so vulnerable in the hospital bed as a nurse installed an oxygen tent about him. The strange apparatus was enough to frighten anyone, no less someone only four years old. "It'll be OK, Jim," I said, trying to reassure him as he began to whimper. "They know what they're doing."

"Don't be too sure about that, honey," the attendant said sharply as she shot a glance at me across the room. It was all I could do not to snatch Jim out of the bed and run home with him. Instead, I prayed through the night and hired sitters to stay with the other two during the day while I sat bedside at Walson.

By the time all three kids were finally healthy again—and stayed that way—we'd been through three cases of measles, tests for cystic fibrosis on the two youngest, a tonsillectomy for the oldest and so many medical bills we were eventually audited by the IRS, who couldn't believe a military family wasn't making some of them up.

It seemed the worst possible timing when, in the midst of all this, Don was offered a Regular Air Force commission and we suddenly had to decide whether he'd accept it or get out and go back to the job National Broadcasting was holding for him. Without realizing what was happening, living nestled in the bosom of a neighborhood of friends had made a difference to me. Even a gypsy existence could be peopled with "family."

Through the first few years of Don's time in the Air Force, I had comforted myself with the knowledge that we could return to New York and a normal life when his commitment was up. I mostly ignored the voice in the back of my head that said we'd be apart as much as ever, just in a different way. Don's daily commute to Rockefeller Plaza in the city, from the Long Island neighborhoods we could afford to live in, would mean few waking hours together but at least we'd be on the same continent, in the same state.

Don was on a trip when his commander called to tell me he'd been selected for a regular commission in the Air Force. For one thing, that meant security. He couldn't be asked to leave involuntarily before retirement. It also meant—and the commander made a point to make it clear to me—that they really wanted and needed him to stay.

The next call that came was from the friend at National Broadcasting who would be Don's boss when he returned. He invited all five of us to his home in North Jersey for Sunday dinner with his family. But first they set a date for Don to visit his old NBC department to look over the office he'd be coming back to.

Don had worked his way through Columbia University as an NBC page, holding back the throngs of teenage girls who tried to reach out and touch Eddie Fischer, whisking away youngsters who said "I need to go potty **now**" when the camera was panning the Peanut Gallery of the Howdy Doody show, and on many a night making his dinner on Hostess Twinkies, Welch's Grape Juice or whatever other edible samples a show sponsor was handing out that day.

Just before we were married, he was selected to join the company's management training program and ended up a ratings analyst. One of the most difficult tasks he had to perform that year was delivering the forecast that ABC's Mouseketeers would outrun Howdy in the ratings. After his time as a page, it was like betraying an old friend. But a letter from the Air Force assigning him a date to begin pilot training made even the fate of Princess Summerspring Winterfall fade into the beckoning clouds of the wild blue yonder.

The week before Don had originally taken his job in NBC's Audience Measurement Department, a Bellevue psychiatric team had come in to take away the almost catatonic man he was to replace, his fingers tracing repeated patterns on a calculator he saw suspended midair. Don had known Frank when he'd hoped to break in as a singer. Somehow the job had broken him instead.

When Don returned home that evening from New York, he painted a grim picture. "If someone gets sick or dies, I guess there's a chance of moving up. Otherwise, it looks like years of status quo if I go back." I tried to see Don in a job that went nowhere but Bellevue and I couldn't.

Sunday dinner with the boss-to-be, gracious and kind as it was, failed to repaint the picture of the situation. Somehow a green cubicle could never compete with the airplane cockpits that now carried Don all over the world. But that was not the most important thing.

The world around us gave us both more than enough reasons to reconsider. By now the Czech revolt had been squelched by Russian tanks and the Beirut crisis saw McGuire helping to put Marines in place. All in all, the Cold War was heating up, and even I could see there was more purpose in what Don was doing than going back to crunch numbers for NBC. We voted down a return to New York.

It was hard for either of us to grasp that I was willing to even consider "staying in." Though still a bit uneasy, I understood Don's reasons for wanting to. Although it was the last decision either one of us had ever expected me to agree to, we were in for the long haul. Had we known what lay ahead, just a few months later, we might have decided differently.

We had meaning in our lives, one of the two things the experts say we all need. Now all we had to do was pin down the other: some degree of control over what happened to us, some check on the Mickey Mouse. It wasn't due to happen anytime soon.

Don was soon chosen to be among the first to fly a new transport plane just coming off the production line, the first new equipment in years. Then he learned that instead, he was one of four people slated for transfer in January to the command's "schoolhouse" in Oklahoma, where he would teach others to fly the old outdated models. His local commanders fought his going, but to no avail. Someone further up the chain of command was running the show. Though we continued to drag our heels halfway across the country, westward ho we went.

When final orders for the transfer came, we tried putting our house up for sale. But it was an impossible time to sell, not only because of the holidays, but because the market had just evaporated with the opening of on-base housing at McGuire. Don said he'd rather rent it out anyway and it proved our only option.

We worked to get the place into tip-top shape for a family that looked like they'd be careful tenants. For the last and hardest task in our preparations, though, we had to wait until the house was completely empty so Don could get at the basement walls to give them a new coating of waterproof sealant. As I cleaned the house from top to bottom upstairs, he labored beneath, wielding a brush so heavy it felt as if it were loaded with cement.

It seemed to be taking forever until Jule's husband Harry appeared on the scene to lend a hand. But even with two working at it, Harry decided he and Don needed more motivation to spur them to paint faster. Explaining that now they would have to cover the wall before our oldest came home from school, he blazoned a four-letter word across the uncoated portion.

Almost instantly a woman from around the block, whom we had known only in passing, showed up on the scene. She had, in fact, never before crossed our threshold. There wasn't even time to head her off at the pass before I heard her bouncing down the basement staircase to say hi to Harry and Don, anxious, she said, to see what they were up to. They didn't have to spell it out for her. There, in three-foot high letters, was "S H—."

We'd gained so many fast friends on Mitchell Terrace, it was easy to shrug off the few who were just "passing through."

Chapter 8:

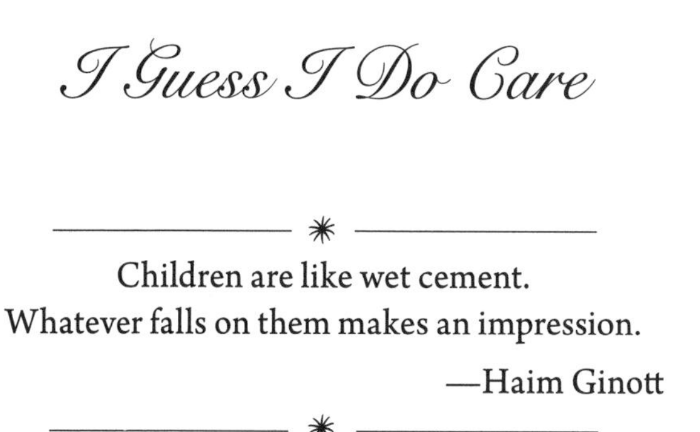

I Guess I Do Care

Children are like wet cement.
Whatever falls on them makes an impression.

—Haim Ginott

By now, in early 1962, the 1953 green Dodge with which we'd started out married life was starting to show its age. But we'd decided to keep it as a second car and Don was determined to drive it west before the rest of us made the trip, to smooth the move by scouting out a rental house for us. We decided to make the car a packhorse to transport anything we could jam into it that either was banned from the moving van or might make us exceed our authorized weight allowance. It was the first time I realized how much we had to start worrying about putting on pounds stuff-wise.

First, we loaded everything heavy that would fit, like the bulky old air-conditioners Don's brother had given us from his business to help get us through the steamy South Jersey summers.

Around them we crammed every other weighty or forbidden object we could find, things like car parts, ink, shoe polishes, spray cans and alcoholic beverages.

Next, Don made a last run with the cargo-laden car into the heart of Mount Holly and back up the steep hill that ran through the center of town to be sure the Dodge would make it.

"If the car breaks down on the way," he said, laughing, as he kissed us goodbye, "I'll just have to sell it and everything in it."

When the phone rang a day later and I heard the alarm that had invaded Don's mellow baritone, I was sure he was calling from a junkyard—or a hospital. Maybe the car had exploded.

"Where are you and how bad is it?"

"I can't believe I did it, Jo. I completely forgot to sign out at the squadron. Officially, I'm AWOL. Call them right away and get someone to do it for me, as of two days ago."

No longer absent without leave, Don and the old green Dodge negotiated the rest of the way, up the last few hills, between him and Midwest City, Oklahoma.

The next call brought the happy news that we had a new address. Shadybrook Drive would be our new Mitchell Terrace, and Cathy could transfer to St. Philip Neri's second grade the beginning of February. The only glitch, and it was a minor one, was that the house had an electric stove. I had never before cooked on anything but gas.

I set about getting transfer papers for our oldest from Sacred Heart School. Sister Mary Cornelius hated to see Cathy leave, she said, relating how our six-year-old had told the class all about having to move, the new house Daddy had found and the fact that "it has an electric stove and Mommy can't cook on it."

Funny as it sounded, it was my first lesson in how much the kids might be influenced by Don's and my reactions. If our heel marks were in the clay halfway across the country as we went, three other pairs would be there right alongside. I resolved to become the best electric stove cooker the state of Oklahoma had ever known.

We drove the younger two children to stay safely in the care of their grandparents while the movers came to pack us out. Since Don was not yet back from Oklahoma by the time the movers arrived, and the house was a split-level with a basement, that left me to supervise the concurrent packing on each of three floors and in the garage. As a result, unpacking at the other end revealed shoes tossed in on top of freshly laundered linens and garbage, lifted from the pail, carefully rolled into wrapping paper and used to fill in a box.

I knew the driver would hand me the long pages of inventory he was annotating with the alphabet soup movers used to indicate marred and scarred, chipped, dented, or scratched—all meant to preclude false claims for damages. At the end of the day, I would have to check it all over, consent to what the illegible M & S's, Ch's, D's and S's said was the condition and verify the sorry state of all our furniture with my signature.

But I was unprepared for the driver's absolute refusal to erase the "mechanical condition unknown" mark he'd put next to the Grundig stereo set that was Don's pride and joy—and which had been playing all during the packing. Grizzled and adamant, he hunkered in on our one remaining chair and would probably still be sitting there if I hadn't gotten the base transportation officer on the phone to convince him to remove the "MCU." I suspect that, in all his years, he'd rarely met a movee who could be more unyielding than himself.

When Don got back from Oklahoma, all five of us finally left together, but not without a wrenching goodbye to what had become a neighborhood family as well as our parents in New York. Excitement replaced tears though as we pointed our station wagon west to begin the journey. Don had described the rancher he'd rented in glowing terms and we couldn't wait to get resettled.

Surprisingly, snow laid down a white carpet for us and the moving van, only to be replaced by a few months of what we—like everyone born in those parts—came to call "gully washers." The one thing our new home did not have was grass. That was a fact muddily brought home to me our first week in the house when five-year-old Jim headed inside from playing in the yard through the back door at the same time two-and-a-half-year-old Nancy appeared at the front, each coated in wet, red clay from hat to boots, like two unbaked ceramics come to life.

Only a couple of neighbors seemed to know we were there, but there was no doubt about it with the people in Don's new wing on the base. I was not only called and invited to the wives' get-togethers, but picked up, taken to them and warmly greeted everywhere at the base at Tinker. It was like being reborn into a whole new Air Force world, one that had yet to embrace me before, and I gradually found myself bonding within its welcoming arms.

To the problem of mud, we said "Seed," to that of cold neighbors, "Patience," and for the difficulty of Cathy's transferring schools mid-year, "Time." Surprisingly, although we'd had to give up closeness to our families in New York, we'd gained much more time together for the five of us. Don might work strange hours, but most of them were there in Oklahoma, and trips away were now only a monthly, rather than a weekly fact of life.

We were learning, too, that there was more to the world than the East Coast of the United States. Trips to Anadarko, southwest of Oklahoma City, took us to Native Americans in a way the movies never did. Some of the few remaining Delaware Indians made their home here. Colorfully arrayed in their native dress, they performed traditional dances at an annual exposition. Here visitors also got to see authentic wigwams, both fully constructed and just framed, thatch-roofed log buildings, animal hides stretched out for drying, and much of the Native culture.

Even a shopping expedition to Oklahoma City had its own revelations as I struggled to understand a new dialect.

"I wonder if you'd have these slacks in a tan," I asked the saleswoman, holding up a pair of size eight black ones.

"Well, yehss, honey, there's a tan rhaat here," she cooed as she handed me a black pair in size ten.

We tossed her "tan" and my "ten" around for a while before we could finally communicate. At least I had shoes on my feet, just as the sign on the door to the department store decreed I must in order to enter.

Somehow, though, we had failed to meet the standards of the optician who lived right next door to us. I knew his wife well enough and his children played with ours. Yet, if I happened to be outside at the same time he was coming or going, he steadfastly refused to return my greeting whenever I tried to say hi. At first, Don said, "Maybe he didn't see you."

"But, he's an optician—an optician who wears glasses."

"Well, maybe he can't hear you."

I gave up talking about it. We were into the "If you can't say something nice about someone, say nothing" mode. Then, Don came home at the same time as our neighbor and boomed a big "Hi!" at him. Zero response.

Now that he had grasped the icicle with his own hands and seen with his own eyes, Don was livid. He couldn't believe I'd actually cut flowers from our garden for the optician when, three months later, he finally came to our door on Mother's Day to ask if his children could bring some to church. "I wouldn't have given him a thing," said the husband that usually found excuses for everyone's bad behavior. While Mr. Cool wasn't exactly friendly, even after that, at least we knew he could see and hear.

But sometimes I wasn't sure I could. One four o'clock get-up day, I carefully laid out the kids' vitamin pills at Don's place. Because he was teaching flying in the C-118, as well as beginning work on his MBA by driving into the University of Oklahoma in Norman two nights a week, he often had to be in for a first period flight.

Early on I had been given a briefing, along with the wives of other pilots-in-training, about the importance of getting up every day to make sure our husbands had a good breakfast of bacon and eggs before flying. Otherwise, we were warned, they risked hypoglycemia and losing consciousness in flight.

Now the fact of the matter was Don's choice of breakfast, before this, had always been cereal, toast, coffee and juice. But I'd listened carefully, and if I had anything to do with it he'd get the breakfast he was supposed to have. His freedom to choose returned only when cholesterol emerged as villain.

Fortunately, we were wise enough to realize that some things which had already become family traditions should remain unchanged, no matter how many times we moved. Pancakes, along with the waffles with which they alternated on our menu, had long ago become a Sunday breakfast staple. It became an ongoing thread that still runs through our family life, giving a sense of continuity.

And, no matter where we were, the things most important to us remained constant. The kids were already picking up on that. We had begun to give each a small allowance, which we encouraged them to save as much as possible. When our kindergartner Jim asked why, I instinctively answered, "So you'll have money to go to college someday."

Not too long after that, following an extended water shortage that had caused us to temporarily limit flushing, he'd keep forgetting to resume doing it after he'd gone to the bathroom. I reminded and reminded until one day, tired and exasperated with his ignoring me, I said, "OK, Jim. I'm going to start fining you a penny every time you forget to flush." With that he threw up his arms and stomped from the room, shouting, "Now I'll *never* get to college!"

Sometimes though, when we got to sorting things out, I found that what I'd always considered important needed to be weighed on a more accurate scale. I'd been very pleased to see that one of our new babysitters, an older woman, was extremely careful about where she put her handbag down upon arrival, so as not to mar the furniture. With all the chips and dings moving had contributed to our décor, I was happy to see such care. What I didn't yet know was that it failed to translate into caring for kids.

At breakfast one morning after Mrs. Careful had been there the preceding evening, Cathy and Jim were all upset.

"Jim committed a mortal sin last night," Cathy said. "When the sitter said he had to go to bed, he threw a block at her."

"I did not commit a mortal sin," Jim immediately protested. "I missed."

As it turned out, Mrs. C. had arbitrarily and abruptly interrupted play far before the kids' normal bedtimes so that she could settle down to read a book. We obviously had to get another recommendation for someone who really liked being with kids when we needed a sitter in the future. In the meantime, we took a little time out to redefine serious sin.

Perhaps because Don was home most Sundays now that we were in Oklahoma, I had also taken to making dinner on that day a special one, fit for company. Along with some great main course, I'd serve what might be considered a "difficult" vegetable for children's—and even some adults'—taste buds. I can't say I remember the maternal logic of this. I probably figured the rest of the meal would be so delicious it would be like Mary Poppins' spoonful of sugar making the medicine go down.

Nancy was about two-and-a-half when, on one of these occasions, I'd served a truly tough one—Brussels sprouts. She sat in her high chair, pushing them around her plate all meal long, with not a bite consumed.

"Nance," said Don. "Eat your vegetables."

Silence.

"If you don't eat your vegetables, there will be no dessert."

Silence.

"Nancy, I'm getting really annoyed with you. I said, 'Eat your vegetables.' If you don't, there's no dessert."

"I don't care," she said brazenly.

As Don lost no time in reaching over to take her out of the high chair and end all the shenanigans, her blue eyes widened and she belted out, "I guess I do care!" faster than he could lift her. It was all we could do to keep from doubling over with laughter. Both Brussels sprouts and discipline had met their comeuppance.

Because I felt such closeness to the community that had made me feel welcome here, I decided to offer to work on the staff of the wives' magazine published each month. I was welcomed with open arms and made assistant editor. Before very long, I ended up in full charge when the editor's husband was transferred. Unlike the bacon and eggs for breakfast routine, though, there were some things people told me I had to do in this new life that I refused to go along with. My predecessor had insisted it was necessary to list wives according to their husbands' ranks, to which I said (to myself), "Baloney," and immediately ceased such nonsense.

There were, of course, those worried about a not-yet-wet-behind-the-ears neophyte and what I might put into print. I was told that pre-publication, I had to take every issue to the general's wife for her to look over and approve. "That's censorship," I told Don. "I won't do it."

After I calmed down and thought about what I knew about the woman, I finally decided to try to go along with it. A single visit was all it took. She browsed through the copy I'd brought, suggested we not print the names of wives in the hospital (at another base, someone sick-listed had passed away before the issue arrived at her home, reopening the family's wounds) and that was the end of her ever wanting to see it. I found her suggestion reasonable. She must also have found me sensible. I never had to darken her doorstep again, except when she gave a thank-you party for all who'd helped out in any way that year. Whenever she ran into me somewhere, she never failed to thank me and had only good things to say about what we were doing with the publication, called *Femme Facts*.

That didn't stop other "senior wives" from calling me, worried when they somehow learned I had asked a psychologist to do an article on the effects of moving on military children. If they'd only realized how reading it would relieve my mind and later, when it was printed, those of countless other young wives, they would have rejoiced at the prospect. Basically, he had written that moving from pillar to post actually broadened the perspectives of our offspring. The only way it seemed to hurt, he had found, was when there were basic problems in the family to begin with, which moving could then exacerbate. After an interim of several years, I tried the idea again, only this time in another publication, elsewhere in the country. The psychologist was different, but the conclusion reached was the same.

Several things came together at the time that helped make it easier for me to become more involved outside the home. One was a notice in our parish bulletin by a dynamic 78-year-old woman named Anna Lambert that she was available for babysitting. We had tried a few days of nursery school a week for our youngest, but that didn't work out, whereas short trial periods proved Mrs. Lambert very definitely did.

Each time she watched Nancy at our house or, eventually, in her own home, it was an exciting adventure for our now three-year-old. I would come back to find Nancy with a new pair of slippers freshly knitted or crocheted for her. Or perhaps they had baked a cake or cookies together, gardened a bit, or done artwork. Anna had even written a book.

At the same time that I was busy editing, I was also home room mother for Jim's all-day kindergarten class now that he had started school. When Don's boss' wife, Molly Scarpato, heard that I would be helping to chaperone a class visit to the zoo, she immediately volunteered to take Nancy for the day. There seemed no end to the kindnesses being showered upon us by people we'd only just met a short time ago.

I still tried not to ask for outside help any more than was absolutely necessary though. When Jim came down with the mumps and I needed to deposit Don's pay in the bank so I could write a check for our rent, I decided the nearest branch was close enough that I could safely pile Nancy into the car and leave our sick son home for a few minutes while I ran that errand. I was, of course, in a big hurry to do it as quickly as possible and so was driving along pretty fast when I noted I was over the speed limit and had better slow down. A glance in the rearview mirror assured me I was lucky there had been no cop behind me.

Just shortly after that, though, flashing red lights and a siren's blast told me things had changed. Puzzled, I pulled over.

"You know you were speeding, don't you?"

"Well, I was—a block or two back, officer. But, as soon as I realized it, I slowed down. I wasn't any more. Could there possibly be something wrong with my speedometer?"

"I have no idea. Bring it in and have it checked," he huffed as he scribbled out a speeding ticket, the first of my driving lifetime.

I was devastated. Not only was I going to have to pay a fine—and appear in court to do it—but the ticket said I had to be there on what was a school night for Don. This meant even more money because I'd have to hire a babysitter. I dreaded telling Don and decided there was nothing for it but to talk to St. Jude. He was supposed to be able to persuade God to do the impossible and fixing a ticket surely was.

"I told you you've got a lead foot," Don said when I confessed to him that night over dinner. "Maybe now you'll slow down."

"But I didn't dare leave Jim alone more than a few minutes," I countered, knowing full well, with twenty-twenty hindsight, I'd have been better to bundle our son up, mumps and all, and just take him with me and Nancy.

As the week went along and my upcoming court appearance loomed, I had just about resigned myself to the inevitable. Then the phone rang.

"Mrs. Brown, I don't know if you remember me, but I'm Officer X, who stopped you last week for speeding."

How could I ever forget you, I thought, as I said, "Yes, I remember."

"Well, you were so sure that there was something wrong with a speedometer that I had my patrol car calibrated and it was malfunctioning. You can tear up that ticket."

At first I thought it might be a joke and didn't dare tear anything up. Maybe someone was playing a gag on me. I held on to it until I was sure no legal repercussions were going to haunt me for ignoring it. But I never did hear another word from the good officer. I supposed it was possible he had a ticket quota to fill, did so and decided to let me off the hook. In my heart I knew, though, that there were other forces at work.

To me, it seemed nothing short of a miracle. But then again, maybe the real miracle was that, as far as our new way of life was concerned, now I too had discovered that I guess I did care.

Chapter 9:

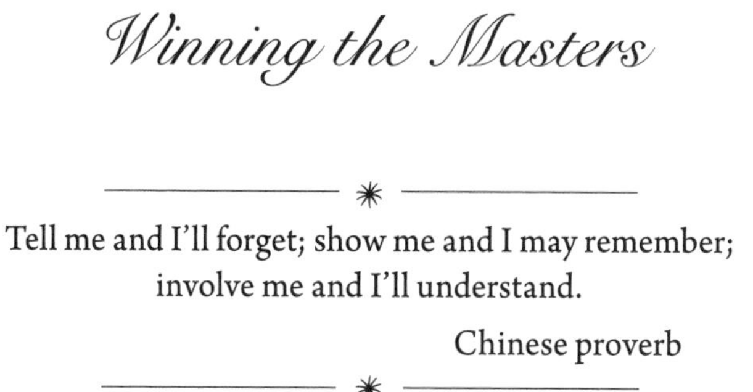

Winning the Masters

> Tell me and I'll forget; show me and I may remember;
> involve me and I'll understand.
>
> Chinese proverb

Sometime during each of our two Oklahoma summers in the early '60s, we pointed our un-air-conditioned station wagon east on Route 66 for a sweaty cross-country trek to visit family. We didn't want the kids to grow up not knowing their relatives and our friends.

Then, at the beginning of what would have been our third year there, Don got word he'd been accepted into the Air Force Institute of Technology program and would spend the next twelve months studying for his MBA at Syracuse University in upstate New York. We had barely gotten over the initial excitement of anticipating a move closer to "home" when a conflicting assignment came in.

A general headed to a command in Anchorage had picked Don to be his pilot. Instead of New York in May, we'd be headed to Alaska in April. It was both an embarrassment of riches and a dilemma, but one which was soon settled by Don's squadron commander, Joe Scarpato, whose motto in life was "No Sweat."

A New Yorker like us, he and his wife Molly had a no-nonsense, do-good approach to life. Joe simply picked up the phone and told the man who'd tapped Don for his pilot about the university assignment. Then he called Don in to tell him the general's message: "Forget Alaska. Seize that chance to go back to school."

With that settled, we decided to pay an Easter weekend visit to friends in San Antonio to say goodbye before we headed east in May. There we visited the Alamo and savored the charm of the city's old Spanish soul, with its picturesque restaurants along the river. It was here that we also got news of the massive earthquake that had just struck Alaska—right after the time we had been due to arrive. That was one "moving" experience we'd been spared, but we felt for all those who hadn't.

A far less traumatic problem faced us when we got to Syracuse that July. We couldn't locate a single house to rent for just the year's time we'd be there. In contrast, the Air Force base at Hancock Field had so many empty duplexes that they were making them available to the families of military not assigned there. How ironic it seemed that, with Don a student at a civilian university, we were moving into government housing for the first time in his nine years in the service.

We became one of a motley crew of student families sharing a T-shaped enclave. Around the corner were the Weisses, Jewish and, like us, from Long Island. The Cades, a black Army couple, lived one door down. Diagonally across the street from them were a couple of Southern white families who had moved in when the husbands were transferred to Hancock, long before the students and their families took over the corner. A few weeks later our ranks increased again when the Fredericks, another black Air Force family, also there for the university, moved into the other side of our duplex.

The day we moved in, the voices of an assortment of the block's kids singing "Here Comes the Bride" in our backyard prompted us to take a break from trying to create order out of the chaos of boxes and furniture in the house and peek outside to see the wedding party. There, arm-in-arm, were our tow-headed five-year-old Nancy and five-year-old Andrew Cade, being feted in what I suspected was the first racially mixed marriage in the neighborhood.

Being new to both military housing and the block, I wondered how this would sit with those around us who'd grown up with total segregation. I couldn't help but recall my astonishment at the priorities of the pregnant Southern gal who lived next door to us in our first New Jersey house who, when she went into labor with their third child, insisted her husband drive her south below the Mason-Dixon Line for delivery.

At Newtown High School on Long Island, where Don and I had met, we'd been some of the very few whites invited to the parties black friends had given in their homes. Even though it was now the mid '60s, with Northerners traveling South to help foster integration there, the New York neighborhoods we'd each grown up in remained very much segregated. If one black moved in, panic over property values drove whites to flee. Yet, here we were, experiencing integration years ahead of the civilian world around us. It was an education far more significant than any we were officially there for.

For the rest of our formal educational needs, we enrolled all three kids in a good Catholic school in nearby Mattydale. Once that was squared away, we headed for a local discount store to take advantage of a sale on carpet remnants to counteract the fact that base housing had cement floors throughout, topped with only a thin layer of asphalt tile. In anticipation of the cold winter ahead, we wanted to put a layer of padding between us and that frigid ground. What in the world were they thinking, we wondered, when they'd built these places? Cars sat in the driveway completely unprotected by even a carport from cold or snow. A heated dipstick quickly found its way onto our shopping list as well.

Cathy had already built a model she called "Why It Snows So Much in Syracuse" for a fifth-grade project at school when we learned we lacked more than a carport. There was little or no insulation in the walls. Circulars advised us to ensure all our faucets dripped whenever there were freezing conditions. Although we dutifully complied, the kitchen pipes froze anyway.

Unlike off-base, though, at least we didn't need to take care of it ourselves or summon a plumber. We could call the civil engineers. They advised using a hair dryer to thaw the pipes under the sink, which we did, to no avail. When they also had no success, they said there was no alternative but for them to break through the wall behind one of the cabinets to get at the line there. But once I'd emptied the cabinet of dishes, the holes they'd broken through revealed not a single pipe.

"You'll have to empty this other cabinet then," they said.

When I suggested they first go back to find the plans for the unit so they could see just where the pipes really ran, they said there were no plans to be found.

As the day wore on, the kitchen became "holier" and the pipelines remained so mysteriously hidden that the GIs called in reinforcements. Along with the uniformed airmen, at least four civilian supervisors in business suits, hats and overcoats crowded into our small kitchen and the adjoining utility area, conferring.

"We need to rip down the ceiling all along here," the head man finally concluded, motioning to a six-foot stretch of ceiling above the washer and dryer. Just as he finished waving his arm to direct the next demolition, a school bus pulled up outside and Cathy came racing in from school.

"Mom," she whispered, grabbing my arm to pull me aside. "We just had this movie at school about the facts of life and I have to talk to you."

To my mind, the deconstruction facts of life that threatened to bring more wallboard down right above our heads had to be settled first. We put the discussion of baby-making and related issues, beyond what we had already had previously, temporarily on hold while I informed the "experts" they weren't ripping down another thing until they found out where the pipes really were.

With that, the boss glanced at his watch and saw it was quitting time for civilians. They beat a hasty exit, leaving behind only the most junior airman, armed with a blowtorch, to try again on the pipe under the sink. It proved to be a lot more than the experts had accomplished.

In no time at all, and with no more holes, he had the frozen pipes thawed. Now the only problem was the copper coupler that broke in the process and had to be replaced before the water to the kitchen sink could be turned back on. The supply area from which the young man could get the part had just closed down until Monday morning. That meant two more days of carting all the water needed in the kitchen across the length of the duplex from a bathroom in back.

Don, who by now had also come in from school, had a better idea. After asking the one-striper to wait, he dashed out to a local hardware store and bought the coupler. We gained not only water in the kitchen but a growing appreciation for a capitalist society. It was a memorable first experience with "silly engineering" other than our own.

For another two weeks we waited through a progression of work orders to get the holes closed up and the walls repainted. Despite the nuisance and nonsense of all that, it was the first time in ten years of marriage we had the use of a clothes dryer. It came with the house. All in all, life in the cold North was proving a warm experience.

Rather than the stereotypical reaction we'd expected to our backyard wedding the day we'd moved in, we found that the neighbor who ran over most to visit was one from Dixie. She worried about us because whenever she got up at night to check on her son she could see our lights burning into the wee hours. It was Don's time to write papers or work on his thesis, mine to type away on it all.

The "groom's" mom had since become Jim's Cub Scout den mother and our adjoining streets had evolved into a close-knit bunch. Since our children were older, I could run in to babysit in a pinch for those with littler ones, a chance to pay back the many times in the past others had done the same and much more for us. Our three kids had acquired so many playmates—the Fredericks had five girls, the Cades four boys and everyone else at least one or two youngsters—that there was always a large group outside doing something together.

I was over in Hattie Frederick's kitchen one morning when we noticed a procession of them parading down the street. Our kindergartner, Nancy, was at the helm, holding a confederate flag someone had brought back as a souvenir of a visit to the South, with everyone else, white and black, stepping smartly behind.

Hattie laughed, shook her head and said, "I never thought I'd see the day when my kids were marching behind a Confederate flag—and I let them."

Embarrassed as I felt, I couldn't help but appreciate the innocence children bring to all things. Don, Cathy, Jim and Nancy might be the ones in school, but I was catching on to a lot of equally important lessons, shedding stereotypes, experiencing a way of life I knew would take years to arrive in the world beyond base housing.

Betty Freidan and the women's movement had already arrived in that world, stirring up waves around each of us, no matter where we lived. People who met you for the first time now asked what you did instead of where you lived or where you were from. Never mind who you were. The Ladies' Room became the Women's Room, but like a "rose by any other name," the places themselves remained cramped and inadequate.

Consciously, I fell back upon the Ursuline nuns' philosophy of service that had been ingrained at New Rochelle and, I guess, right from the womb. To be honest, though, deep inside I felt inferior to those who pursued careers. It was bad enough to get no respect from some men, but when women joined the fray it made it all the harder to value my life as a stay-at-home mother.

Within myself I continued to fight the newly declared war of lost respect for myself for the choices I'd made. Why didn't anyone acknowledge there was no right decision for every woman about working outside the home?

It wasn't just women's lib. Somewhere along the line I began to realize that it had long been important to me to show others the outfits I'd made for the kids, to have a spotless house, to be a great cook. Somehow I'd ingrained the message that what I could do was what mattered, perhaps as early as when I'd received oohs and ahs as a four-or-five-year-old who, on demand, could recite the alphabet backward with ease.

Ever since Lubbock I'd put to use my years of piano and high school training as a music major, along with a year of weekend courses at the Julliard School of Music, by giving piano lessons in our various homes. I reasoned that, with a trustworthy babysitter, I could even try getting back to the classroom and maybe feel less isolated. I experimented by substitute-teaching when we were in Mount Holly.

After only a week I discovered that the caregiver I'd thought so competent really preferred boys to girls, inciting an uncivil war between our toddler daughter and her baby brother. Nothing was worth that. How things went at home was one thing I could do something about, and I felt that far more important than anything I could contribute in a classroom. There were other babysitters out there, I knew, but if there were capable full-time caregivers anywhere we lived, I never heard of them. With all the other instability in our lives, the last thing I wanted to do was to add more.

On top of everything, the pronouncements of psychologists who declared our children's futures all depended upon those first five years in their lives reigned supreme in my decisions. I drove Don crazy by agonizing over whether I had already single-handedly messed everything up for our three.

When our fifth-grader began rebelling while we were in Syracuse and I felt completely lost about what to do, I consulted a priest-counselor who advised easing up at the controls, letting the kids begin to take more responsibility for the results of their own actions. For someone who had been raised to feel responsible for everything in life—and who still lived in terror of incurring my mother's wrath, worry and hurt if I were late answering her letters—it was an important step in a new direction. Maybe it was time to stop letting others pull my strings as well.

Don was at the university to learn about production management but he also brought home the revelation that, contrary to our belief, the Air Force was light years ahead of the civilian world in management procedures. We had always thought it the other way around and were so used to hearing everyone deride all things military that it was refreshing news, especially coming from a civilian professor.

An even bigger surprise emerged from our mailbox. We were on our way out the door the day Don stopped to pick up the newly arrived mail and opened a letter that notified him he'd been selected for early promotion. It would take a year for it to actually happen, but such a complete and joyous surprise couldn't help but astound us.

That made it all the more puzzling when the Air Force suddenly stopped paying him altogether. Then, when he thought he'd finally succeeded in getting his messed up finance records straightened out, he found that the next check was made out for the princely sum of thirty-eight cents. It wasn't only the engineers that could be silly.

But we weren't the children of parents who'd lived through the Depression for nothing. We remained basically frugal do-it-yourselfers at heart, especially when it took a couple of months to get paid again. At least we weren't reduced to borrowing from the kids' piggy banks for the cash to make it through to the end of December as we'd had to when the first two kids were toddlers.

This Christmas the extent of our conservation was to insert a bar in the blue two-wheeled bike that Cathy had outgrown and paint it red to hand down as a present for Jim. The only problem was that, with freezing temperatures outside, snow on the ground and no garage or basement to work in, there was no place warm enough to spray it except our postage stamp of a utility room. There was no place to safely hide it, either, so Don waited to do it until after the kids went to bed the night before we headed south to be with family for the holidays. At least as far as some of our brood were concerned, Santa Claus still delivered. And somehow he always seemed able to locate us, no matter where in the world we happened to hang our hats.

To avoid getting overspray on anything, Don carefully closed all the doors he could while, last-minute-Annie that I was, I sewed away on doll clothes. He was still at it long after midnight when I decided I might as well wash my hair too. I was in the middle of drying it, some fifteen feet away and around the corner in the next room from where he was working, when I noticed the red paint that had been sucked into the dryer housing.

It had also drifted under closed doors on the other side of where he was spraying and settled on the carpet remnants we'd bought, as well as on the asphalt tile and woodwork in the front hall and the utility room itself. This was one version of "painting the town red" we could easily have done without. While we marveled at the physics involved, Don spent most of the little remaining night getting every last bit of stray paint removed before it could set in.

Our other projects proved a little less complicated. As students, except for those like Don who had to keep current by flying a couple of weekends a month, the guys were at least around for us to have get-togethers. Toward the end of the year, as assignments began to come in for friends we'd made, we hosted farewell dinners with menus based on the place to which the departing couple was headed. Things got very elaborate in our kitchen as I borrowed ethnic cookbooks and experimented on the family first, even daring to try baklava from scratch for those on their way to Turkey.

Entertaining had been a big part of our lives ever since we were first married. I liked to cook and it meshed with Don's growing up in a family that had always had lots of company. But that hadn't made him an easy husband to cook for in the beginning. Then, even onions were an exotic food to him. When I'd had the audacity to experiment with Mexican cooking while we were living in North Carolina, he'd minced no words in declaring he never wanted it ever again.

"You'll just have to finish the rest of this stuff yourself," he said, pushing it away as he got up from the table in an uncharacteristic huff.

It had taken "flying the line" all over the world to accomplish what I could never have done. On one trip he'd been horrified to see a tourist throw food across the room, ugly-American style, loudly refusing to eat it in the venerable Botin's Restaurant in Spain. Don had at least tried everything ever since—and found he liked a lot of foods that went far beyond his family's British cooking heritage.

In his classes at Syracuse there were several students from South America that he'd gotten to know well enough to want to have them to the house. It seemed the perfect occasion for a party when, toward the end of the year, we read in the paper that classical guitarist Carlos Montoya would be in the city to give a concert. Don suggested we invite the South Americans and others to join us in hearing the classical guitarist play, ending the evening at our place with a late-night dinner of the paella dish Don had enjoyed so often when his flying had taken him to Madrid.

There remained just one little catch. While Don had been out sampling the world's cuisines, I was cooking things like hamburgers, chicken and spaghetti for the kids and myself in New Jersey and had no idea how to even begin. I'd never even heard of paella—except from Don. In desperation, I decided to search the *Reader's Guide to Periodical Literature* at the library. I retrieved not just one but several versions in the *New York Times'* food sections and incorporated what I considered the best of each into one recipe.

The next stumbling block was finding the ingredients. In 1965, Italian food and its makings abounded on the East Coast. Just the opposite was true of Hispanic cuisine. In place of the chorizo called for, I finally had to substitute spiced Italian sausage. Along with the paella, we planned sangria and other dishes from Spain that I'd researched, but the rice dish with everything in it but the infamous kitchen sink reigned as focal point of the menu.

I was to serve this dish I'd never made before to a group that seemed to grow daily. In the meantime, before I presented it to our guests Madrid style at ten o'clock at night, the family became my paella-eating guinea pigs. They wouldn't be the only ones.

What happened next brought back memories of the day in Oklahoma we'd invited a base pediatrician and his wife who'd become friends, fellow New Yorkers Mike and Judy Stein, for dinner. I certainly hadn't counted on opening the "Living" section of the newspaper that Saturday morning to find Judy smiling up at me from over a wok atop an article about her prowess in Chinese cooking, the lead feature in the food section that day.

And now, despite the fact that my own culinary skills had never evoked headlines of any kind, Don had such confidence that he not only added the base chaplain Father Stawasz, a paella aficionado, to the guest list but invited him over as the quality control expert to sample beforehand. Father, you see, had just returned from an assignment in Spain. Much to my relief, he—and everyone else—liked my neophyte efforts. I'm sure the sangria wine punch we served helped but the party was, in fact, a rip-roaring success.

By now I knew this would not be the last of Don's bright ideas. The hardest thing about the man I had married had always been that he seemed congenitally unable to see what there was to worry about in life, like the possibility that I might not be the very greatest cook in the world, as he thought I was. Don was almost hopelessly happy, having no sense of the Irish Catholic's need to have a strong sense of tragedy to sustain him through periodic moments of joy. It was the cross I had to bear.

I hadn't yet realized that it was precisely Don's total trust in my ability to do something that gave me the courage to try.

Chapter 10:

California, Here We Come

> The world of children and child-rearing is social history writ small but indelible.
>
> —Anna Quindlen

A few months later, following the graduation ceremony at which Don was awarded his master's degree, I found out we were being transferred coast to coast to March Air Force Base. En route to Riverside, California, we'd make a vacation of the almost 3000 mile trip, visiting Yellowstone, Jackson Hole, Yosemite and San Francisco.

We'd recently upgraded our second car from the old green Dodge on which the driver's door kept swinging open every time we turned the corner, replacing it with a Volkswagen bug. But, instead of driving two cars, we decided to all go together in the station wagon, one happy family for the continental crossing we had planned. We acquired a proper tow bar, and mile after mile the VW trooped faithfully behind us.

Other than the crankiness too much togetherness can bring, everything went well until we began to navigate the steep, winding cliffs that lead to the groves of mammoth redwoods in Muir Woods, just north of San Francisco. Looking out from the passenger's seat over sheer drop-offs at trees that were millions of years old, the ribbon of road seemed to head in only one direction—straight down. We had arrived at a place that took our breath away for such a multitude of reasons that the only way we could possibly continue demanded an immediate and complete separation.

It was short-lived. As soon as we were out of the Woods, we hitched right back up again.

Exactly one year in New York had intervened, but like the characters in Steinbeck's *Grapes of Wrath* we Okies had come to California. Except for the fact that we too were once again homeless, the similarities ended there. We weren't in a struggle for our very existence; we were feasting on a wealth of national treasures. Even the terror we had felt as we found ourselves towing in the midst of sheer hairpin curves dissipated as soon as we'd disconnected cars. We couldn't believe how lucky we were to have the chance to see so much of our beautiful country. I just wished the vacation part could somehow have come after the resettling was behind us.

More than a coast-to-coast change of address for all of us, this move radically altered what Don would be doing in the Air Force. Instead of flying full-time, he'd now become a base supply officer. After all his years in what was then called the Military Air Transport Service, he'd be assigned to the Strategic Air Command.

First priority, as always, was finding a place to live. We began by looking into base housing but found it to be in such a state of disrepair we persisted in searching elsewhere. When we'd finally located a house to rent in nearby Arlington, there was a wait to get into it—meaning additional expense and the crowded conditions of a small furnished apartment for at least a month, to say nothing of double change of address notifications. We had to get by with only the clothes and things we'd packed into the cars and no access to anything that had gone on the moving van.

By the time the house was finally available, school had already begun and Don had received an assignment to leave for a three-month supply course in Amarillo, Texas. Now that all three kids were in school, there was no way we could go with him.

It was still swimming pool weather in Southern California, but, from the kitchen window of our new home, I found it fascinating to look out on the breathtaking beauty of the nearby San Bernardino Mountains' snow-covered peaks, only an hour's drive away. It helped to focus on the serenity of that scene our first day in the house because, otherwise, I spent it in a single corner of the kitchen, just scrubbing grease from the walls. Such poor housekeeping in a home the owners themselves had just vacated flabbergasted the Mrs. Clean in me.

I would return often to that window in the days ahead as the movers delivered the majority of our household goods but not the small overage they'd had to put on another truck. Since the leftovers included mattresses for some beds, box springs for others and the bed frames for all, we were reduced to sleeping on the asphalt tile floors, with whatever we could cobble together for mattresses laid out on the flattened cardboard cartons they'd been packed in.

With Don due to leave soon for the next school, we were impatient to get things back to normal. But repeated calls to the moving company reaped only hollow assurances and zero results. Finally, in desperation, I stormed their office, threatening to come back with all three kids and picket signs if they didn't get the rest of our shipment—and beds—there pronto. I figured two can play the game of making promises with no intention of keeping them as well as one. And it worked. Now we could really settle in to enjoy the house and California living.

We delighted in eating out on a large covered patio that, in the mild climate, we knew we'd be able to use a good part of the year. A picnic table soon joined our list of purchases, along with a humidifier to put some moisture into the extremely dry house air. The yard itself was huge but everyone pitched in to do much needed weeding of all the flower beds. The kids were thrilled to have the company of a large tortoise who waddled in from a neighbor's yard to visit through an opening in the back fence. They also found the large, sprawling tree in the front yard an ideal perch in which to sit and read. For my part, I was excited to have orange, grapefruit and lime trees growing right in our own backyard. It was months before I realized the "limes" I'd picked early on were really lemons that had not yet ripened. Even I knew there was no such thing as a lemon and lime tree.

The owners had appointed a couple that lived next door to us as our surrogate landlords. A bachelor police officer lived on the other side of us, but even when it came time to move again we'd neither seen nor met him. A municipal park across the street featured a large public swimming pool. On previous moves, when the children were younger, I'd always scouted the neighborhoods we moved into to make sure there were no private pools, lakes or streams one of them might fall into. Now that they each could swim, I felt a lot less panicked about living that close to a body of water.

All in all, we couldn't wait to explore all there was to do in Southern California. But first, Don had to learn Supply 101. We were grateful he had the Volkswagen to get him to Amarillo and happy he expected to be able to get a hop back to be with us for some weekends.

The first of these held more surprises than either of us expected when he checked in with his new squadron by phone to see what was new.

"Orders just came in for your next move," the voice on the other end of the phone informed Don.

Talk about planning ahead. Almost a year to the day from when we'd left Syracuse, we were already scheduled to depart California and cross not just the country this time, but the Pacific Ocean, on our way to Guam, our new sultry island home. We were alone in the family room when Don relayed the news and I erupted in laughter.

"I'm so glad we just bought a humidifier!"

We talked about all that this transfer would mean, like shots for typhoid, cholera and the like that we'd all have to get in a spaced series over the coming months.

"I don't want to tell the kids yet though," I said. "We just now got into the house and they're going through all the adjustments of the move, new friends, another school. We just can't tell them yet that they're going to have to do it all over again in a few months."

"Absolutely," he agreed. "Let them enjoy this year. We'll wait till we have to."

I'd just have to figure out some way to begin getting our shots before they knew why we needed them. Exhausted from all the heavy cleaning and weighty news, I'd actually drifted off to sleep over the Sunday papers when it seemed someone or something began shaking me awake. It took a minute for me to realize it was the floor beneath me that was doing the moving.

"Our first earthquake," Don said. It seemed a fitting conclusion to a day that had managed to shake up even the temporary stability we thought we'd finally settled into.

The rest of Don's weekend trips home over September, October and November proved somewhat less eventful. Even the time he couldn't drive the car when he got back to Texas until I'd dashed out to overnight him the VW keys he'd left home in California paled in comparison—a mere inconvenience.

While Don was still in Amarillo, I began to take the kids out to the base to begin our shots, being careful not to let slip what was really going on. To allow the right spacing, I had to begin right after Halloween.

Much to my amazement, I was able to pick up Cathy, Jim and Nancy from school, take them out and pull it all off without raising a single suspicion or question. So far so good.

But only up to the front door of our house. As I put the key in the slot, I realized it was already unlocked. Never one to leave a house without closing up and, even more obsessed with security when Don was away, I knew I was looking at a more serious problem than shots or even another move. Someone had been in the house while we were gone.

Inside, nothing seemed disturbed. At first. Then I discovered the lingerie I had gathered into a bag to take out to the washer in the garage lay scattered about our bedroom floor, the bag itself gone. A quick walk-through the rest of the house revealed nothing more. Had some kind of pervert gained entrance?

I was almost relieved when the kids reported their Halloween trick or treat bags had been rifled too, with much of the candy missing. It didn't take long to figure out it had to be kids who had somehow gotten hold of the key from the house's caretakers next door and raided the candy, using the bag that had held my laundry to carry off their loot.

I got on the phone to report to the next-door neighbors what had happened, and to my relief they arrived to change the locks right away. Perhaps they realized their own kids had to be somehow implicated but I couldn't be sure they did. So it continued to gnaw away in the back of my mind that the new lock was equally vulnerable. I could only hope the people next door had come to the same conclusion and would be more careful now about where they kept the keys and who had access to them.

Because we had found the local parish out of touch with contemporary Catholicism, we decided to put the kids into public schools for the first time. We soon found ourselves telling our ten-year-old sixth-grader Cathy that, contrary to what "all" the other girls in her class were allowed to do, *she* couldn't wear lipstick yet and no, she *couldn't* smoke or go steady. I was astounded to find parents sending kids her age to beauty parlors and allowing, if not outright encouraging them, to date. When I'd been teaching in upstate New York, we'd been distressed to have one pregnancy in the entire high school. Here there seemed to be an abundance of teenage mothers who soon evolved into single parent high school drop-outs.

I was unloading groceries from the car one afternoon when I noticed a huge crowd involved in a watery melee in the park across the street. Right after school let out, hand-to-hand combat over a boyfriend had begun between two young girls, prompting park officials to turn on the sprinkler system to cool things down and break it up. Privately, Don and I almost began to look forward to the upcoming move so we could stop saying, "No, we don't care who else is doing it. YOU can't."

We realized how very far off our world view was from that of those around us when the woman everyone knew was Don's married commander's mistress (and who worked in the same office) was seated at the head table with him at a squadron dinner party, as if they were husband and wife. Whoever had made the seating arrangements was following a protocol we'd never heard of.

During our more family-oriented Oklahoma experience, I'd become so busy with volunteer work and in Syracuse with typing Don's thesis and other papers that at first I thought I'd take a year off in California and relax a little. But I found that I missed the community involvement, and as soon as I stopped flitting around like a bird whose nest had been disturbed, redistributing every last twig and feather—something I instinctively did each time we were uprooted and resettled—I went back to "work."

At one of the first get-togethers for the wives of the people Don worked with, I volunteered to write the monthly news feature for our group. That seemed simple enough. But next thing I knew I was in charge of all publicity for a huge Games Day to raise funds for the various charities the base wives supported. This was followed by the revelation that, allegedly, for the past ten years, no base group had succeeded in getting a single line of coverage into the local off-base newspaper because of some long-standing ill will between a former commander and the publisher.

I wondered what I had gotten myself into now. About the only in-town contact I had was a civilian pediatrician who'd lived in the community for many years. Being such a new kid on the block, I decided to ask him, while in his office for one of our kids' checkups, if he knew of a contact person on the paper. Armed with the name of the features editor he kindly supplied, I called her, submitted the news release and amazed one and all, but most of all myself, by getting complete coverage. Gathering the facts first though proved almost as much of a challenge.

Games Day featured both contract and duplicate bridge as well as mahjong. Because neither Don nor I enjoyed it one bit, we had finally stopped even trying to play couples bridge with groups of friends that got together for that purpose. And both mahjong and duplicate bridge were total mysteries to me. I nevertheless went after my story, unaware that when I was told where I could find the person in charge of duplicate bridge on the day that the group met, I'd be a fool rushing in where angels knew better than to tread, even if I tiptoed into that cathedral-like domain during play.

Life went on anyway and nobody fired me. Then we came up with the idea of inviting Mrs. Curtis LeMay, wife of the retired Air Force Chief of Staff, as a guest speaker. Her presence would be sure to draw attendees. Because of that and my burgeoning confidence, I was also successfully seeking television and radio coverage for our big day and needed background materials on her to supply the stations and newspapers. After receiving no response whatsoever from repeated calls to the information officer on the base, I explained to his gatekeeper that I was going to miss my deadlines if he didn't furnish the information.

When he finally took my call, he began our conversation by asking, "Which Mrs. Brown are you anyway?" If he was looking for my husband's rank, I figured it wasn't part of my job to tell him—nor was it his to ask. He finally gave me the information anyway and we ended up with a terrific turnout—even when Mrs. LeMay had to cancel at the last minute and reschedule for a later time.

A few months later, as a special thank you to all the volunteers who'd contributed to the welfare of the community, I was invited, with Don, to an exclusive showing of the new James Bond movie, *Goldfinger*. The importance of such a tangible expression of recognition and appreciation for volunteer efforts was a lesson I would carry with me from then on. And I began to grasp how much it meant to treat volunteers with the respect too often reserved for salaried employees.

On the school front, when Jim's third-grade teacher heard I'd taught English, she suggested I work with her class to help them put together a class newspaper. It proved to be a successful and fun experience, even though I was dismayed by the discovery that the teacher routinely misspelled words she wrote on the blackboard and told me she considered spelling unimportant. Perhaps because she couldn't seem to master it herself? Again I was learning, this time about what was going on in the kids' classrooms.

Throughout the year, other wonders of California's late '60s progressive teaching methodology came to light. At a parents' conference just after the holidays, Nancy's first-grade teacher quizzed me about where and how we'd found the phonics workbook that had been a last-minute Christmas stocking stuffer. Nancy had brought it in for Show and Tell and the teacher spoke of it as a kind of gold mine for teaching reading she had no idea existed. I liked her and she seemed to want to do her job well but the incident underscored all that appeared to be lacking in teaching training and resources.

We were delighted to hear from Cathy's sixth grade teacher that her scores on the standardized reading tests were beyond those of a senior in high school. But she also wanted to know where in the world Cathy had gone to school before coming to California because she stood so far above the rest of her class.

Perhaps this was why, on the day I met a woman who had just come back from living two years on Guam, the first question out of my mouth was "What about the schools?" She advised I write ahead as soon as possible to the nuns at the Cathedral School in Agaña to enroll all three kids there. I made haste to do exactly that. By writing early, I hoped we'd ensure slots for all of them and have one less thing to worry about when we arrived on island in mid-July. I also jotted down all her other tips, like where to get the kids' school uniforms made once we had them enrolled.

In the meantime, we were determined the five of us would see and do as much as we could to enjoy all that Southern California had to offer. Once Don was back from school, we began to explore all the areas and sights we could possibly fit in.

Christmas Day was a serendipitous seventy degrees and we didn't miss a white Christmas even one little bit. In keeping with "when in Rome" we hung a Santa piñata in the backyard for the kids to swat at, blindfolded, with a baseball bat. We all eagerly anticipated the shower of candies we'd seen so many times since our arrival in California when piñatas finally broke open.

"There's nothing inside," Nancy said, looking at the colorful papier-mâché shreds hanging from our clothesline.

"No candy," Jim was the first to put the catastrophe into words as I added, "Oh, my gosh. I thought they came already filled."

Trying to make me feel better, Cathy patted my arm with a simple, "That's OK."

One can only hope it didn't take too many years of therapy for each of them to recover from the trauma.

It was April before we finally found a weekend to drive south and enter the magical kingdom of Disneyland. The timing proved perfect. For lunch, we stepped into a tropical paradise alive with birdsong. Beneath a canopy of palms and banyan trees lay an understory of ginger, ti plants, hibiscus, orchids and plumeria laced with lava rock and flowing waters. Even the kids enjoyed the flavors of fresh pineapple, papaya and coconut blended into our Pacific Rim lunches. With everyone caught up in this enchantment, Don asked the three of them, "How would you like to *live* in a place like this?"

"Wow, Dad, that would be great," they enthused, with unanimous excitement at the thought of such a wondrous location.

"Well," he announced triumphantly, as though unwrapping a belatedly discovered Christmas present, "we'll be able to do just that in July when we move to the island of Guam."

I was married to the Pied Piper. Instead of working behind the scenes at NBC, Don should have joined the ranks of Captain Kangaroo and Mr. Rogers.

From then on, the books on Guam that Don and I had been surreptitiously reading could be brought into the light of the kids' days too. It was fascinating for all of us to learn about the history and flora and fauna of our Pacific destination and discover that, even in these late '60s, Japanese soldiers still occasionally emerged from living in the boonies, bewildered to learn the hostilities of World War II had long ended.

As the months went on, it began to look as if our families in New York were all so used to having us come home every summer that it would be too late before they finally grasped they were each really going to have to make the trip to visit us this time. We couldn't possibly drive all the way cross-country and back between the end of school and the date Don had orders to depart for Guam.

Finally, everyone descended upon us at once. Both our mothers and fathers and Don's Aunt Ina from Montreal all arrived at the same time, at the very end of our year there. We shuffled beds, listened to countless family stories, took trips to Sea World, Disneyland again and everyplace they wanted to see. The hard part was finding out when any of them was planning to leave. It would be two years before we saw each other again and no one was in any hurry to pull away.

Savoring the time together and seeing all they could, after their long drives to get there, became their agenda. For our part, though, we also had to get ready to move, and despite its condition when we arrived, get the house shipshape in order to retrieve our security deposit. This time relocating was far more complicated because all our earthly possessions had to be sorted four ways.

There was what would go into storage, which included all the furniture we owned; the "hold baggage," meant to include everything needed in order to live for several months but severely weight-restricted because it would come by air; the main shipment, also weight restricted, but not as much so, because it would travel by very slow boat; and lastly, all we could stuff into the couple of suitcases each that went with us.

As a packrat, weight allowances had long been my nemesis. We had to pay for transporting every pound over the authorized amount, an added expense we certainly didn't need. It was bad enough putting up with all the damages that occurred and things that were lost, for which we needed to find replacements. The time spent getting the required number of replacement and repair estimates, then preparing all the substantiating claim forms, made it a long, arduous process. For this move, we also had to dispose of the disallowed items like alcoholic beverages, paints or flammable materials and anything that might stain if spilled that we normally squeezed into the car to take with us.

Then there was the car to be shipped—we were only authorized to move one to Guam—and the need to do it sufficiently ahead of time so that it would be there as soon as possible after our arrival. We needed to schedule pick up dates too for each of the three categories of shipment that we weren't lugging on the airplane in suitcases. Each day that we didn't know when our families were leaving—and therefore when we could begin sorting—it became harder and harder to know when to tell the transportation office to schedule. We had even received our date to be on an airplane before it dawned on us that maybe everyone planned on staying to see us off at the plane, unaware of how much had yet to be done in preparation. It just wasn't possible in a house jam-packed with company, even if it was family. Yet we didn't dare hurt them by asking bluntly, "When do you plan to leave?"

By the time we finally got the unspoken message across and said a tearful farewell, Don couldn't get a single day off from work to be there with me for the movers. I struggled by myself to estimate poundage, weighing things on our bathroom scale, as I sorted out the very limited amount we'd be allowed to ship "quickly." But it was all so new to me, a poor estimator—compared to Don anyway—and there was so little time left before pickup that it fast became the most daunting change of address yet. To prevent our going overweight, the movers ended up having to change categories and repack some boxes at the warehouse. In the process, quite a few of the kids' toys disappeared, perhaps finding their way into someone else's home. In any event, they never got to ours on Guam.

Now we just had to sell the Volkswagen, much as we would've

preferred to keep it. On one of his countless trips overseas, Don had saved money by making arrangements to buy it direct from Germany. But neither of us had any idea what havoc the fact that all the ownership papers were in German would create when he went to sign the car over to its new California owner the morning of our flight.

As it got later and later and Cathy, Jim, Nancy and I waited for Don to get back, I paced the temporary quarters, wondering what in the world we would do if we missed the plane. Finally, he came tearing in and we took off for the Ontario airport, a little the worse for wear, but on our way at last. The hours flying to Honolulu were a welcome respite from any more glitches, allowing us to unwind and anticipate the magical introduction to island living Don had had the forethought to plan.

To help transform the current year's upheaval of hearth and home into a joyful adventure, he'd requested a few days' leave en route. We would spend them on Oahu. Bathed in the lush warmth and beauty of Hawaii, just off the beaches of Waikiki, we didn't even mind our barracks-like accommodations in Fort DeRussy, or the concern that our kids' room was quite a distance from ours.

There were no chocolates on our pillows and Tom Bodett hadn't yet emerged to leave the light on for anyone, but it was the lap of luxury as far as we were concerned. From Diamond Head, Pearl Harbor and the Punchbowl to the Polynesian Cultural Center, we explored, walking our legs off, immersing ourselves in the aura of aloha.

One night as we paused long enough to rest on a bench on Kapiolani Boulevard, I fell immediately sound asleep sitting up. Jim took one look at me and said, "Hey Dad, look at the lady bum, asleep on a park bench!"

Maybe I really had joined the ranks of the hoboes. Throughout our Hawaiian respite, I'd even forgotten about the fact that we'd still not heard a word from the nuns on Guam about school for the kids.

CHAPTER 11:

Education is the most powerful weapon
you can use to change the world.

—Nelson Mandela

The massive green "Christmas stocking" shaped island afloat below us in some of the deepest waters of the Pacific Ocean riveted our attention as we got ready to make our descent. Although only about a quarter the length of Long Island and a third to a half as wide, it was the largest of the Marianas Islands—as well as the most populous. And we were indeed in the middle of the deep blue sea, farther from the Hawaiian Islands than they were from the mainland.

When our plane finally touched down at seven in the morning on the northern tip of Guam in mid-July of 1966, we stepped off into what already felt like a sauna. With little sleep and only one brief stop on Wake Island to break up our eight-hour Pan Am flight from Honolulu, we were overjoyed to finally be on Andersen Air Force Base, the site of our home for the next two years.

Waiting in the terminal to greet us, our sponsors, Ritzy and Ernie Preston, made us feel more like returning relatives clasped to the family bosom than unknown newcomers. We were so grateful for that, as well as all their help with luggage, that we hardly noticed the sump pump-drained marsh that sat just below our end of a poured concrete single-story duplex. Or, for that matter, the frogs and other critters scooting around the sidewalk and plantings outside.

Once inside we discovered Ritzy and Ernie had not only stocked our cabinets and refrigerator with welcoming food and liquor, they'd even made up each of the beds so we could throw ourselves into them. After the long, noisy flight through several time zones and the international dateline, the first order of the day was to catch up on sleep.

The only thing missing was the means to keep cool and dry. Although the rules sometimes varied, at the time of our arrival it was mandatory to remove all window air conditioners from base quarters between occupants. There was little debate about the fact that you needed them. There were no central units to cool or dehumidify the homes and it took two window units to do the job.

But, since there was no way for departing families to coordinate with those not yet on island, they almost always sold their air conditioners before departure. Unless the newly arrived were lucky enough to find someone leaving who still had one, you just had to hope the base exchanges had them in stock. As it happened, there were none to be had anywhere when we arrived.

That was the first of many phenomena of island life we had yet to learn about, like the fact that availability of everything, from frozen green beans to undershorts, depended upon the timely arrival of supply ships. Even though the *Guam Bear* had sunk en route some three years before, many a shortage was still attributed to its untimely demise.

Lack of air conditioning or even fans meant we had to leave all the windows and metal storm louvers wide open so that any available movement in the air could waft through. This afforded a quick introduction to the so-called "canary" of the islands, the ghostly lizard that slipped in through doors and windows faster than you could say "Watch out for geckos." Considered good luck by islanders because of their bug-devouring abilities, these colorless creatures clung to walls and ceilings with suction-cupped feet. And their black beady eyes could startle the daylights out of you as they unexpectedly met yours from behind a wall-hung light fixture or some other nook or cranny.

A more significant talent was their ability at the least sign of danger to instantly shed their tails and leave them wriggling on the wall behind, as the gecko itself got out of town fast. As we lay in the freshly made beds the morning of our arrival, soon bonded to the sheets by the humidity and our own perspiration, I whispered, "Hon, can those geckos fall off the ceiling on us?"

"Of course not," he assured me and, hearing just the answer I'd hoped for, I promptly drifted off for an hour or two's sleep with the rest of the family. Lucky for Don, it was months before I found out otherwise. When one fell into a pot that was cooking on a friend's stove, I realized even geckos occasionally lose their footing.

At a compulsory first week briefing for the newly arrived, both military and family, we learned of the island's beautiful beaches and reefs as well as the need to wear sneakers in the water when we went swimming. Both sharp coral and stonefish could inflict painful injuries. Speakers also briefed us on procedures to follow if a typhoon headed our way and suggested we soak the lettuce flown in from Japan in bleach water before serving it, presumably because of the use of night soil as a fertilizer. We soon found out on our own that power outages happened almost as regularly as if they'd been scheduled. A sign near the generating plant that the Navy maintained proudly proclaimed:

"SIX DAYS SINCE LAST POWER OUTAGE."

I tried to imagine what it would be like back in New York City if every few days the power or water went off without warning for an hour or more. True to Murphy's Law, it was always when you were just about to rinse something (and it needed to be done immediately or your hair or tile floor would never be the same), were in the midst of preparing dinner for company (electric stoves again), or trying to make an important phone call.

For us, that included repeated attempts to talk to someone in Agaña to get the three kids enrolled in the Cathedral School. It proved more frustrating than the wait for air conditioners to arrive in a shipment. I seemed doomed to be unable to reach anyone by phone any better than I had by mail.

When we finally succeeded, Sister said, "I'm sorry but we have not received any letters about your children. We can take the oldest in seventh grade in the Cathedral School. There's no room in either fourth or second for the younger two, but we can fit them in at St. Anthony's in Dededo." The upward island inflection of her voice seemed ironic, given the content of her message.

Still puzzled as to why they had never received my letter, I accepted the slots as offered, resigned myself, and since I did not yet have my sewing machine, headed with offspring in tow for measurement, to the dressmaking shop in Agaña I'd been told about by the gal in California. There I explained to Edwina Jose, the owner, that Cathy would need the pink-checked jumper that was the Cathedral School girl's uniform, but Nancy's would be the brown and white one for Dededo. For Jim, it was white shirts and khaki slacks.

"What, you have only three children and they can't take them all in the same school?" Mrs. Jose asked, sounding shocked. She muttered on about it as she wielded the tape measure, told us when we could expect the uniforms to be ready, and sometime after we had left must surely have put the same question she had just asked us to the good Sisters of Mercy.

Within a day one of the nuns called to tell us a couple of slots had just opened up for Jim and Nancy, along with Cathy's, at Cathedral. This time the upward lilt sounded more than appropriate. Excitedly, we called Mrs. Jose to share the good news that there'd be no need for two different colors of jumpers after all. But, of course, she already knew. Smiling at another island revelation about power,

I thanked the Lord for leading us to someone who could open the lines of communication and get us the school miracle we needed.

Meanwhile, back at the duplex, our "fast" shipment finally arrived, complete with vacuum cleaner, but not one dust bag to put in it. In the last minute California confusion and haste to get all the various categories sorted, I'd removed and discarded the dirt-filled one as I included the vacuum in the fast shipment. But, contrary to what I thought I'd done, I'd somehow sent every last replacement bag in the hold baggage, still locked away on some boat, months away from reaching us.

Gathering up scissors and tape, I tried refiguring other brands I'd found on island to fit, but nothing lasted long before popping a hole and spraying dust and debris all over the motor and inside the machine. Next, I tried to bring some in from the States, but the process of finding, ordering and getting delivery from thousands of miles away failed to beat the boat that eventually brought in the ones I'd shipped in the first place. We just had to manage with mops and brooms in the interim. It was all in learning to adapt.

Before we'd left California, I'd trained to become a Girl Scout leader, having promised myself and Cathy that I'd take on a junior high troop when we got to Guam. At first I was turned away. Andersen Air Force Base already had a Cadette troop and the Girl Scout decision makers didn't see the need for another. But there was no room for Cathy in the existing group and they soon realized there were so many incoming scouts that they really did need another junior-high-aged troop. Before we knew it, there were thirty-five girls enrolled and the chapel staff agreed to let us use the annex near base housing one night a week, provided we cleaned up thoroughly after each meeting.

Julia Chavez, the mother of one of the other girls in the troop with Cathy, soon came forward to be the assistant leader and another mother who knew a lot more about both scouting and camping than I did volunteered to help with the outdoor activities. I had never been a scout and still considered staying in a motel about as close to camping as I liked to get. But, with a family totally immersed in scouting, I was determined to get myself past that mindset. Don was on the pack committee for Jim's troop and Dee Simmons, another wife of a supply guy, also became a leader, taking on the new Brownie troop that Nancy went into.

Between scouting, school activities and the camaraderie of the people Don worked with, it seemed no time at all before we felt very much at home on our Pacific island. Although we were still basically night people, the need to get up early brought with it such breathtaking sunrise views that I felt these had to have been what Homer himself had in mind when he immortalized the "rosy-fingered Dawn."

We couldn't have asked for a community with more generosity of spirit than this one showed us. It included names as diverse as Shinohara, McWey and Hillman, every one of which frequently hosted us at parties in their island homes.

Mary and Matt Hillman both worked in Base Supply. Born and raised on Oahu, Mary had met and married the ruddy, red-haired Texan, Matt, on Guam, where they'd lived and worked ever since. Somehow Mary found time to host luaus in the floral backyard paradise that she'd created, to whip up matching muumuus and shirts for many of us and to pamper the two or three dogs that gave her so much joy. Her regimen of canine care including almost daily tooth brushing and bathing. Mary even added bluing to the white-haired dog's bathwater to keep her fur from yellowing.

At one point she had to leave for a two-week school off-island and entrust the care of the dogs to Matt, who wasn't about to go to the lengths that Mary did to groom them. Not wanting to be caught at what his wife would surely deem neglect, he decided, just before her return, that he'd better add a bit more bluing to the white dog's bathwater to make up for all the baths he'd skipped giving. The cat was out of the bag, so to speak, as soon as the now true-blue dog ran, tail wagging, to greet her mistress.

We loved the camaraderie of sharing such stories as well as expanding our culinary horizons at the frequent fiestas and get-togethers we were included in. New favorite foods included Guamanian and Philippino favorites such as Shrimp Kelaguen, Lumpia, Pancit and a flatbread called Lavosh. We even found we enjoyed pickled papaya when Cathy brought it home from school.

"Sister made it and brought it to class," she said, going on to describe the refrigerator that had stored it, which she'd noticed had to be tied closed with a rope, all experiences unique to being immersed in another culture.

Not everything, of course, was idyllic. The kids were also learning what it feels like to be in the minority and occasionally discriminated against in subtle ways. During our second year there, Cathy was chosen to be yearbook editor for the graduating eighth grade class. But, despite my protests that I had no problem with taking her back and forth to Agaña to work on it outside of school hours, Sister insisted that was too much and appointed a Guamanian instead.

For his part, Jim, born right at the peak of the baby boomers' generation, was caught up in an overcrowded classroom entangled in the New Math curriculum. While struggling to understand a teacher with a heavy Philippine accent, he was also learning more about base two and clock arithmetic than the basics of multiplication. On balance, though, Guam was good and good for us, especially as we got to know more and more of its people.

One day Sister Mary Benedict, a nun who taught first grade across the hall from Nancy's second grade classroom, asked her to bring home a cake for the Air Force Catholic chaplain's parents who lived with Father on base. We lived just around the corner but I thought it best to call first to make sure they'd be home when we got there with it.

"Oh no, dear," Mrs. Bush insisted. "You keep the cake. We get too much of that sort of thing. You just hold on to it and enjoy it." It was the first of many of Sister's cakes that we received, whether as direct recipients or as emissaries to others. Unanimously, they all refused to accept them. We soon found out why. Sister's baked goods were either rock hard on arrival or turned that way almost instantly.

But Sister herself became such a solid friend that it didn't matter to us whether she could bake or not. Her smiling face, lilting voice and generous heart brightened our days and opened many doors to us throughout the island.

Soon tropical living became second nature. We'd learned not to leave shoes and other things that might mildew on the un-air-conditioned lanai, to watch for geckos as we went in or out and to always bring large sheets of plastic to the outdoor movie theaters on base so we were prepared to hold them over ourselves when rain began to pour down on us in the middle of the feature.

Since Guam was a U.S. territory, there were also many of the usual overseas adaptations we *didn't* have to make, like learning or boning up on a foreign language, figuring exchange rates for currency or converting sizes to the metric system. "*Hafa Adai,*" pronounced "half-a-day," the Guam version of "hello," and singing some hymns in Chamorro at the Cathedral was about as exotic as our native language needed to get.

The Girl Scout troop decided it would be thoughtful for us to learn some carols in the native language so we could visit the local hospital in Agaña to entertain Guamanian patients at Christmas time. When we had sung our way through the building, we asked the nurse who'd accompanied us if we'd done OK with the pronunciations we'd worked so hard to get right.

"I don't know," she replied. "I'm from the Philippines and I only know Tagalog."

We hadn't thought of that. Like Edwina Jose, there were many on Guam from the Philippines. Others had emigrated from Samoa, Fiji and various locations in Polynesia, Micronesia or Asia. Heaven knows how many of the patients couldn't understand a word we sang—but they all showed great appreciation for our efforts, whether they understood the Chamorro or not.

Another holiday surprise was the chance to go to a live Bob Hope Christmas Show on base. Even more of a thrill for our kids was their success in getting the great comedian's autograph. After the show they got on their bikes and headed right over to the quarters in which such celebrities were usually billeted, waiting outside in hopes that they'd see him drive up. Much to their delight, he graciously stopped the car he was being driven in to give it to them.

Part of immersing ourselves in island life included exploring the territory and participating in life beyond the military base. Because we had always done that wherever we were, we were surprised to find that our regular attendance at the Cathedral School's PTA meetings never failed to amaze the staff. We enjoyed the colorful religious feast day processions that the school children participated in as well as liturgies at the beautiful Cathedral for which the school was named.

At one of the first of these, our fourth-grader, Jim, noted the absence of screens on the open windows and the fact that birds flew in freely and perched atop the main altar.

"Boy, this is what you call a really High Mass," he whispered in my ear.

Chapter 12:

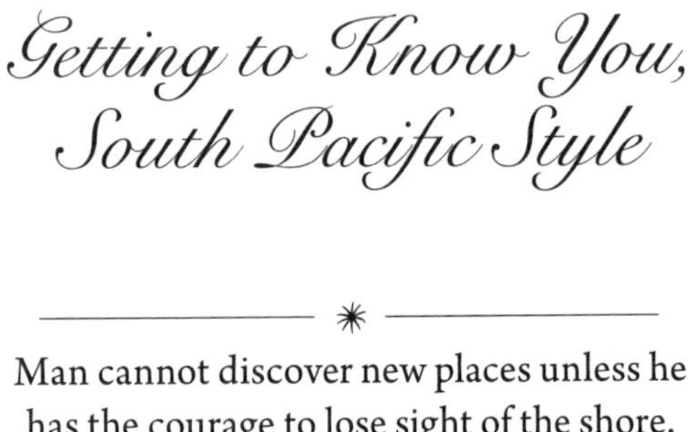

Getting to Know You, South Pacific Style

Man cannot discover new places unless he
has the courage to lose sight of the shore.

—André Gide

So much of what was normal here evoked wonder. Cathy brought home stories of the nuns' stapling fresh orchids to the bulletin boards for decoration, and we delighted in finding remnants of the ancient latte stones on which palm-thatched houses had traditionally been built still scattered about the island. In the red laterite soil of our backyard, we planted three palm trees, one for each of the kids to climb and call his or her own.

One Sunday on a family hike through "the boonies," we even came upon a pond with a rope swinging high above it from a tree. Not many kids get to be Tarzan or Jane for an afternoon as ours did that day.

Despite the fact that Don was working at least six full days a week, we tried to keep Sundays for church and family, heading down to Tarague Beach with our snorkels, goggles and fins for the afternoons. Floating in what felt like a colossal tropical aquarium, time stood still, mesmerized as we were by the rainbow-hued beauties that darted beneath us. Inevitably, one of us would have to tap Don on the back and tell him it was time to go home.

"But we just got here," he'd protest.

"Dad, you've been in the water for three hours," Cathy reminded him.

Other weekends, we drove as far as the roads went around the island, exploring Merizo, Inarajan and other island villages, discovering historical markers like the monument at Umatac Bay that marked the site where Magellan first landed when he discovered Guam in the early sixteenth century.

But the biggest exploration of all was the one to Talofofo Falls that our Girl Scout troop undertook. Just a couple of weeks before we set out to go, I read in the local paper that a troop of Boys Scouts had become lost in the boonies and had to be rescued. Given my non-sense of direction, this seemed an even more likely prospect for us. In Syracuse, our own kids had loved to drive with me because they said it was always an adventure. They never knew where we'd end up. The last thing I wanted was for our hike to end up like that, with our troop the subject of the next helicopter rescue. We decided to be on the safe side and enlist a few local boys to keep us headed in the right direction.

As we made our way along the densely overgrown muddy trails, I tried not to worry that the betel nuts our Chamorro guides were chewing away on would muddle their heads as well. And there were enough other things to be concerned about to distract me. A wide stream that we came to at midday had to be crossed, but fortunately someone had rigged a raft there for just that purpose. In turn, each small group that boarded propelled it across by grasping an overhead steel cable hand over hand until reaching the other side.

Although we had been forewarned of mosquitoes, nothing prepared us for the fact that they were denser per square inch than even the heat and humidity. Mosquito repellent, long shirts and pants did a fairly good job of protecting us until one girl caught her jeans on a branch, tearing a hole in the seat of her pants. She was so concerned because of the teenage male guides accompanying us that, without thinking, I took off the shirt I'd borrowed from Don and handed it to her to tie around herself to cover the gap. With only a skimpy sleeveless tee on underneath, I became fair game for every biting insect on the island but we got there and back and none of the girls got hurt in the process.

When Cathy and I finally crawled in the back door at home, a muck-covered, disheveled pair, Don ran for the camera to memorialize the day and my well-bitten hide, suggested we take turns soaking in the tub and brought me a martini to celebrate our having made it safely to the falls and back.

Long after that we decided one Sunday to take a family hike to another site that sounded historically interesting. After church we headed out for a midday trek to the "Tank Farm" where we understood a battle had been fought between American and Japanese forces in World War II.

Unaware of how far we would have to go, high up on an elevated plateau in blazing early afternoon sun, we found ourselves in a world of hurt. Unlike our trip to Talofofo Falls, that I realized beforehand would be formidable, I had no idea what we were getting into this time and had not even thought to bring drinking water for us or basic protection from the sun.

Nevertheless, we kept pressing on, thinking surely we were almost there. When we finally came to a place strewn with a few rusting Japanese tanks, it appeared to be more the site of their abandonment than a battlefield. And now we were faced with the long, scorching journey back to the car, still with no fluids, shelter or place to escape from the sun and regain some strength. By the time we had finally panted our way back to where we were parked, Don and I were growing more and more alarmed about dehydration.

Then we opened the station wagon and discovered a six-pack

of beer that had been left in the back from some previous shopping expedition. I truly hated beer and it went totally against the grain for us to give anything like that to the kids. But those half-dozen cans now took on the aura of an oasis in the desert. Desperate to get some kind of fluid into us, we decided to split the beer among us until we could locate something more suitable. The first roadside stand that came into view loomed as a kind of sanctuary. And the extra tall lemonades we all but inhaled took on the aura of the nectar of the gods. If nothing else, the day drove home the necessity of planning ahead.

The weekends we camped out on Girl Scout Beach with our troop, either Don or Julia's husband slept over in a station wagon, just in case one of the infamous wild boars in the area gave us any problems. A few months later we decided to hike the beautiful palm-lined base beach called Tarague to view historic beehive ovens, which dated back to the Spanish. They were strewn throughout the boonies north of there on private property, and we were careful to apply for permission to venture into the area. Not only did the family that owned it OK our coming, they even volunteered to send someone to guide us through its dense undergrowth, hacking a path for us with a machete to help us locate the ovens. We never would have found them on our own and we were immensely grateful for their kindness in leading us in.

Just as when I was in a classroom, leading a troop meant following a kind of curriculum, preparing for each meeting or outing and assembling and storing materials. At weekly meetings we might be practicing first aid, preparing for a fashion show or brushing up on the basic skills we'd need on camping trips. An assigned place in the chapel storage closet held our big box of supplies for knot tying, making trench candles and whatever might be needed for current projects such as making batiks, along with the usual scout songbooks and handbooks.

After getting the box out week after week for our current projects, we were shocked to return after Christmas vacation one year to find the entire thing gone. And no amount of searching by the chapel staff managed to turn it up.

Ever since World War II, the rescue squadron at Andersen Air Force Base had been doing Christmas airdrops of food staples to the outlying small islands of Micronesia. Since our things had disappeared right after the annual holiday flights and all of those boxes had been packed and stored in the same closet that we used, we could only believe ours had been mistakenly dropped at Christmas. What in the world did the recipients of our rope lengths, pieces of wood, candles in tin cans and songbooks make of these strange contents?

Much as we missed our families, particularly when we knew we could not be there for a cousin's wedding or my grandfather's funeral, our lives were so all-consuming with fun, friends and family that time seemed to fly by.

Don was the only one in his group authorized to fly, and about once a month he took a plane to Hong Kong or Japan, carrying military and their families off-island for rest and relaxation (R and R). For the passengers, that translated to vacation time and the chance to see still another part of the world. For Don, it meant the role of super shopper. For me, it meant becoming the "egg lady."

Inevitably, Don carried a long list with him of all the things unavailable on the island, like fresh eggs, that people wanted him to buy and bring back for them. After he'd arrive home late on a Friday night, it was my task first thing Saturday morning to bag up the eggs that came 200 to a case and deliver them to all those who'd ordered them but hadn't yet picked them up. It took half the day and there was always someone who said, "Gosh, Joan, I don't have any room in my frig right now, but, as soon as I do, I'll be over to get them."

I wondered what made them think we somehow had been supplied with a refrigerator large enough to hold a case of 200, along with our own perishables. Somehow we always managed though. Maybe I was learning more about adapting than I realized.

Even Don was amazed to find when he landed from some trips

that no one waited at planeside to pick up items like huge mamasan or papasan chairs they had asked him to buy for them in Japan. We didn't have access to a warehouse anymore than a large refrigerator. But these were minor annoyances compared to the feeling of being part of a close, sprawling family that might not be perfect but didn't expect us to be either.

We too were eligible to take a trip off-island twice a year but our first trip, to Hong Kong, could not include the kids. According to R and R age restrictions, they weren't yet old enough. Don was as excited about sharing the colony's great shopping, Star Ferry, floating restaurants, gourmet food and all the other wonders he had come to know on his trips there as I was to get to see them. Once we found a great husband and wife who would fill in for a week at a time for couples while they were away, we were all set to take our trip in February at the time of the Chinese New Year. "*Kung Hay Fat Choy*, Happy New Year, hon," he said, as he hugged me. "We're all signed up and set to go."

But, as I was busy vacuuming one day, I felt something pull in my neck and reached up, surprised to find I could feel a lump there. Later in the week, when I mentioned it in passing to Jane Senger, the nurse who lived next door, she advised me to have it checked out by a doctor.

The plot thickened when the base GPs thought it was beyond their expertise, referred me to the docs at the Navy hospital and the first of these to examine me described it as something like a fish's gill.

"You'll have to have it removed," he said. My reaction was, "Fine, but not until after our trip to Hong Kong."

When I dutifully reported in as scheduled, to have the surgery right after we'd returned, another doctor saw me and came up with a completely different diagnosis.

"This is a growth on your thyroid. The first thing we do is put you on meds to see if we can shrink it without surgery."

That was a relief. I happily swallowed the prescribed pills for a couple of months until it became obvious the darned lump wasn't about to budge. Again, I was scheduled for surgery, this time for a thyroidectomy.

"If it's cancer, that's the best place you can get it," the surgeon reassured me. "Thyroid malignancies are very slow growing."

Even so, I still couldn't believe this wasn't one big mistake, just like the fish gill thing. No one in my family had ever had thyroid problems. But I was no doctor, so I went ahead and arranged coverage for the Girl Scout troop meetings I would miss and any other commitments I'd need covered.

I worked so hard to get ready that by the time I had to enter the hospital the evening before surgery I'd developed a sore throat. Although I mentioned it to the surgeon who came by that night for a chat, he saw no reason to cancel.

It proved to be a short sleep night. First a lab tech woke me up to draw blood in the middle of the night, then lost the specimen and awakened me again to retake it. Next it was time to shave my neck and swab it with antiseptic. By morning I began coughing with a vengeance. They began sedation anyway and rolled me into the hall on the gurney to await my turn in the operating room queue, but only until one of the anesthetists walked by and heard me hacking away. He took one look at my throat and said, "We can't operate on you in your condition."

"But I told the surgeon last night I had a sore throat and he said it was OK," I protested. I'd come this far. I just wanted to get the whole thing over with.

"Well, maybe it was last night, but it sure isn't today. You'll just have to go home, get well and reschedule."

When they rolled me back down, neck unbandaged, past where Don was waiting just some twenty minutes after I'd left, he said, "Boy, that has be the fastest surgery anyone ever had."

When the nurse explained what had happened, the next words out of his mouth, much to my amazement, were, "Well, now that we're down island this far and I have the time off, let's go to the Navy commissary and exchange. I've never been there."

Thinking maybe I was delusional from the IV sedation they'd given me, I protested I was in no state to go anywhere but to bed. Instead, I ended up staggering around the stores behind Don. By the time we got home, I felt normal enough to make supper and head out to the Girl Scout meeting. There I was greeted by cries of "What happened? I thought you were having surgery today." The part that made me feel worst was all the friends who had already sent flowers to the hospital and then went and did it all over again two weeks later when I really had the operation.

The great thing was they'd found only a benign adenoma and were able to leave in part of the thyroid. Covering the scar even gave me the excuse to acquire a beautiful string of pearls on our next R and R, this time to Japan with the kids.

Chapter 13:

Sayonara

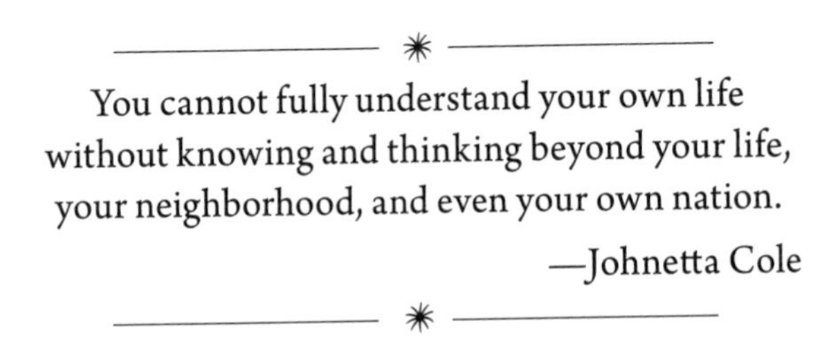

Like Hong Kong, Don had planned every detail of this trip down to the nth degree. We began in Tokyo, traveling on a bullet train into the countryside where he'd made reservations at a traditional resort. To get all five of us to the train station took two taxis and I wasn't looking forward at all to one of the kamikaze rides through Tokyo traffic that I'd heard so much about, Don in one cab and me in the other. But when I heard Don tell the lead driver of the cab he was riding in with one of the kids that we were a little behind schedule for the train—which we well knew was never, never the slightest bit late—I wanted to take out the beads and start praying. If we didn't break speed records that morning, we did for heart rates.

The first place we were staying offered rooms with alternating Western and Japanese style sleeping arrangements right next door to one another, but each had its own typical Japanese bath with a shower and deep tub. While the kids all thought it great fun to spend the night on the floor on straw mats called tatami, we slept equally soundly next door on our Western-style bed.

From there we headed to Kyoto and stepped back centuries in time, visiting temples, shrines and an ancient castle whose "nightingale" floors sang beneath us, the samurai's early version of a security system, our guide explained.

Before leaving Guam, we had borrowed stacks of books from the library and read up on the country and the places we'd be visiting. The kids had even taken out Japanese language records to help them prepare further. Don and I had peeked into the girls' bedroom and found all three kids sitting cross-legged on the floor around the phonograph, busily taking phonetic notes on what words they thought they'd most need when we arrived in Japan.

It was when we were on Lake Hakone at a small Japanese amusement park and faced with a long wait for a boat to take us to our next stop that we were very grateful someone had thought to do this. "*Benjo doko deska*?" our tow-headed youngest asked one of the women collecting for rides. It didn't matter that she'd just asked for the male version of a bathroom. Our needs were understood and we were pointed in the right direction. The girls and I were even prepared to find just a tiled hole in the floor in ours.

But we hadn't anticipated what happened when it was time to return to Guam at the end of our week there and our plane left without us. There had been a seasonal change in flight schedules but, upon our arrival, someone had given us the reporting time from the old one. To be there in time, we'd gotten up at four in the morning to catch the train from Tokyo to Fussa in the Kanto plains where we were to fly out of Yokota Air Base.

Now we'd have to wait until the next day for a flight. Traveling all the way back to Tokyo with all our luggage wouldn't be much help because we had no reservations there for the night any more than we did locally. While Don checked periodically with the billeting people to see if a room or two on the base might open up to accommodate the five of us, we spent the entire day in the terminal. Finally, late in the afternoon, after reservations appeared to be accommodated, Don got word from a kind sergeant, who recognized him as a regular Guam crew member, "We'll put you and your family in the general's quarters. But if a VIP unexpectedly shows up, you'll have to vacate."

Don cautioned Cathy, Jim and Nancy and me that we'd have to be really quiet and not call attention to ourselves. We didn't want to get anyone in trouble over our being someplace we shouldn't. I felt like a jittery fugitive, skulking in and out of the gated area as we came and went, shushing the poor kids every two seconds and altogether overwhelmed by the risk the good sergeant in charge was taking by letting us stay there. The rooms were furnished like those of a good civilian hotel, but compared to what we were used to that seemed quite plush to us. Other than my own overwrought worries, the evening proved uneventfully peaceful. No one evicted us.

When we returned the next fall for our second R and R in Japan, we opted to stay at the Sanno, the military hotel located right in the heart of Tokyo, since we planned to spend all our time exploring the city. Our week took us from the serenity of the Meiji Shrine with its exquisite gardens to the culture-shock and sensory overload of making our way through the Ginza shopping area, where the number of choices suddenly available to us felt overwhelming.

It was in one of the large department stores like the Mitsukoshi that Nancy decided she wanted to spend some of her saved allowance monies on her very own kimono. The saleswoman helped her try them on, fussing over her as she fitted each one and demonstrated how the obi should properly be tied. Nancy's blonde head seemed to emit a kind of call sign that brought Japanese women trotting from all directions to view the blue-eyed eight-year-old anomaly in their midst so that they too could join in the process, chattering in seeming disagreement about how things should be done. One even decided she had to redo things, altering the way the wide pink obi sash was fastened atop the long, flowing wide-sleeved blue-flowered robe Nancy had chosen.

Like the origami Japanese paper-folding the kids had already learned to do, as evidenced in the endless chains of Japanese bubble gum wrappers that Cathy had carefully created, it was all part of discovering another culture.

We enjoyed our dinners in the local restaurants Japanese style, seated on the floor, all of us adept by now at using chopsticks. Each time I picked them up though, it brought back memories of a meal while Don and I were visiting a Hong Kong restaurant with a Chinese friend who had left the table for a few moments to use the restroom. Don grabbed the opportunity to hurriedly brief me on the process of holding and eating with chopsticks. Starting out as I did that first time with the slippery ivory kind certainly made the more prevalent wooden ones seem almost a cinch.

We also experienced a late night cab ride through Tokyo after Jim accidentally opened his head up on an old-fashioned radiator next to his rollaway bed at the Sanno and we had to get him to a Japanese hospital for a doctor to stitch him up.

The last six months on Guam before we'd be headed home we excitedly looked forward to one last trip together, this time to Hong Kong *with* the kids, who were all now allowed to go with us. We were doubly saddened when we learned a plane had gone down in the ocean, not only because the pilot appeared lost, but also because it meant cancellation of our flight in order for that plane to be used on a search mission. Unfortunately, he was never found and we never got to go to Hong Kong as a family. For the kids' sakes I felt deep disappointment, but it was also mixed with guilt. How could one even compare missing out on a trip with the loss of a life?

The chance to vacation off-island included only the Pacific area. We couldn't get a free ride back to the States, even for a family emergency. Thank goodness the need never arose but that still left us unable to be there with the rest of our families at the funerals of grandparents who passed away or the weddings of the cousins who married during those two years. Missing those pivotal moments in the lives of our families back on the mainland made the distance between us really hit home. It seemed so cold to just hear about the death of a loved one in a letter.

My dad was working *Fiddler on the Roof* at the time on Broadway and, as always, got to know prominent actors like Harry Goz, then playing the role of Tevye at the Majestic. When Goz jokingly complained to my father that he didn't have anything on his dressing room to indicate he was playing the lead, Dad obliged by mounting a Star of David on the door, further cementing an already special friendship.

That was how it happened that, when my father poured out his sorrow over the fact that he and Mom couldn't come to see us in his own revised version of "If I Were a Rich Man," Harry's voice was the one we heard singing it on tape. With it was a framed wall hanging of the rewritten lyrics. The electrician and stage hand I called Dad harbored the soul of a Celtic poet.

Even on Guam it seemed I found more than I'd expected to remind me of my roots, like the afternoons I sat in traffic jams in downtown Agaña, looking out over the vast seas around me, wondering if I were really chock-a-block in a bottleneck of vehicles in the middle of the Pacific Ocean instead of stalled back home on the Grand Central Parkway.

The day I decided to answer an ad that appeared in *The Guam Daily News,* seeking substitutes to cover for teachers throughout the island who would be taking multimedia training for six weeks, Cathy, Jim and Nancy's comments again carried me back.

"Hey Mom, did you read this article about the New York City sanitation workers? They're striking for increased salaries, and they already make a lot more than you're going to get teaching."

Out of the mouths of babes come many facts of life. It felt good, nevertheless, to get back into the saddle and adapt, one week at a time, to situations that included teaching a multi-aged special ed class, a senior English class at the Academy, the Catholic girls' high school, and finally to the Quonset huts on Andersen Air Force Base that housed the elementary school. That experience and seeing rats running across the rafters there at an evening meeting made me even more grateful the kids had all gotten in at Cathedral.

Part of learning to use or make do with what you couldn't change was a soggy bog on the side of our house that made it difficult to cut the grass there. When a friend suggested that bananas flourished in moist areas and offered us four or five small trees, we decided to put the site to good use. Our very own banana trees grew by leaps and bounds, even faster than the three palm trees we'd planted on the other side of the house. Even though we were disappointed to find they were cooking bananas, rather than the kind we were used to, it was a sad day when civil engineering discovered and came to fix the broken water pipe that had apparently been there beneath the lawn since before we'd moved in. Adios bananas.

But there was another surprise more difficult to take than anything else we'd yet had to face in our fourteen years of married life. Don's next assignment would send him back to the cockpit on an unaccompanied tour in Vietnam. It was something you knew could happen, much as you hoped it never would. We had been happy on our Pacific isle, unlike some who complained of island fever. Our response had always been, "Hey, at least it's not Vietnam!" And now it was.

I wondered how I was ever going to make it through the year and a half—when you added up Don's time away from us retraining in new aircraft and a year in-country—that we would be apart. And where?

We were definitely not moving in with Don's or my parents. We were too independent for that. Besides, we'd been warned by families who had tried going that route that moving yourself and your children back in with parents was just too hard on all three generations. Maybe it was a good thing that we still owned a house.

Much as I hated the thought, the only option that seemed to make any sense was to go back to the home in Mount Holly that we had rented out all of the seven-and-a-half years since we'd left New Jersey for Oklahoma. The problem was I just didn't want to be anywhere without Don. But, despite our decision to stay together whenever possible, this time we had no choice in the matter.

There, we'd be close enough to visit our families on Long Island often. It also put us nearby in case of an emergency but far enough away from the more rampant antiwar sentiments of New York, we thought, to spare our children some of the backlash we feared they would experience. It was back to Mitchell Terrace, only this time we'd live there apart from Don for months and months instead of days and days at a time.

As our remaining months on Guam came to an end, I tried to pull myself together and make the best of what couldn't be changed. The Prestons had already rotated back to the States to an assignment in D.C., and Ernie was planning to have Don assigned there once this nightmare was over. Both Don and I began the process of taking care of all the things involved with the complicated move we were about to make, hoping that somehow it would make it all go faster and, if it couldn't go away, at least seem to be over with sooner.

We had the station wagon to sell as well as the two air conditioners we'd bought, arrangements to make to allow us to get back into our house and scads of yet another address change to send out to friends, publications and others. It didn't hurt either that every remaining minute seemed to be taken up by farewell parties our friends were throwing for us.

The morning we stepped on the plane that would carry us back to the States, what we really needed most, short of cancellation of Don's orders to Vietnam, were necks as lofty as those of a giraffe. Sister Benedict had sat up half the night in a convent closet, stringing together stacks of beautiful orchid leis for each of us. Another friend put together garlands of martini miniatures and olives for Don and me while the kids' gifts included snacks, puzzles and things to make time pass on the long flight.

So many flowers and gifts encircled each of us that our tears didn't have far to fall to spritz them and keep them fresh. And if the tears of joy at the love that embraced us proved insufficient, the ones we were already shedding over our upcoming separation stood all lined up, ready to take their place.

Chapter 14:

Stuck Between a Clock and a Hard Place

> To grow up is to accept vulnerability.
>
> —Madeleine L'Engle

Anticipating how long it would take our hold baggage to reach us this time, I insisted we each carry with us in our suitcases every last piece of clothing we might need for several months. In the case of the kids, I figured they might outgrow any clothes we shipped by the time they got to us. For once I was right. On top of the logistics involved with things traveling all the way from Guam to the East Coast, the longshore workers went on strike the summer of 1968, just when our hold baggage had finally arrived in port.

When we first landed back in the continental U.S. from Guam, we could have used some of those longshoremen to help us hoist the hefty bags we were each dragging through customs at the San Francisco airport. The officer in charge of the screening line in which we waited took one look at all we had packed in the first couple of suitcases he opened—and how long it took to mash everything back in and close them up again—then waved all five of us through with no further ado.

Just as when we visited Japan, we found ourselves overwhelmed with all the choices now available to us in the form of malls, department stores and supermarkets. It felt a bit as if we'd just emerged from being on some desert island instead of a detached part of the United States.

From California we flew to Michigan to pick up a new Pontiac that Don had preordered at a good price. Since we'd sold our old station wagon on Guam, we were switching to a sedan and planned to add a small second car after Don returned. From Flint, we began the drive the rest of the way home to New York. Seeing our families for the first time in two years made it a joyful reunion, even though overshadowed by the realization that Don would soon be headed away again, this time to a war zone. Playing in the back of our minds was the need to leave as soon as possible for New Jersey to get our Mount Holly house ready to move back into.

As soon as we'd decided that was where the kids and I would go to live while Don was gone, we'd written to the realty firm that had been haphazardly collecting rent and handling repairs during most of the seven years since we'd left for Oklahoma. In fact, when we got back to Mount Holly, we discovered things were even worse than we'd imagined. The realtors had moved, without notifying us, no longer to be found at the only address we'd ever had for them. We finally tracked them down and were thankful to be able to take the whole thing out of their hands once and for all.

To give the kids more time with our parents, we decided to leave them on Long Island while we checked out what kind of shape our home was in and got it ready for us to live in again. We borrowed a couple of camp cots from Don's folks and headed south, all set to roll up our sleeves and begin cleaning and painting.

But even low expectations about the condition of a house that had been rented for so long couldn't have prepared us for the shock. At least a hundred dart holes perforated every bedroom wall and girlie magazines and cigarette butts had been stashed away, perhaps by someone's teenager, on top of all the heating ducts in the basement. Then there was the fenced-in backyard, where a good part of our lawn and shrubs had been swallowed up by so-called "living rose bushes," planted by the people who'd bought the house behind us while we were gone. Where did we start first?

While I began deep cleaning inside, Don tackled the thorny hedge that had overrun our fence, destroying shrubs and lawn across a ten-foot-wide swath that stretched across the entire backyard. By the time our next door neighbor, Ada Gleba, came over to say hello she found Don out there, bleeding so profusely from his arms and hands that he looked like he was already in combat.

"This isn't right, Don," Ada said, her Polish accent emphasizing the degree of certainty she felt in the matter. "You have to go talk to those people. They should be doing this, not you. It's their hedge. On your property. You go talk to them."

It sounded reasonable. Though a bit uneasy about it, we walked around the block a day or so later and very politely made the request. The response was more subtly put than "hell, no" but not much. Taking one look at Don's hands, arms and legs, we could see why.

The husband, who taught school during the year and was now on summer vacation, unenthusiastically painting the outside of their house, gave us one of our first clues to what the next year and a half would hold in antagonism. Disapproving of the war in Vietnam meant scorning everyone ordered to fight it. As a military man, Don was a "bad person" for living up to his sworn commitment. And that went for the rest of his family too. To many people we were just itinerants anyway. We'd already seen hints of it in New York with some of our friends. That hurt more than the hostility of strangers. We'd see a lot more of all of it before the war was over.

After calling the base to seek legal advice on whether we had a leg to stand on about the living rose, we discovered we actually had a valid case. Rather than get into a lawsuit, though, we "compromised," with Don taking the very short end of the thorny stick.

For days he labored at cutting down the barbed branches while the people whose plantings had caused it all merely arranged for large sanitation containers for him to put them into. If it weren't for the attitude of most of the rest of our neighbors and the fact that we had so much to think about and do before we could go back up to get the kids and move in, I think I for one would've just given up.

Once again Harry and Jule Steinberg had come to the rescue. What tools we didn't yet have with us we'd borrowed from them, even their vacuum cleaner, then quickly set up our beds and got to work. We were oblivious to time when Harry came to the door with our first day's lunch.

"Jule and I think it's absolutely stupid for you to stay in the house, eat out and make do here. You're to come to dinner as soon as it's too dark to see what you're doing anymore. And then you'll stay with us. No arguments."

"No, Harry, we can't do that. We have everything we need right here. You've already done enough."

"Look, I can squat on these darned cots till morning. You won't be able to sleep on them. Now that's that. You're coming down to our place. It's air-conditioned. Yours isn't."

And that indeed was that. Our early morning getups began with the breakfasts that Jule had laid out the night before so that we could just eat and run without disturbing them. Each lunchtime brown bag lunches appeared, hand delivered by Harry. And at nightfall there was the inevitable phone call at dark, summoning us up the block to a waiting martini and dinner. It got us through the nightmare of day after day of bushwhacking, cleaning, scrubbing and painting. By the time we were ready to head up the Jersey Turnpike and out the Long Island Expressway to pick up Cathy, Jim and Nancy, we were feeling a lot better about everything.

But we still had to figure out what to do about transportation. Soon Don would have to leave for the Florida panhandle to train in the C-123 cargo planes he'd now be flying. He needed a car. But then, so did I. His mother came to the rescue on that one. At sixty-two, she had recently learned to drive for the first time and had acquired a small car of her own that she generously agreed to let me borrow for the two months that Don was away with ours.

For his part, my dad wanted to make sure that before Don had to leave we caught up on some of the best shows currently on Broadway. He'd already made arrangements for us to see *Man of La Mancha* and *Fiddler on the Roof.*

The last Sunday on Long Island before we began the moving-in process, the five of us were also invited to dinner at Joe and Molly Scarpato's, the home of Don's "No Sweat" commander in Oklahoma, now retired in Massapequa. Don commented on the familiar looking car already parked in their driveway when we pulled up. Inside, we discovered that when Joe and Molly had learned both Don and Frank Griffith from Joe's old squadron were headed to Fort Walton Beach and Vietnam at the same time, ever thoughtful, they had engineered this as a surprise reunion.

Newly returned from Germany as we were from Guam, Pat Griffith and their four kids had made the decision to wait for Frank in Levittown, Pennsylvania, just across the river from us in New Jersey. By the end of the day it was all arranged that Don and Griff, as all the guys called Frank, would drive down to Florida together.

Don and the kids and I returned to Mount Holly early the next week, very much looking forward to taking delivery of all the furniture we'd had to put into storage in California and do without for the past two years because Guam quarters had come furnished. We felt a little as if it were Christmas in August, getting to again use our very own beds, living room furniture, refrigerator and table and chairs after so long. Fortunately, there was enough in the way of good china and other kitchen things for us to make do until our everyday stuff arrived in the delayed hold baggage.

We certainly had plenty of sorting and putting away to take care of in the meantime. While the rest of us dug into boxes that needed unpacking, Don tackled the job of adding flooring in the attic to enlarge our storage space. But, just when the Welcome Wagon lady rang our front doorbell, we heard a giant crash as Don's leg emerged through the ceiling of the stairwell just off the living room. A misstep on the rafters had left him dangling above us. Thankfully, nothing was hurt except his pride. But the to-do list had just grown by another job.

As if we needed more, the night before both our families were to come down for the weekend and a big farewell pre-departure dinner on Sunday for Don, the seal on our upstairs bathroom john failed, pouring water through the ceiling of the tiny powder room below. It seemed the fun would never end.

Pat Griffin and I didn't know it the weekend we met again at the Scarpatos' but in September we would see our husbands off together from Philadelphia International Airport on the same flight, both on their way to survival school in the Philippines, en route to Saigon. Right after they'd boarded, we even found we'd each taken refuge in the same ladies' room to finally let down and cry. The clock of separation had begun ticking.

Since they were already back in school for the year, the kids, thirteen, eleven and nine, had already said their goodbyes at home. Cathy was now a freshman in Rancocas Valley Regional, and Jim was in sixth grade and Nancy in fourth at Sacred Heart. The younger two were also back in school uniforms, a lot more staid than the pink-checked jumpers and khaki pants on Guam, but at least they left no room for daily clothing disputes.

Cathy, on the other hand, was now in public school after three years in the warm climates of Southern California and Guam, the last two in uniform. I wasn't looking forward to taking on the role of sole dissenting parent in all the possible clothing purchases and debates that could emerge throughout the year with a teenager who suddenly needed a completely new multi-seasonal wardrobe.

Before Don left, we had talked it over and, remembering a concept I'd picked up from scouting or an article I'd read, we agreed to institute a clothing allowance. Other than gifts, which didn't count against the total, Cathy would have sole discretion over the allocation of the extremely modest fund amount agreed upon. This put the decision-making monkey where it belonged, a concept we went on to use as well for Jim and Nancy as they entered their teenage years.

When my father heard about it he seemed to think us a bit heartless and decided to help out a little. In addition to his work backstage on Broadway at night, he still carried on his own electrical contracting business during the day and knew one of his customers had some connection with a fabric mill. Always the Irish storyteller, Dad regaled him with the tale of all the sewing his older granddaughter was doing in order to live within the meager clothing allowance her parents had negotiated. Before long, boxes of mill ends started to come our way to help her out. In the months ahead, it kept her as busy turning out her own clothes as I had been making baby things for her when she was still in utero.

Don had asked Jim to take over as much as possible of the chores he himself generally did. We bought a power lawn mower, the first we'd ever owned, and Don instructed him on its safe operation, adding, "When you're not busy cutting and trimming our lawn, Jim, feel free to use the mower to earn some money cutting lawns for the neighbors if you'd like."

Our son had already shown himself an entrepreneur early on, coming home from kindergarten in Oklahoma one day to show us the change he'd gotten from another kindergartner for the shiny brass key to an earlier house we'd lived in that he'd "sold" him. So it wasn't too surprising when Jim soon built himself a regular clientele on the block. It included the older childless couple who lived across the street and regularly read the riot act to cul-de-sac kids whose balls or bodies landed on their property during a game. For some reason, though, they'd taken a liking to our three youngsters and praised Jim for his care of their lawn.

The Steinbergs were quick to employ him, too, but no one was too surprised when Jim came home and told us about Jule's trying to tell him how to do it. Since her instructions went contrary to those his father had given him on the safest way to mow a hill, Jim stuck to his guns and his mowing direction.

Young as she was, Nancy too pitched in, learning to iron small pieces and pitch in with the other two on snow shoveling and whatever else needed doing. Early in the year, she'd also asked if she might begin piano lessons. All that activity, on top of school, extra curricular activities, and writing or taping daily messages to Don, made for full days. But we all seemed to instinctively sense that in busyness lay the path to our salvation, a way to distract ourselves and make time seem to go faster.

When we were finally fairly well settled in, I applied for a paying position with the Girl Scout Council, which I'd been given to think on Guam was a strong possibility after we returned stateside. I hadn't anticipated that, despite glowing recommendations about the work I'd done with the Cadette troop in the two years prior, I would be unable to get a paying scouting job of any kind. The interviewer thought I wouldn't be living there long enough to make it worthwhile to hire me. The likelihood of Don's getting orders to go elsewhere in a year to eighteen months from then was certainly real and I couldn't lie about it.

Disappointed, I decided to return to the classroom. Although accredited to teach English on the secondary level in New York City and State, I lacked the specific New Jersey credentials to teach full-time. Since I also wanted to avoid being assigned to classes in either of the schools our own kids were attending, I limited myself to subbing in grades K–8 in Mount Holly's public schools.

We had also begun a marathon of producing baked goods to send to Vietnam for Don's Christmas. If we were to be sure of its reaching him in time, we had to get everything together and into the mail soon after he'd left for Vietnam. The carton grew to such a size we had to pay extra to ship it. Then, right after it finally arrived, Don was transferred from Tan Son Nut to Phan Rang Air Base.

"There was just no way for me to take all those goodies with me to the new base, Jo," his letter said. "I took it all to a nearby orphanage so the kids there could enjoy it." In the long run, that was an even better destination.

Like Cathy, I also spent a lot of time at the sewing machine, putting together some of the new clothes we all needed now that we were back in a four-season climate. Once it looked like he'd be staying at Phan Rang, I also got a request from Don for some kind of window coverings for his room in the "hooch" there. I even lined the plaid drapes I turned out. They were bright and cheerful, an effort to lift all our spirits.

As the months dragged by, though, I wasn't always sure I was going to be able to hold it together through all of this. But I was giving it the best I could, taking one day at a time for Don's and the kids' sakes.

I wasn't sure if I was going to be able to hold our old washing machine together much longer either. Over the years Don had already fixed it more times than I could remember and had lined up someone to take care of repairs in his absence. But one day, rather than again call Joe about another leak the old Speed Queen had developed, I decided I could save some money and troubleshoot the problem myself. My inquiring mind was now trapped between the loaded washing machine and the legs of the laundry tub.

When you're in a tight spot like the one I'd now gotten myself into, crazy things race through your mind. I remembered they said fire engines had rushed in to rescue my father as a young boy when he'd caught his head between the bars of an iron fence. And there was Don, stuck in Vietnam, with no one prepared to hurry in to end that emergency. Nor was there anyone here to help or, for that matter, even know where I was.

I tried again to raise myself up from the cold slab of basement floor I was kneeling on to see if there was any more room up top, between the washing machine and the laundry tub. Rotating my head as much as possible, I tried to flatten my ears as I told myself not to panic. The kids would be home from school in a couple of hours.

But what would they say when they finally found me in the basement, head caught between an unbudgeable washing machine full of clothes and water and a stone laundry tub bolted to the floor?

I knew what Don would say: "Why didn't you call Joe instead of trying to do it yourself?"

I'd been so sure I could easily find the source of the trouble. Careful to turn the machine off so its spinning vibrations wouldn't bang it against my head as I pinpointed where the water was coming from with my flashlight, I'd never even thought of the possibility of getting stuck.

Just picturing the ridiculousness of my position and imagining telling Don about it on tape that night made me finally relax enough to try one more time to extricate myself. Back and forth, up and down, I was never more aware of the shape of the human head than I became for the next twenty or thirty minutes. Miraculously, it seemed, a slightly wider spot between tub and washer finally converged with a narrower part of my skull, held at just the right angle to allow it to back out. Slowly, I pulled myself to my feet and teetered up the stairs, a bit woozy. I'd have to call Joe after all. The heck with saving money. At least the substituting helped bring in a little extra.

Teaching had started as a way to make the time pass faster and help with the extras brought on by living apart but it was also helping me to save for a summer trip to meet Don for R and R in Hawaii. By then we'd need "rest and relaxation." Summer still seemed such a very long way off as I led Joe to the basement to look at our ailing washer.

Most school breaks or holidays since the day I'd put Don on the plane, we'd packed ourselves up and headed for a visit with each of the grandparents, a chance to be with family as well as talk freely about the person we all missed so very much. When I got too lonely, I sometimes called just to talk.

To my mother, who never seemed to quite get over having lived through the Great Depression, long distance phone calls were only for dire emergencies. It always jarred me when I called her, she heard my voice on the phone and gasped, "Oh my God, what's happened?" right after she said hello. My heart said that enough, all by itself.

So did the news, to which I'd become addicted in all forms. Behind the door of our bedroom I kept a large map of Vietnam on which I located and marked the places all over the country where I knew Don was flying, bringing in supplies and taking out prisoners and the wounded, some mortally and in body bags. I carefully culled the information from each of his letters or tapes as it arrived. Whenever a place was mentioned in the papers or on radio or TV that I knew he flew into regularly, I listened and read all the more intently.

I felt like an intelligence agent trying to piece together what was really happening from the unanticipated enemy of a media who, although I didn't know it at the time, in many cases "reported" from bars well removed from where the real stories were. I waited to do my piecing until the kids were in school or in bed. No need to let on to them how frightened I was.

The house was quiet at night when I finally sat down in the family room to listen to the eleven o'clock news. Trouble in Phu Cat today. "Oh God, don't let him be flying near there." How I longed to hear Don's voice reassuring me.

It was already bedtime, and with all the washer fiasco earlier I still had not added my own voice to that of Cathy, Jim and Nancy's on the tape they'd started a day ago for Don. The kids and I each took turns recording messages in a room by ourselves so it would be a private time for each of us with him.

"Hi, hon," I began. "You won't believe what happened today," I said as I told the tale of the washer.

When I'd finished, I pushed the rewind button to replay what I'd recorded to make sure it wouldn't worry Don. By the time I realized my knack for messing up mechanical things had resurfaced, I had rewound too far. Instead of hearing my own voice, I was listening to that of Nancy and words to which I should not have been privy: "Daddy, I miss you more than anyone can miss a person."

CHAPTER 15:

Spiritual Galoshes

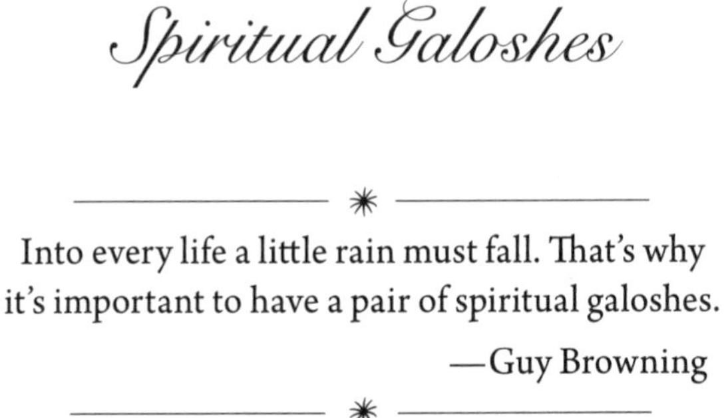

> Into every life a little rain must fall. That's why it's important to have a pair of spiritual galoshes.
>
> —Guy Browning

My heart ached for Nancy and the void she was describing. We all felt it. But I wondered how much harder it must be if you were only nine years old.

It was a far cry from World War II when the climate on the home front was one of support for those overseas. People like my father had taken care of the heating and electrical needs of customers who had a family member in the service completely free of charge. Instead, it was as if we were fighting a kind of guerrilla war on the home front as well as in Southeast Asia. You could never be sure when you'd take a bizarre incoming round from some unexpected source. To my surprise, even some of the people who lived on our block or fairly near us were hostile.

One Saturday while Jim was out cutting the backyard lawn, he came in, holding up a woman's bra, and said, "Mom, I just found this on our back lawn. What should I do with it?"

I thought for a minute or two about how it might have gotten there before I remembered the clothesline for the living-rose-bush neighbors was just over the fence. It had to have blown off.

"Just toss it back into their yard, Jim," I said. "It probably blew off their clothesline." I wasn't about to make him march around and ring their doorbell to return it.

He had hardly finished cutting the lawn when a livid Mrs. "Living Rose Bush" arrived instead at our front door with both her daughters. "My girls tell me your son just threw this over into our yard," she shouted.

"Well, yes," I began, taken aback. "I told him to do that when he came in and asked me what to do with it. I figured it must've blown off your line."

"But how could you possibly think it was mine? Surely I don't look like just a 34B?"

I bit my tongue rather than say that I really hadn't examined it or her that closely. Having left me temporarily speechless, she stomped out of the house with her daughters.

Now I was livid and in dire need of venting. If Don had been there, I'd have unloaded instantly. But this wasn't something to talk about with other friends in the neighborhood. I couldn't believe the ridiculousness of the whole thing. Still fuming, I made lunch. The phone rang about an hour after we'd finished eating. It was our apparently well-endowed-and-proud-of-it neighbor.

"Mrs. Brown, I just finished speaking to my girls again and the older one admitted that she was the one who found the bra somewhere and threw it over the fence when she knew your son was cutting the lawn." It was the next best thing to an apology that I'd heard in months. And one more good story to tell Don in a letter that night.

At the end of every day, we talked as we always had, but in those days, before e-mail and cell phones, we were limited to letters or tape recordings and the delivery time of the postal system at either end. Whatever was said, even the insignificant, took on immense importance.

Depending on the flow, it was the peak or valley of our daily existence. The silence of the times when mail was held up somewhere along the line seemed deafening and we lived for the joy of regular deliveries. On those days, we had at least "talked."

From Phan Rang Don told us what it was like to have Pat Nugent, President Johnson's son-in-law, as a loadmaster on his C-123 flights, shooing live cattle on to the cargo planes with a broom and cleaning up after them once they were delivered. Lacking refrigeration of any kind, the Army's Special Forces depended on these deliveries for their meat supply.

We even heard Pat's response to squadron beautification and the flowers he'd been saddled with trying to plant in the rock-hard laterite soil around the unit's building: "My mother-in-law," he said, "would sure eat this s--- up."

In Mount Holly we carried on our own fall and spring beautification, restoring the lawn, planting, weeding and watering. The winter included its own busywork, shoveling our way out of more blizzards than we'd ever had before on Mitchell Terrace. What really seemed ridiculous, though, was the fact that I might be wearing woolen slacks to keep warm while we shoveled the car out of the driveway, but then, if I were on my way out to the commissary to buy food, I had to first go and change into a skirt. Blizzard or no blizzard, at the time they wouldn't admit a woman wearing pants.

This assignment was one I would have dearly loved to see cut short, even if it involved another move. But the only van that pulled up to our door during month after endless month of waiting was one that was delivering, rather than taking away. It left our family room stacked to the ceiling with cartons of Girl Scout cookies. It also gave Nancy and me, as troop cookie chairman, one more thing to help keep us occupied. That helped a little to make the time go faster.

Once summer arrived we all tackled the chain-link fence that enclosed our backyard. I got more paint on me than anywhere else, and when they weren't actively painting too the kids documented all this in pictures to send to their dad. But we finally restored it to almost as good as new.

Of course, no one was lobbing incoming rounds over our fence as they were at Don and his cohorts, and in contrast to their situation we got to sleep all night, as best we could, on top of our beds and without flack vests. The only alarms going off at home were mainly inside me.

Out of wariness about advertising the fact that we were alone, we made a point of not talking to strangers about the fact that Don was in Vietnam, but there seemed to be enough craziness out there that paranoia had a way of setting in anyway. Like the night the phone kept ringing and no one was ever there when one of the kids picked it up to answer. I finally grabbed the receiver myself, determined to put a stop to whoever was harassing us. "Mount Holly Police Department," I said with as much authority as I could muster when it rang still another time, about ten that night.

There was silence, then the sound of a rather confused but recognizable voice of an old college friend: "Oh, I'm sorry; I was trying to reach Joan Brown." Trying to plan a New York reunion, she had been having trouble getting through. The phone would ring and seem to be answered, but she could hear nothing. I felt like a dingbat as I tried to explain what had happened at our end and hoped word would not get around that I was "over the edge." Visits to and from those old friends and family helped so much and all the efforts involved in just doing things with others distracted me from worry.

Any excursion we came up with among ourselves also helped. In the spring, we headed down to Atlantic City one weekend, just to walk the boardwalk, eat cotton candy and play a few games. We could stay only as long as our short end-of-the-month cash supply held out because we had to keep running back to the car to keep the parking meters fed. Somehow "beat the meter before we get a ticket" became a silly game in itself, all the more fun because we had invented it.

We finally had a pet, albeit a tiny one. We'd never thought a dog or cat would make a lot of sense, what with the kids' allergies and all the moves, but Norma Elser, my best friend from college, had given the kids a hamster to whom they gave the name Sam, short for Samantha or Samuel—because we weren't sure whether it was a he or a she. Sam was duly installed in a cage in our basement, atop the big table we sometimes set up the trains on and amidst the shelves of games and other toys stored down there.

Periodically, metal balls from a pachinko machine we'd brought back from Guam would spill out all over the floor, and we'd have to crawl around the basement trying to retrieve them. But that was nothing compared to the occasional hunt for the hamster when Sam tired of squeaking round and round on his wheel and somehow escaped from the cage. First of all he had to survive the long drop from the table, which he thankfully always managed to do. Then he was home free because box after box of storage items piled along the walls on shelves Don had built made ideal hiding places.

When we learned that the rat snake Jim's Boy Scout troop used in the Native American dances they performed had escaped in his scoutmaster's house, never again to be found, I was very glad I'd said no to the request that we give it a home and feed it live mice and other animate delicacies. All we needed was a snake loose in the house, even a benign one. A hamster was enough.

In July it was finally time for a hiatus. Cathy was going to the Michigan peninsula to visit one of her best friends from Guam, Diana Chavez. Jim and Nancy were off to the grandparents. And I was leaving for Hawaii to meet my beloved.

Rather than be upset that we couldn't all just go and spend the week together, the kids had been great, even secretly baking me a send-off cake. I felt as excited as a newlywed. We would start out on Oahu where Don was to join me at the Ilikai hotel on Waikiki. The next day we made the short flight to the north end of Kauai and a honeymoon-like site where they'd filmed *South Pacific*. Our idyllic cottage, in walking distance to the beach, was one we could afford because the hotel management was making it available at special discounts for guys from Vietnam.

Unlike the months before, the days of our week together raced by until it was suddenly time for Don to go back. Now I was faced with walking around Honolulu alone for the day, watching other couples still together and waiting for my red-eye nighttime flight to carry me back to the States. All I could think of was how much I already missed Don and would I ever get to see him again? The old fear and worry were again blazing on my mind's marquee.

I was to rendezvous again with Cathy in Michigan, where I'd meet her puddle-jumper flight as she came in from the Upper Peninsula. We'd reversed the process on the way out. But her return flight was so late that it looked as if we'd miss our connection. I couldn't believe it when she finally landed and United whisked the two of us and her luggage in a cart, direct from her gate across the runway to our fully loaded and waiting flight to Philadelphia. "Welcome aboard, we're so glad you could make it," the flight attendants chorused as a plane-full of waiting passengers gaped at us making our way down the aisle to our seats.

Soon after we all arrived back home, Don's Auntie Ina, as the family called her, came down from Montreal for a visit, sweeping in like the Lone Ranger to rescue us from loneliness and bring cheer with her jokes and Canadian "ehs" all "aboot the hoose." To show her a little of our own local color, we piled into the car and drove to the Amish country in Pennsylvania for the day. But we returned home to a sweltering Mount Holly as a wave of heat and humidity swept over the Delaware Valley and our un-air-conditioned house. There was nothing for it but to head for the movies or a mall for relief while it was at its worst.

Aunt Ina had also picked up a new card game that she was eager to share with us, and her stories, so much like Don's, punctuated our days with so much laughter that we hated to see her go when it was time for her to return to Canada.

Before I knew it, the kids were back in school for another September, and in a few months, God willing, we'd have Don back and be moving again, this time probably to D.C. Now a sophomore,

Cathy was nominated for class office but told me she thought she'd have to withdraw her name because she knew she wouldn't be there to serve. I gave it a lot of thought before saying, "No, Cath, I don't think you do. We don't know for sure that we'll be going anywhere, and until we do there's no reason for you not to run."

I stalked the mailman for letters from Don that would give us the word on when and where we were headed next and the mailman cooperated, as he had all year, ringing the doorbell when he had a batch of letters piled up for me after none had come in for days. The first one we got about the new assignment was one of the last Don had written about it, leapfrogging the one that told us what was actually going to happen. It sounded as if we were staying put, but until the earlier one arrived we didn't really know.

"Well, hon, they want me back in the cockpit. We're not going to D.C. after all. I'm coming back to McGuire to fly C-141s." I couldn't believe it. No move. We'd be staying right here in our house. Now, if only Don could stay safe until November.

When the day for him to return finally came, the kids lettered a huge "Welcome Home, Daddy" banner that they strung across the outside of the front of the top story of our split level, right over the garage, where he'd be sure to see it. He was due in about an hour after school got out and we'd worked for days to get everything ready. I'd even gotten my hair frosted a bit as a special surprise.

But just as the kids got home from school and it was time to leave for the airport, I realized it would be too dark by the time we got back for Don to see the sign the kids had hung. I dashed over to Grant's and bought a spotlight that we hastily installed to shine on it. Now late, I lead-footed it most of the way to Philly International Airport, arriving just in time to meet the plane.

There was so much to talk about all the way home that Don didn't even notice the hair. The one thing that no one could miss, though, as we pulled into the driveway, was the crunch of broken spotlight glass beneath our tires, and the darkness where light should have been on the kids' "Welcome home, Daddy." Next door a couple of teenage boys sat in the driveway watching and snickering.

But even our fury at these adolescent addle-brains couldn't take away our joy that Daddy was, in fact, home—nor our relief that it was only glass, not Don that lay shattered.

Chapter 16:

How Do You Do and Shake Hands

Crises are definitely invitations to growth,
and those who courageously accept these invitations will
find a new and fresh dimension in their love-relationship.

—John Powell

Cleaning up the glass strewn all over the driveway was easy. Shrugging off our disappointment that the happiness of Don's homecoming had been fouled by some dimwits wasn't as hard as we'd first expected it to be either. But we soon discovered we were embarked on another totally unanticipated task—that of putting our lives as a couple and a family back together again. In some ways it proved even more difficult than surviving our year apart. Yet, neither Don nor I had had the slightest clue that once we were all reunited we might feel anything short of euphoria.

We were ecstatic that we could at least be together over the holidays before Don had to leave again. He had enough leave time to keep him home with us until just after the New Year when he'd have to report to Altus Air Force Base in Oklahoma to begin training in a new airplane. In the meantime, school was in session for the kids, along with scouts, extracurricular activities and everything else that required life to go on at its normal pace. The only cloud on the horizon that loomed for us now was the reality that we'd soon face another two months of separation.

Compared to many who'd gone through Vietnam assignments, we had counted ourselves fortunate that we'd always divided our labors on the home front in ways that made it less difficult for me to manage for the year alone. Perhaps because Don had always been away so much, I'd routinely written the checks for the day-to-day bill paying. He managed the income taxes and long-range financial planning. It was especially comforting that the troops weren't required to file their income tax returns until they returned home from Vietnam. We knew that. The IRS, as it turned out, seemed to have forgotten.

For at least a year following Don's return, they kept dunning us to pay a penalty for not having filed the year before. We wrote letter after letter that apparently no one could read. So we tried phone call after phone call. Finally, they agreed that we owed no penalty but continued to bill us for the interest on the unpaid, admittedly not due, penalty. In frustration, I finally found out where the closest office was and drove to Camden to talk to someone, nose-to-nose and toes-to-toes. That worked, and at last the whole ridiculous cycle was interrupted and billing ceased.

We had thought it would make things so much easier that we didn't have to face another move when Don got back. But, as he was quick to point out, the house that had seemed so adequate when we'd first bought it now appeared to have shrunken in inverse proportion to our three children's growth. Repainting, refurbishing and rearranging, we decided, would go a long way to help the situation. And there was no doubt we'd soon need a second car.

While we worked through all of this, preparing for Don to leave again in January and celebrating his homecoming with our families in New York, even the tiniest disagreements between us seemed to mushroom from a pimple to a boil on the face of the happiness we each felt at being together again. In the first few weeks I would find myself in tears for no discernible reason except that they were tears of relief that Don was actually finally home safe. I had held in the terror of losing him for so long that the dam seemed determined to burst.

To my horror, I also had to admit that I had begun to crave a "They also serve who only stand and wait" citation for keeping the home fires burning. It wasn't that Don didn't appreciate me. It was just that no one else seemed to "get" anything about our lives, especially when the subject was Vietnam. And if anyone was aware there was a home front, they held those who manned it in equal contempt with the veterans.

Above all, there was the reality that, for a year, we had walked separate paths and were now struggling to get back into step. The dynamics of things like discipline and having two parents again to do what one had done for so long also screeched for a tune-up. Come January it would all require renewed tinkering when Don went out the door once more and would only come home for the weekends he could manage a hop from Oklahoma.

Adjustments even carried over to the car. The twenty-five to thirty-five miles an hour speed limits Don had lived with on base in Vietnam for the past year had stuck with him. Soon the kids began to complain, "Dad drives so slowly now. Can't we speed up!" We were all far from agile at trying to bend, but we didn't give up trying.

Despite the fact he was just back from four continuous years of tropical living and it was November in New Jersey, Don braved a campout with Jim's Boy Scout troop on his first weekend home. It proved to be a bitterly cold outing but he shivered his way through it to be with Jim.

In contrast, Don was constantly tossing the covers off in bed at home, freezing me out. I couldn't figure out why this was happening but finally threw down the gauntlet: "We're either getting an electric blanket with dual controls or a divorce!"

At first, even the new blanket didn't work. No matter how far I upped the temperature, I almost froze to death the first night it was on the bed. The next morning Don was equally upset that he'd been roasted alive.

"No matter how much I turned up the temperature, it just kept getting colder and colder," I complained.

"I even turned the thing off altogether but it got even hotter," Don countered.

Miserable as we both were all night long, neither one of us had been awake enough to figure out we'd reversed the controls until the next morning over breakfast.

We were hardly the first couple in the world to do that and it was easily fixable. But we hadn't yet figured out that we were having just as hard a time reconfiguring controls in the rest of life. And that it was all perfectly normal, given the circumstances.

One of the weekends that Don was home from Oklahoma, we headed for D.C. because Cathy, aware of how fast we could be relocated, was starting early to think about where she might want to go to college and wanted to check out Trinity College while we were still on the East Coast. It was fun for all of us to get away together, but at the end of it Don had to catch his hop back to Oklahoma from D.C. Knowing me, he worried about my ability to find my way home alone. Ever the thoughtful planner, he carefully listed the routes I should follow to navigate the drive back without a single missed turn.

Since not even Cathy was old enough to drive yet in the state of New Jersey, all three kids were engrossed in books as I made my way through Maryland, toward Delaware and the New Jersey turnpike. It wasn't until one of them looked up from reading and said, "Mom, we just passed a Pennsylvania post office," that I had any hint something was amiss.

"We can't be. I've been following Dad's instructions line by line," I protested. "We don't even go through Pennsylvania."

"Mom, I saw it. I'm sure it said some town in Pennsylvania."

"OK. We'll head back. We're supposed to be going over the Delaware Memorial Bridge."

But as we drove on and on, retracing our route, it became more and more obvious I had bypassed an entire state by so many miles that it made no sense to continue. I finally pulled over and, after finding the name of the town we were now in on the map, figured out the only thing for it was to turn around again, forget Delaware and drive home this convoluted way instead. Clearly, I had neglected to read down to the next line on the instructions after Route 295 north, but it still didn't explain how I had missed seeing any signs to the bridge.

That night Don called to make sure we had arrived home safely, as he had to Oklahoma.

"Well, everything went fine until we got to Philadelphia International Airport in the middle of rush hour."

"You what? What the heck were you doing there? That wasn't on the route I gave you."

"I know, but there wasn't one sign for the bridge and I didn't read down to the next line on the instructions."

"Of course there are signs for the bridge."

"Hon, I'm telling you. I didn't see a single sign."

On our next round trip to D.C. we checked, of course. There were at least seven.

By the beginning of March Don was finally home to stay—more or less. He was back flying the line again. But before long, he was tapped to be executive officer to the Wing Operations Officer. That meant he worked at the base and, although he still flew, at least he wasn't gone quite as often as the last time we were at McGuire.

The same was true after he moved on to become director of Wing Current Operations. It was a fun group of people that loved to ride one another about their ethnic diversity. At Christmas time we decided we'd host a big holiday office gathering at the house. The kicker was that I had to be the one to drive all the way to the Philadelphia Naval Yard, which was at the time the closest place we could find the reasonably priced alcoholic beverages we'd need for the occasion.

Don drew up a substantial list and I made sure when I tucked our checkbook into my purse that it showed a balance that would cover it all. I wasn't sure what to do if they didn't have the brands Don had specified on the list in stock, but he said, "Just ask someone who works there for help." That proved to be the least of my worries.

It began on the way over when I vaguely remembered reading something in the newspaper about crossing state lines with alcohol and wondered what I would do if a state trooper pulled me over somewhere on the way back and asked to look in the trunk. I decided to cross that bridge if and when I came to it and the trip over proved lengthy but uneventful.

When I got to the Class 6 store at the Naval Yard, I was greeted by the large sign, "Patrons limited to purchases of one liter per person." A quick glance at the people protesting at checkout told me it was being enforced. What in the world was I going to do now?

Desperate, I approached the man at the door who seemed to be a manager of some sort and explained my dilemma, brandishing my list. I thought maybe I had heard him wrong when he said, "Oh, that's OK. Just go in and come out again until you have the whole order." Did he realize how many trips that would have to be? Would the clerk at the register let me get away with it?

I began by finding out what to get as a substitute for the Lauder's Scotch Don wanted that wasn't in stock, then paid with cash. But that was all I had the cash for. Next, I had to find my way to the Officers' Club to cash a check for as much money as the daily limit allowed. There was no way I had enough checks with me to write a dozen or more, one for each bottle I checked out.

I couldn't help but feel uneasy at what I was doing. All around me, other people were being turned away from buying any more than one bottle of wine or spirits. And, in the middle of all this coming and going, the manager at the door who'd told me what to do was replaced by another. Would this one agree to let me keep adding to this liquor litany, one bottle at a time?

I decided to play it safe and try to alter my appearance each time I came in and out. Raincoat on; raincoat off. Enter bare-headed; tie a kerchief around my head. Rain hat on; rain hat off. Don sunglasses; remove them. In place of my normal glasses, I did without, squinting to read the labels. When I was finally done marching in and out, I was absolutely certain there'd be a trooper waiting for me. It had been that kind of a day.

Instead, it proved a blessedly peaceful drive home. And, despite all the readjustments we'd all had to make, home life itself finally settled into as close to a normal routine as it had been in a long time.

CHAPTER 17:

Gypsy Caravan

The truth is that it is natural, as well as necessary,
for every man to be a vagabond occasionally.

—Samuel H. Hammond

While Don had been away from 1968 to 1969, a new priest, fresh out of the seminary, had been assigned to Sacred Heart and brought a breath of youth into the parish. Father Flood worked hard to help out the Boy Scout troop and eventually employed each of our kids to answer the phone in the rectory on weekends when there was otherwise no one there to take messages. They loved the little bit of extra money and Nancy would even occasionally convince Father to hire her to wash his Volkswagen bug as well.

After Don's return we began to invite Père Deluge, as Don insisted on calling him, to dinner occasionally and it was always great fun to have him with us. Everyone in our family had an opinion about everything and, perhaps because the kids had grown up hearing Don and me talk so freely to one another, no one was afraid to express it. "Listening to the conversations at this table," Father said, "is like trying to keep your eye on the ball in a fast tennis match."

Often after Mass on a Sunday, he'd invite all of us to dinner at the rectory, something we'd never had a priest do before. The evenings of good food and even better conversation always seemed to end with a phone call from one of the parish youth groups though, summoning Father away just in time for us to take over the job of doing the dishes.

Before we knew it, it was 1971 and almost three years had gone by without a move. Jim was progressing toward Eagle Scout in his Scout troop and doing well in the same great high school in which Cathy was now a junior, while Nancy had entered the junior high grades at Sacred Heart.

Instead of the hand-me-down or baby furniture they'd all had before Guam, the kids now enjoyed teakwood knockoffs of Ethan Allen furniture that Don had bought for them during the flights he'd made to Taiwan. And we gradually acquired new living room furniture as well as drapes that, for the first time, I hadn't made myself. We even found time for the time-consuming do-it-ourselves project of repainting the entire outside of our split-level house.

We were also able to actually plan a summer vacation that didn't have to get changed because of some world emergency. The first year Don was back home we headed for New England, alternating our days between camping and staying in motels. Now I was hearing so much about young couples going Space Available from McGuire to Europe that I wondered out loud to Don why, after all these years at this Air Force base, we had never tried to do the same.

"Well, for one thing, there are five of us," he answered.

But I persisted. "So, if we don't all get on, we just go camping again. At least we could try."

Cathy was away for much of the summer between junior and senior year of high school at Rutgers University, having been chosen to attend an advanced math program. At first when we related our Space-A vacation intentions on a weekend visit, she thought we planned to go right away, before she got home, and without her. Of course, there was no way we would've done such a thing, and as soon as she came back in August Don signed us up on the list to try to get five seats to anywhere in Europe.

Things were looking very good for our getting to Germany until we found out it was also already time for all the Department of Defense teachers to fly over for the beginning of the new school year. On top of that, the day before we thought we had a good chance, a commercial carrier originally scheduled to carry a sizeable group of educators had broken, leaving a huge backlog to be accommodated on the next flight, the one we'd thought we'd be able to get on.

But all was not lost. We could have five seats on a lumbering C-121 Constellation scheduled to go to Goose Bay, Labrador, then on to Madrid. Were we interested? Don assured us that, while it would take a little longer, it would be fine. Besides, it offered the chance to see a place in which Don had spent a lot of time over the years when his airplanes broke down there.

When we called our folks from the terminal to tell them what we were doing, my dad said, "You're going where?"

"To wherever we can get to in Europe."

The voice at the other end was incredulous. "You're gypsies, nothing but gypsies!"

Once we arrived in Goose Bay, we didn't have long to wait. The next day we'd be on our way again. Meanwhile, we were able to stay in temporary quarters on base, with the kids right next door to us in typical G.I. metal bunk beds. Don described the snow tunnels through which we might have had to walk to the mess hall to eat, had it been winter. I wrote out postcards that pictured polar bears to each of our folks, telling them of our safe arrival. But I neglected to mention the gypsies were already booked on another flight the next day, this time to Spain.

It was two in the morning when we finally landed in Madrid, and even later before we were safely ensconced in hotel rooms. It concerned me that the kids were on a separate floor, but they seemed OK except for the spring sticking up right in the middle of Jim's mattress. It was the same place that the crews from McGuire usually stayed, and in the small hours of the night we couldn't afford to be too fussy.

Despite the fact that Don and I were the only ones interested and the kids came under protest, we began our sightseeing the next day with the Prado Museum. Little did we know that, in just a year or so, Cathy would end up an art history major in college. Then it was on to the bullfights and all around town to places like the Plaza Major and favorite restaurants that Don was eager to share from his own experiences flying the line.

Cabs were cheap but so small they were not supposed to take all five of us in one vehicle. At one point we were almost reduced to four as the door next to Nancy suddenly swung open just as we rounded a corner. Had it not been for her sister and brother's instantly grabbing her and then the door, we would've lost our youngest for sure. There wasn't much Don could've done that fast from the front seat and I was useless too, at the opposite end of the back seat and consumed with panic at what had happened. The cab driver just about had a stroke himself.

In the time we were there we even managed to fit in a train ride to tour the city of Toledo. Then Don got word that we might be able to fly to Germany by way of Turkey.

"There's the chance we could be bumped off in Turkey, though, so what do you all want to do?"

The kids unanimously voted to go, saying: "No matter what, we'll get to see another country." Maybe we *were* gypsies.

As it turned out, the only sightseeing in Turkey was in an Air Force base cafeteria before we reboarded for Frankfurt. From Rhein Mein Air Base, where we landed in Germany, we decided to contact my cousin Jean, her husband Bill and daughter Susan who were living on the Army base at Fuerth. When they'd come through Mount Holly on their way oversees, none of us had even suspected we'd ever be able to take them up on their invitation to come and visit.

We were a kind of oddity in the large Irish McAndrews family in which our fathers had grown up. Born just a little over a month apart, the two of us were the only ones who had any military connection. Even during World War II, only one uncle by marriage had been in the service.

Another cousin, Ann, who'd been the flower girl at our wedding, was there too, on her way home from a college graduation trip. Although we didn't get to see her for long because she was just leaving, we knew news of our visit would travel fast in our family. Before we were home, my father had already gotten word of our mini family reunion. We were no longer gypsies.

Even on the home front. We remained in place for still another year, much to our astonishment. When, around 1972, I ran into the woman from Girl Scouts who'd interviewed me for a position when Don was in Vietnam, she stuttered, "Why, you're still here." I just smiled and said, "Yes," really wanting to add, "And isn't it a shame that you didn't take a chance and hire me?"

Cathy, who'd attended seven schools from first to twelfth grades, had actually gotten to remain in the same high school for all four years. All the moves seemed not to have hurt her education. She was accepted at Princeton and selected as one of only two Presidential Scholars from the state of New Jersey. Don and I were invited to the presentation ceremony in D.C. at which Vice-President Agnew officiated in place of President Nixon. She spent the summer working at the base, and before we knew it we were watching the first of our kids solo from the nest.

In June of that year, Don had changed jobs again, taking command of the 30th Military Airlift Squadron, then an imposing family of some 500 people. As in our first time at McGuire, people made their homes as far away as Long Island, North Jersey and the Jersey shore. But, looking back on our own moving experiences, Don and I were determined to see that everyone was welcomed in some way, no matter where they lived.

We soon had all the help anyone could want. Joe and Winnie Lemyre, a wonderful couple, raised in nearby Philadelphia, had just been reassigned from Italy and bought a hundred-year-old house in nearby Lumberton for their new home. The only problem looming on the horizon for us now was the very real possibility that Don's new job would mean our having to give up our house again and move to base housing. Eventually, even that threat went away and we were able to stay put.

Don and I, along with Winnie and Joe, were the "oldtimers" now and tried to put to use all the good and bad things gleaned from others in the past. I found that typing the roster of wives' names and phone numbers myself helped reinforce my memory of people's names. If newcomers lived too far away to visit them, I tried to at least call on the phone to welcome them. I kept notes on what I found out about children and family to help me remember people and really get to know them.

The wives got together monthly for coffees and the squadron as a whole for cocktail parties. As a group, we were always being called upon to help with fundraising or other volunteer activities like the Red Cross, Thrift Shop and Family Services. Then there was the question of who would host our various events.

I'd always hated it when a commander's wife passed around a sign-up sheet at functions to get people to fill a slot. It seemed like putting it all on the backs of those who came out to things. And maybe the job you were coerced into signing up for wasn't even the kind you liked, no less excelled at doing.

As we got to know people, I tried to match requests to talents and interests, making private one-on-one conversations the basis for finding volunteers, rather than passing around that infamous piece of paper. The last thing I wanted to do was push anyone. Somehow, the more we all got to know one another, the more fun even the work became.

It seemed natural, too, for Don and me to host a fair share of things ourselves. I had several gals willing to help with the baking for the first coffee I had at the house. But as the appointed hour drew closer and closer, I became increasingly nervous because no one else on the committee had arrived with the rest of the food. Would everyone be able to find our house? If they could, where were they?

When the first wife finally showed up, I practically knocked her over as I rushed out to greet her, saying, "Thank God, you're here."

It didn't seem to matter that I was often, at least at first, that blithering worry-wart, terrified of getting up and speaking in public, even on the relatively small scale that I now had to do. As soon as I calmed down about the whole thing, I began to enjoy the challenge. And the Lemyres were right there with ideas and assistance every step of the way. Winnie volunteered their house for the wives' holiday party and Joe proved one of the most conscientious Ops Officers anyone could want. Our closeness made it all the more traumatic when, after months of working and playing together, Don called from the Army hospital that provided our medical care to tell me Joe had just had a massive heart attack.

"I'll be right home to pick you up so we can go together to get Winnie. She doesn't know yet. I didn't want to call and tell her on the phone." Their youngest child, Dan, was only four at the time.

The damage was sufficient that Joe was medically retired. A heavy smoker, he had a family history of cholesterol problems but was eventually able to return to work as an accountant for the state. Both we and the Air Force had suffered a tremendous loss.

It would not be the last. A few months later, in June 1973, we got the call from Don's mother that his dad had had a heart attack. I thanked God that Don was home and Cathy back from college so we were all able to get right up to Long Island for a weekend with the kind and jovial man that I called Dad, just as I did my own father. We never suspected it would be our last time together. In mid-July, while Don was away on a trip in Japan, his mother called again, this time to tell us Dad had suffered a fatal coronary while cutting the lawn.

The squadron summoned Don home, being careful to wait to break the news until he was on the ground, rather than flying an airplane. Again we hurried to New York, this time to help plan his dad's funeral. We were all devastated—and concerned as well. His mother had never had anything to do with their finances. And, to make matters worse, we soon discovered that, other than social security, the pension from the British publishing firm Dad had worked for for so many years, a pension he believed would continue after his death, was no more. Secured by a handshake, there was no paperwork to back it up now that the company had been taken over by a conglomerate. Handshakes were passé. No paperwork? No pension.

Our only consolation was that, although Don had just been promoted, he'd been told there would be no move. He'd have to give up the squadron but he'd be reassigned at McGuire.

The assurance lasted just long enough to allow Nancy to graduate from Sacred Heart, us to sit down with his mom to go over things like how to write a check and balance a checkbook and Don to swear Father Flood into the Air Force as a chaplain.

Everything changed when someone at Military Airlift Command headquarters discovered Don's previous logistics experience and instantly tapped him for a non-flying headquarters' supply job at Scott Air Force Base. He'd have to be in Southern Illinois in just a matter of weeks. And, under new regulations, he'd no longer be able to fly. Despite the promotion, it meant a cut in pay as well.

We had planned all along that the next time we were transferred we'd sell the house. On top of our concern now at having to leave Don's mother, we were faced with getting the house on the market, taking the two younger kids out of a good high school and leaving Cath behind in college.

Should we think about buying another house in Illinois or move on base? What were the high schools like out there? There was so much to do and so little time. We quickly contacted a realtor to start showing our house, got the kids' records from school and made another trip to New York to do what we could before we left.

In the process of getting things together for Long Island, I told Don we needed to touch up the paint that had chipped in a few places in the rec room in case the realtor we'd contracted with started showing the place before we got back. His reaction was swift: "Jo, you're being ridiculous, and besides, there's no time."

Stubborn as always, I decided I could get to it before he even knew I had gone ahead anyway. Rushing to start and finish before he could discover what I was up to, I upended the can, spilling paint all over the rug and tiled floor. Now we really did need to do something. Despite the fact that the paint was latex, it took forever to clean up, even with Don pitching in to help. He didn't even tell me, "I told you so."

The more the five of us talked about where to live in Illinois, the more we leaned toward taking base housing this time. That way we wouldn't have to come up with the money for another home before this one had sold. We decided to combine a quick trip west to look over the situation while Jim was at a long-scheduled Boy Scout Jamboree in Pennsylvania. We were to pick him up from it on the way back.

Once we got to Scott, we accepted a duplex available on base in what were called the Colonials. It wasn't great, but we figured we could manage. We always did. We went ahead and bought the living room and hall carpeting and some yellow and green striped kitchen curtains from the last tenants in hopes that it would make the two apartments that had been spliced together to form each unit look more welcoming when the kids first laid eyes on it. We visited the high school in Mascoutah to deliver their transfer records. From what we heard, the school had been an award winner a few years back, but we didn't get to talk to anyone who had much to say about its present status.

Then we began the drive back, calling the Boy Scout camp, as agreed, to find out where and when to pick Jim up. Instead, we were told there was no way we could reach him directly. All we could do was leave a message for him to call us back in a motel along the way. That was the beginning of the nightmare.

No call ever came. When we checked at the house to see if he'd left a message there, Nancy told us he hadn't. As the hours dragged on and we kept phoning the camp in the hopes of finding out what to do but getting nowhere, we checked one more time at home before deciding there was nothing for it but to drive the rest of the way home in hopes that he'd be coming in the next day on the bus instead. Nancy's distress mirrored our own. All of our imaginations were working overtime. Why couldn't the camp officials tell us where Jim was?

The drive home became the longest we'd ever had to make. We prayed all this was just because Jim had never gotten any of our messages but we were both holding our breath the next day as we drove over to the bus station in Philadelphia for what was our last hope at finding the son we and the Scouts had somehow lost track of.

He was one of the very last to step off the bus, never having gotten a single one of our messages. "Oh, Jim," I stammered, choking on the tears that started as soon as I reached out to hug him. "Not now, Mom," he said, embarrassed at my emotional display, motioning with his chin to the scout friend he'd been sitting with on the bus. I was so grateful to see him safe and sound, I didn't even argue.

After five years, it was suddenly moving time all over again. School in Illinois resumed the last week of August and we didn't want Jim and Nancy, who would again be the new kids on the block, to be latecomers as well. But we were soon reminded that the end of summer is one of the busiest times of year for moving. There was no way the people on the base could schedule a door-to-door move for us before school began. And I didn't want our stuff going into storage. That was how you incurred more damages.

Since Don also had to report in at Scott, I suggested he head out in the larger, air conditioned Pontiac with Jim and Nancy so they could all get there in time. Cathy didn't yet have to be back to college so she could stay behind to help me handle the move, then drive out in the Volkswagen with me before we had to put her on a plane back to Princeton.

It was no picnic. After the other three had left, Cathy and I rushed around washing windows, mowing and edging the lawn, weeding the flower beds and, for my part, worrying incessantly about going overweight on our shipment. After five years in one place, that could prove an expensive proposition. At dark each day, we'd finally drag ourselves to the kitchen to make supper out of the dregs of food left in the house. Even the half-spent candles I lit for fun—and to disguise what we were eating—didn't make it any more palatable.

Don and the kids called to say they'd arrived safely. But they waited a day to drop their bombshell. The teachers had gone on strike in the Mascoutah district. No one knew how long it would last. And, oh, by the way, it was so hot and humid the three of them had spent the last two days at the swimming pool.

Cathy and I had been spending ours in a pool, too, but it was filled with our own perspiration. When, at last, we were ready and the movers arrived to pack and load, I was still so obsessed with weight that I begged to accompany the van to the scales and stood there praying. Much to my relief, we were still within the allowed limits. After a good but short night's sleep at Howard Johnson's, we jumped into the VW to begin our trek west. It was only then that I remembered there was no air conditioning in this car. And there was no one to blame but myself.

Chapter 18:

The Winter of Our Discontent

If the world seems cold to you, kindle fires to warm it.

—Lucy Larcom

Despite the heat, humidity and our fatigue, Cathy and I enjoyed the drive, savoring it as a rare chance for just the two of us to be together—and vowing to never let the others forget how easy they'd had it.

But the Volkswagen's lack of air conditioning proved to be not the only thing I'd failed to give any thought to. Since Don and I had been to Illinois to find a place to live, another layer of chalky paint had been added to all that had long ago sealed most of the windows shut in the jerrybuilt house we would now call home. You could trace the forty-year history of the government duplex in the layers. As a result, the kitchen and utility room curtains we'd bought—and their warmth—were nowhere in sight when we went to move in. Although at first it seemed they had been trashed by the painters, we finally found them stowed away in one of the upstairs hall closets.

By the time the van arrived on Labor Day weekend of 1973, the movers could find no temporary labor to help them unload. At first we feared they would wait until the following Tuesday to begin. Eager to get settled, we were much relieved when they decided to go ahead and hired Jim to help. As in every move, we all pitched in to try to at least get boxes into the right rooms, make sure everything we'd shipped arrived and note any missing or damaged items.

It was a strange house, made up of what originally were two units, now merged into one. All the rooms were narrower than twelve feet wide, and most were mere cubicles. But the living room and master bedroom above it, formerly the living room for the second-floor apartment, were each twenty feet long, giving them a kind of bowling alley effect.

Weeks later I was still trying to unpack and find a place for everything, particularly in the kitchen, repeatedly taking things out and rearranging them in the hopes of coming up with a more efficient way to store them. Stacks of pots and pans perched precariously on our one kitchen counter, waiting to be put away on the metal racks that served as cabinet shelves. The feet on the electrical appliances kept falling between the wires, where they hung, awkwardly stuck, a little like every one of us seemed to be this time round.

Most days it was the creaking hinges of the rusted screen door as it opened and swung shut that announced one of the kids was home from school. Before I could get there, Jim would already be bolting up the stairs to his room.

Since the move and changing high schools, our son had become a different person. He didn't look anyone right in the eye anymore. Strands of dark blonde hair hung in his face, always covering half of it. At home he closeted his tall, lanky frame in his room and read, stereo earphones permanently attached to his head. Underneath the sullen blue eyes that used to sparkle, a volcano smoldered, ready to erupt.

Even Nancy no longer fit the nickname "Sunny" given her by New Jersey friends. I sighed as I remembered her happiness early last summer, when she'd volunteered in a veterinarian's clinic to see if it was a field she was interested in pursuing someday. We'd all roared with laughter at her demonstration of how to take a goat's temperature, as she pantomimed lifting its tail in the air and thrusting a rectal thermometer beneath.

But that was then, and we had to deal with now. I climbed the steep steps upstairs and knocked softly on Jim's door. No answer. Of course, the earphones were in place. Pounding harder I pushed firmly on the warped door, enough to budge it to signal to Jim I wanted to talk to him.

He twisted the controls to "off," spun round in his chair and tore off the headset. "What do you want?" he bristled.

"How was your day, Jim? You didn't even stop to say hi when you came in."

"Terrible, as usual. Guidance says there will be absolutely no third year French. So I'm stuck with starting over again in Spanish One. I need four years of one language, not two and two. I hate it here. I wish we'd never left Mount Holly."

Don's endless optimism was taking a beating as well. We lived near enough to the runway for him to hear the roar of the jet engines and see the planes taking off without him. A seemingly dead end, non-flying job at less pay seemed an odd way to treat someone who'd just gotten promoted. And our beautiful New Jersey split-level still sat empty. A sale was pending but we were told it would take weeks for the VA to grind out the paperwork for the sale because the husband in the family that wanted it was overseas.

"Hon, I am really worried about the two kids," I told Don that night. "They go right to their rooms when they come home and just stay there. They don't seem to be making any friends. They hardly talk to me anymore.

"Jim is so crushed by the move I'm not sure how he's going to get over it. I can't break through to him. It's as if even God isn't listening." I longed for miraculous solutions to pour from Don's lips.

"Jo, you know you always worry too much. Give us time. We'll be OK. You can't expect everyone to adjust overnight." I wanted to believe I was just being impatient but we were talking weeks, even months, not days.

Maybe having a taste of all that time in one place was a very real part of Jim's problems. Finally, after years of moving every year or two, we'd been able to stay put and our oldest had gotten to graduate from the same high school she'd started out in. In his two years in the same high school Jim had also planted deep roots. I was sure he was feeling the pain of their being abruptly ripped up. And the soil in which we had replanted him and his sister was poor by comparison.

As I lay awake at night trying to figure out what we could possibly do to make things better, I could hear the lonely train whistle whining clearly in the night. My mother had always said that meant rain was on its way. Were we too in for stormy weather?

The man who had held Don's job before him had lost a sixteen-year-old son to that train, on the tracks that crossed the road between town and the area where we lived. The boy either hadn't heard the warning or had tried to beat the engine. Or so the story went.

I shivered as I got into bed. Were we not hearing our children's lonely mournful warnings either? Was our family headed for a crash?

"I hate it here. I wish we had never left New Jersey." Jim's voice echoed and stayed with me all that night through a fitful sleep and for the months to come.

During the day I continued the struggle to find places to put everything away. Packrat that I was, I was now faced with all the boxes of memorabilia I'd saved. Too much, but how could I part with these links with our past?

The articles Jim had written for each issue of the school paper topped one carton, and reminded me of the shy pleasure he had taken in bringing each one home as it appeared. In the last issue his picture was on the front page with the announcement he would be editor the following year. An incoming junior, he'd been chosen to fill what had always been a senior's position. That newspaper had been a big piece of his world.

Now that world was bounded by corn and soybean fields. It seemed ironic that, amidst all that, our house sat right behind that of the four-star commander of the whole Military Airlift Command.

Noting the old clothes I usually wore to work in around the house, the kids surprised me one day by suggesting, "Maybe you'd better dress up more here, Mom. You never know who might see you."

I was again playing musical dishes, with everything strewn all over the small dining room table, when a knock at the front door and a quick glance in the mirror made me wish I'd listened. There stood Helen Carlton, the four-star's wife, in her Family Service uniform, calling to welcome me.

Flustered, I invited her in, amazed that she would be personally greeting newcomers. I was in such a dither that I think it rubbed off. About five minutes after she'd left, Helen Carlton was back at our door. She'd left her purse.

She'd left something else behind as well. Her visit had made an indelible impression on me and, I'm sure, on many other people over the years. She believed in family support and unconsciously mentored by example. Much to Don's and my wonderment, we were even invited to the Carltons' home for a welcoming party for newcomers to the base. It was heady company for us.

Carlton himself was a roaring lion of a general who cowed many. In fact, none of the colonels ever left the headquarters building at night until the "all clear" was sounded by his executive officer, lest the general call someone for information and find him already gone for the day.

For that reason alone, to say nothing of the exalted rank, I checked the etiquette book before writing a thank you note for the party at their home and came across a discussion of the importance of reciprocating every invitation, even if not in kind. How in the world were we going to do that?

Don thought nothing of it, though, and found a way at Christmas, when we were again involved in hosting a holiday gathering for his office. We'd just include the Carltons, he said.

What we hadn't counted on was the blizzard that hit, first delaying Cathy's flight home from college and then snowing out many of the invitees the night of the party. Neither snow, nor rain nor dark of night stayed the Carltons, though. Mushing over from next door in the snow, they were the first to arrive.

When Don went to get the general the bourbon and Fresca he knew he always drank and so had carefully stocked, he found we no longer had any Fresca. Snowed in and completely oblivious to the problem they'd be creating, the kids had drunk every last drop of it that we'd brought into the house. And there was nowhere still open in the storm for us to replenish supplies. Don's only alternative was to offer the general the potent Artillery Punch he had concocted.

But while this and other minor crises were averted, the most important ones involving the high school had so far completely evaded solution. There seemed no way to broaden the focus of a high school that we now knew had slid far downhill from the excellence that had once won it awards.

Perhaps because the state funded remedial and vocational courses more lucratively than college-prep subjects, the school was quick to drop what they called singletons, the more advanced courses in language, math or history. Discouraged, the best teachers were leaving. We also heard stories of racial discrimination. And, even though base kids made up the majority of the school population, they were treated as annoying outsiders.

Frustrated, Don and I began attending school board meetings, along with several of the other parents. One evening, after we had explained why third year languages were so vital to students who needed them for college, the principal countered, "I don't know why you all think foreign languages are so important. I never had any—and look where I am."

One evening, the day after one of the board meetings, the base commander parked his staff car in front of our quarters, waiting for Don to walk home from work.

"Hi Don," he greeted him. "Hop in for a minute."

"What's up, Sharm?"

"I understand you and your wife were at the school board meeting last night."

"Yes, we sure were."

"You know, we have a really great relationship with the school system in Mascoutah and we want to keep it that way."

His message was clear. We were to stop pressing, stop rocking the boat. The base commander didn't know us very well.

There were some things you just put up with, like the fact that there were no after-school buses for the extracurricular activities base kids were involved in. Like the long distance phone call from a pay phone every time Jim or Nancy was ready to be picked up because the town had a different phone system from the surrounding communities. You could bear inconveniences. It was the substantive stuff we worried about.

I was on my way as usual one day to get the kids in the late afternoon traffic. Straddling the lane ahead of me as if it alone belonged there, its green cab rising high above the traffic, a tractor blocked passage on the two-lane road that followed the fence rows from the base to the high school. I was on the alert for a way around, ready to scoot by if I could just find a safe place to pass. At this rate I'd never be there for Jim and Nancy before they were done with their practices. It was almost as frustrating as being unable to really be there for them with the whole school situation.

Icy rain was starting to drop from clouds that hung low overhead, suddenly darkening everything, the sunset only a glimmer on the flat, brown Midwestern horizon. I prayed the blacktop wouldn't get too slick. Like our lives, the road back to the base had become a "slippery slope" before we would finally be able to make our way safely home again.

Home. It was altogether different now. In the middle of this seemingly endless expanse of winter-bare fields, would we ever really be there?

Sundays were the only days we seemed to spend any time together anymore. But could you call it together when we seemed partitioned off from one another by even more than the boxlike cubicles of the house, each of us imprisoned in our own dilemmas?

It all came to a head one Sunday morning, right after we had come home from Mass and found ourselves crowded into Jim's tiny bedroom, screaming at one another. It had begun in the car on the way home, everyone talking at the same time, a somber liturgy of discontent.

"I can't even go to the dance because of this stupid thing about driving," Jim protested. At sixteen he was enrolled in Driver's Ed a full half year later than others his age who were allowed to drive earlier in Illinois than New Jersey. He couldn't get a driver's license until he'd completed the course. "Here, everyone else already has his license."

"Of course you can go to the dance," Don countered. "Mom or I will take you."

"Not on your life! I'd rather wait forever than have to be driven to a dance by my parents!"

We were stripping the bandages from all the wounds that had failed to close, even after months, and it smarted.

"If you're that unhappy here, Jim, that's it. I'll resign my commission and get out of the Air Force. We'll go back to New Jersey."

Don's words stunned me. He had only a year to go before he could retire. But I knew he meant every word of it.

We were all in tears now. Even Jim couldn't hold back. His face contorted as he grabbed his father, hugging him, and sobbed, "That's not what I want!"

Clinging to each other, they both wept. For all that we had lost the summer before, we all did. Together, now maybe we could begin to heal.

Spring in the Midwest can come suddenly, like the ninety-degree day that surprised us in mid-March. I was hosting a coffee at the house for a bunch of the logistics' wives and needed to open a window because it was suddenly so hot. When I finally found one that would open, I had to prop it with a ruler to keep it from tumbling back down because the sash cord was broken. But housing glitches seemed minor now compared to where we were in the rest of our lives. Like the countryside, our family had blossomed with an early thaw and all was again well that spring of 1974.

As the days began to lengthen, we awoke more mornings to rays of sunshine than gloom. All around us the huge farm machines lumbered in the fields and the rich, black soil was ridged in precision formation.

On the same ground that had been covered with snow all through an interminable December and January, forsythia, redbud and fruit trees blossomed, relieving the unbroken flatness with their burgeoning branches.

Soon we were finally on our way downtown for Jim to take the road test to get his driver's license. Jim's hands grasped the steering wheel firmly. "I'll be able to help with the driving when we go to see Grandma in Ronkonkoma this summer," he said with a grin that told me he was confident of passing.

By mid-August, the flourishing tomato plants we had planted had almost reached the second story of our house. Out front, red salvia and dusty miller brightened our flower bed borders. We'd even managed to make the lawn thrive in the steamy 100+ degree weather. The house we'd dubbed a bowling alley was finally home.

Jim's lifeguard job at the pool was a lot like the one Cathy had had in New Jersey the year before. It had been an amazing spring, with his ending up editor of the high school's newspaper and the newly elected president of next year's senior class. Somebody Up There had been listening after all.

Almost everywhere you looked that summer it was green. And the long rows of shiny, tasseled cornstalks that now lined our way as we came and went stood like plumed sentinels signaling we too were putting down roots, finally, in the heartland.

Chapter 19:

Back to Nuts and Bolts

Hope is an orientation of the heart; it transcends the world that is immediately experienced, and is anchored somewhere beyond its horizons.

—Vaclav Havel

For one member of the family, though, the summer that followed proved less than idyllic. With no friends from high school or college in the area, Cathy had felt as uprooted as the rest of us had earlier. Her summer job on base had done little to fill the void and she couldn't wait to get back to school and friends her own age. As it turned out, that summer between her sophomore and junior years in college would be the last Cathy would spend at home.

The next year, already Jim's last in high school and Nancy's second, seemed to fly by. Other than the normal concerns that the teenage years bring to parents, things remained relatively stable. Then the kids brought home the news that the school was shutting down the student government. It appeared to be a battle that would drag on all year until the banned group finally got help to take it to court and won.

Despite all this, both were doing well in school. In the spring we saw Jim inducted into the National Honor Society and listened proudly to the speech he delivered as class president at his graduation in 1975.

As usual, Don had thrown heart and soul into his job, calling a spade a spade about parts problems, even when it was an unpopular message. Because he had done his homework well and had his facts together, he was heard and something was done about things that needed fixing. Although at times he came home sure that this time he'd be fired for the message he'd just delivered, instead he kept acquiring more and more responsibility, finally moving up to the number two logistics position.

Jim was just about to leave for his freshman year at Washington University in St. Louis when we also found out that Don's new job entailed a move. Another base house went with it. Could they maybe let us stay where we were anyway, I wondered?

Even though this bigger and better duplex was just a couple of blocks down the street that ended in the cul-de-sac from which we were moving, the process of schlepping all our worldly possessions from one to the other remained a four-letter word in my book. But it seemed there could be no exceptions to the rule without messing up designated housing for those who came after. Right after getting Jim settled into college, we found ourselves in the throes of yet another un-settling.

Unfortunately, the new, bigger place was also a mess. The couple in it had repeatedly failed the housing inspection we all had to go through when we vacated government quarters, but the husband wouldn't pay anyone to help set things right. Finally, his wife cried so hard that an inspector let them go and we were stuck with it.

I felt like crying myself when confronted with window tracks brimming with dead leaves, mold in the freezing compartment of the refrigerator and a yard all muddy and dug up from the dog kept chained there. Meanwhile, we were held to rigid standards on our own vacating inspection. It didn't seem fair, but at that point I just wanted to get it over with.

At least, I thought, just moving down the street would surely mean that this time I wouldn't have to notify all the magazines of a change of address. Not true, I found out—even for a move from one part of B Street to another.

Happily, there were things we could do ourselves, ahead of the movers, like carry everyday dishes down, along with some pots and pans, and put them in place. Plus, instead of having to empty all the drawers and cabinets to repack the contents in boxes to eliminate loss and theft, this time we could just let the movers leave most of the drawers intact, eliminating a slew of work. The snag proved to be that the movers tried to cram the entire formidable move into a single day, a task that ended up being just too much for them—and us.

Late in the afternoon I gasped when I saw one of the pair of celadon pottery lamps that Don had bought for us in Japan begin to topple when the rear end of an exhausted mover bumped it off the end table as he set something else down. As the lamp tottered, I tried to race across the room to save it, but it was already gone before I could get there, lying in pieces right next to the sofa it had coordinated with so well.

We were able to take one of the carpets we'd bought two years ago with us. But the rest had been installed wall-to-wall and stayed with the house. We decided to take advantage of Jim's discount as a summer Sears employee to replace it, as well as our ancient washer and dryer, in a late summer sale. As soon as I could get everything else in some semblance of order again, I'd start the project of making and altering drapes to fit the new windows. The laws of moving dictated they all be a different size from the last ones.

Right after we'd moved in, Don left on a ten-day trip around the command with General Carlton and I worked like a madwoman while he was gone, determined to get things where they belonged as quickly as possible.

In their rush, the movers had apparently ignored both the markings on the boxes and what we said about where things belonged because I kept finding cartons of heavy books stacked in the basement instead of on the second floor. And, as if to complete the process, they'd filled the attic with cartons that now had to be lugged three flights down to the basement. I felt like a moving man myself as I ran up and down the stairs, hefting boxes, trying to sort it all out. As the final "ta-da" to my efforts, I even installed some shelves in the basement to create a place for some of the tools and things.

By the time Don finally came home, I couldn't wait to show him all I'd accomplished. We began in the basement with the shelves, which unfortunately came tumbling down just as I stood proudly pointing them out. So did my hopes that he'd instantly notice all I'd accomplished and tell me what a great job I'd done settling in. By now, I was on a pretty short fuse.

Then Don began asking questions. Had I gone to Mass that weekday morning? Had I said the rosary? Made a novena?

"Come on, Don. You know what I've been doing. What are you talking about?"

He produced a *Time* magazine article that cited a study showing that the most religious women were also the most interested in sex. We had a good laugh over that as I reminded him that he'd always found me quite devout.

It wasn't until about a week later, when I was at a wives' coffee with Don's boss's wife, Jennet Spillers, that I thought of the article again. Nursing a runny nose and cough, Jennet confided, "I've been such a bitch to Harry all week because of this darned cold." I told her Don's story, took her by the hand and said, "Just pray, Jennet. Pray." It became an inside joke for the four of us.

I found it great fun to turn the tables on Jennet and make her laugh. She was the one who could crack me up with her stories, no matter where we were, even walking along in a driving Midwest rain. I enjoyed doing things with her as much as Don did working with her husband. We were both surprised and disappointed to learn General Spillers was planning to retire at the end of the upcoming summer.

But that was nothing compared to our amazement when General Carlton called Don into his office shortly after that.

"Have you heard your boss is leaving this summer?" he began. Then he went on to explain that, although he'd been planning to transfer Don to the West Coast as a Wing Vice-Commander then, he couldn't have his number one and two headquarters' logistics guys leaving at the same time. So, we were going to have to transfer as soon as possible, whenever Don thought he could be ready to go.

"Just as soon as you want me to, sir," was Don's reply, despite the fact this would be our second move in six months.

"Now don't you give me that brave soldier stuff," Carlton growled. "You have a little girl at home. You go home and see what she says."

This was the same Carlton whose gruffness was legend. The one from whose office all awaited the all clear when "the old man" finally went home for the day.

Underneath the gravelly surface, General Carlton was a straight shooter. He might huff and puff, but he wasn't one of those guys who smile at you one minute and knife you in the back the next. The rough exterior concealed a much gentler side.

That "little girl" still at home was the same one who, when we'd first moved to Illinois, had informed us she didn't want to have to wait to move again right at the beginning of her senior year in high school as a normal three-year-tour there would mean.

"Can't we leave before the end of junior year so I won't have to be a newcomer as a senior?" she'd asked.

"Well, squirt," Don said. "I'm afraid you'll just have to speak to Someone higher up than me about that." Apparently Nancy had.

Don's "bigger" gal at home just laughed. "Well, I just finished the last hem on the last drape. I guess that'll teach me. Never finish the drapes. It means another move."

We were to leave for McChord Air Force Base and Tacoma, Washington, just before Easter, leaving Jim behind as we had Cathy on the East Coast. It seemed we were dropping off kids like bread crumbs, clear across the country, each time our caravan moved on. Now our offspring would stretch from coast to coast. For this trip, houseplants would replace much of what we'd loaded the last time we'd towed the Volkswagen westward.

Initially, all that we could find out about the school system awaiting our youngest in Washington was that it operated on a trimester, rather than a semester system. We'd just have to work around that. In the meantime, Nancy was too busy with a trip to D.C. for Model UN and applying for summer fellowships with Earthwatch and Telluride for us to worry much about it.

A recent dental checkup that I'd just completed detected a cavity. I felt lucky to find I still had time to get it filled before we left rather than have to hook up right away with a new dentist in Washington. Once we'd gotten past the need for babysitters, good beauticians and dentists seemed the hardest thing to find in each new location.

But this time, something went haywire, causing me to have an extreme allergic reaction. Before I'd even driven home the ten minutes it took between the dentist's office and the base, my nose was running like a faucet, making me stop to buy a box of tissues just so I could drive the rest of the way home.

It took days for whatever was causing my gushing nostrils to abate. As a result, when it was time to go to my last coffee, the monthly "Hail and Farewell" for all those wives who were coming and going from the base, I still had a box of tissues in constant tow.

It was hard to be inconspicuous about it so it seemed understandable that one of the wives would ask me about my nasal hyperactivity. A kind and pious woman, my questioner apparently had reason to believe she had the gift of healing. Before I knew it, she had laid hands upon my nose as she prayed aloud for it to stop running—all this in the midst of the very large crowd of several hundred women who were at the well-attended coffee that morning. Grateful for her concern, I tried to slip away as gracefully as a geyser could.

Jennet had picked me up and driven me there in the Spillers' pickup truck and, as we made our way home, asked me what all that had been about. She had only one comment after I explained.

"I sure am glad you didn't have venereal disease."

Along with everything else, like two of our three children, I was surely going to miss that sense of humor and the friendship that went with it.

Chapter 20:

Emptying the Nest

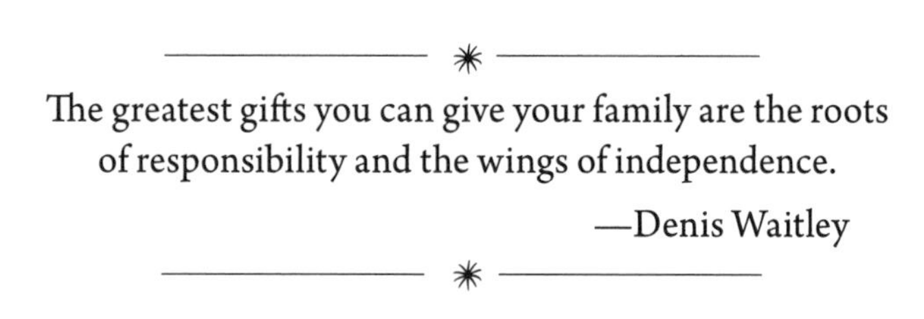

> The greatest gifts you can give your family are the roots of responsibility and the wings of independence.
>
> —Denis Waitley

Almost everything we'd read and heard about the Pacific Northwest to which we were headed sounded idyllic: snow-covered mountains, water, gardens. We couldn't wait to get there, to see and live amidst all that beauty. Despite the fact that it teemed rain every inch of the way as we drove in along the Oregon Dalles and Columbia River Gorge, the vista before us still took our breath away.

We'd allowed time for a stopover visit with Elayne and Dave Brown, friends from Oklahoma who'd since returned to Portland to retire. They might not have been as happy to see us had they known they were going to put up forty houseplants as well as the three of us. But, as if there were nothing to it, they helped us carry them all in from the VW lest they get too cold in the car overnight.

They'd not quite finished the arduous task of building their own home, but that didn't stop Elayne from dropping everything the next day to drive us all the way to the shore so we could see Cannon Beach, with its monolithic Haystack Rock rising out of Pacific coastal waters. While we strolled along Ecola State Park, beachcombing, Don came across a Japanese fishing ball that had been washed in by a storm, something even lifetime residents rarely discovered anymore.

Like most newcomers to the Northwest, we succumbed immediately to its magic. But we had to learn patience too. It would take a couple of months from our arrival just before Easter of 1976 before we'd finally get to see Mount Rainier in all its tantalizing glory. When it did finally doff its mantle of clouds to appear, we excitedly exclaimed, just like long-time residents, "The mountain is out!"

Ironically, now that there were only three of us, our new home was the largest and loveliest we'd ever inhabited, with two stories and a full basement. It was one of only three at the north end of the base, planted between the runways and Interstate 5. Originally, each of the houses had been built as doctors' and nurses' quarters for a tuberculosis sanatorium that was no longer standing. Beneath the grass you could still make out the outlines of the sidewalks that had linked all the buildings.

Majestic firs surrounded us and, I was soon to find out, coyotes. The tranquility of our park-like setting was something of an illusion in other ways as well. Traffic noise from I-5 was so intrusive that even closing our bedroom door against the din did little to reduce it. I lulled myself to sleep at night with the power of suggestion, repeating, "It's the ocean; it's the ocean."

Not too far from the other side of the house were the runways on which all the planes took off and landed, making what Don called "the sound of freedom." But, on occasion, the decibel level grew so high we couldn't even hear on the telephone.

One day shortly after we'd moved in I was startled by still another sound. A gunshot rang out nearby. I found out later that a neighbor had asked the base police to try to eliminate the coyotes because of the danger to pets. But the pregnant female apparently escaped unscathed. Baby coyotes soon scurried through the area, at first looking for all the world like innocent pups rather than predators.

We had hit the ground scurrying, too, at first between our house and the high school, where we were keenly disappointed to find how much it left to be desired. Nancy had to give up a class period for typing, which she'd long ago mastered, in order to fulfill a local requirement. Each extracurricular activity also meant forfeiture of a class period. There was no way for her to continue with all the academic subjects she had been taking as well as things like the newspaper staff, band and tennis. Nothing we or she said made any difference to the school. Take it or leave it.

For my part, the commander's wife, Marge, wanted me to become involved immediately. It always took me weeks to unpack, hang drapes and pictures, and settle in, but as a result of the instant involvement, time to do that had to be begged, borrowed and stolen the best I could from a dawn to dark schedule. There seemed to be almost daily board meetings or other functions, both on base and in the community, as I learned how things worked here and got to know people. As always, getting to know the people was the best part.

By now, I had come to realize that we'd acquired a vast family of friends over the years. Despite the fact that we had grown up in all different parts of the country before we got to know one another and would too soon have to say goodbye again, we kept in touch, no matter how far apart we were scattered about the globe. To me, that was the most surprising discovery of our vagabond lives and one of its greatest joys. To find one of that "family" passing through long enough for a visit was a very special treat. And usually it was as if we'd never skipped a beat. Who knew, back in those first lonely Air Force days, that it could be like this?

Not long after our arrival in Washington, a young officer we didn't know but who now worked for Don's former boss in Illinois came to McChord as part of a group visiting on business, making it a kind of proxy visit from the Spillers. Over lunch, the captain became very serious as he announced to us he'd had a message given to him by them, with very particular instructions on how it was to be delivered.

As he took my hands in his and said he'd been told to ask, "Are you still praying?" he was obviously completely unaware of the *Time* magazine article and the sex connection. We laughed so hard I'm sure he thought he'd done something wrong, but by then I was blushing ten shades of red and Don quickly changed the subject.

When we called Harry and Jennet later that day, they were getting things ready to leave for retirement in Texas but said they'd wanted us to know they'd already packed the Praying Hands picture we'd given them as a farewell present before we'd left Scott. It would, they said, forever hang in a place of honor over their bed. To laugh with them again made our day.

Some of the things I was now involved with gave me the chance to try to do a little of that for others, supplying a boost to newcomers. I'd volunteered at Family Services all the while we were at Scott and knew how it ticked. Happily, that was where Marge particularly wanted help.

The job I'd most loved at Scott was visiting temporary base quarters to welcome the newly arrived with a packet of area and base information. So it seemed a natural thing to bring that to McChord too. Some just took the packet. Others had questions and invited me in. One wife was so elated that her little son, who'd been somewhat developmentally delayed, had just succeeded in tinkling in the pot on his own that she couldn't wait to share the news with someone, even a stranger who'd just knocked on her door to say "Welcome."

At home, we were dealing with our own newcomer adjustments, plus figuring out how to get all of us back to the East Coast for Cathy's upcoming college graduation now that three of us were a continent apart.

As the academic year wound down, we realized we'd have to arrange for Nance to finish her semester a little early in order to be there. Jim was completing his freshman year at Washington University and would fly into Philadelphia directly from St. Louis. Finally, all five of us would rendezvous in New Jersey. We also had to throw our parents into the equation—mine, coming in from Florida where they now lived, and Don's mom from New York. As usual, the path from A to Z zigged and zagged.

Don was flying to the East Coast on an Air Force mission, then taking leave in order to be able to get there. Because he had to leave home before Nancy and me, we'd had to take a bus to Seattle-Tacoma Airport to catch the commercial flight to meet Jim.

When we landed at Philadelphia International, where we were to get together, we discovered that the terminals at which each of our flights arrived couldn't have been further apart. Nancy's brand new luggage had also been damaged and we were advised to make a claim right away. Before we could even set out to look for Jim, I had to first rent a car, something I'd never before done on my own.

The worst of it was that the rental company claimed the tiny two-door vehicle they offered us was all they had left. It barely held the three of us, no less a summer's worth of stuff for each of two kids.

That included most of the contents of Jim's dorm room, which had to go with him for the summer. And, for Nancy, everything she'd need for the next two months while away studying the migration of the Cape Cod shoreline with Earthwatch and at a Telluride program at Cornell.

When we finally got the car and picked Jim up, we tried in vain to squeeze things into a trunk so miniscule we could barely fit Jim's guitar case into it. The two kids ended up perched atop most of their luggage in the back seat. The rest was squeezed into the passenger's seat up front.

It was already quite late and dark, which didn't make it any easier to find my way though an airport under major construction, including exit and entrance revisions. I guess it was inevitable that, after intense effort just to find our way out of there, I also became instantly and hopelessly lost in Philadelphia's streets.

I finally decided it would be safe to stop to ask directions from a man and his daughter I saw out walking a dog. After the father had finished explaining where I needed to go, he added a few more words of advice, "This is a dangerous neighborhood, lady. Get out of it as quickly as you can."

That was all the grist the duo in the backseat needed. Jim and Nance had already begun a debate on the relative safety of city streets in general and where we were driving in particular. It did little to calm my already frayed nerves.

When we got to McGuire Air Force Base, where we were to meet Don, it was already past eleven o'clock at night, and at first I couldn't even pick out the billeting office among the dimly-lit buildings. Then we learned that Don wasn't there yet, a worry because he was quite overdue. But we went ahead and got ourselves into the building in which we were staying and were much relieved when he showed up an hour or so later. The plane he'd been flying had had problems along the way.

All would've been fine if we could've just slept in. Instead, Nancy had to take her French Achievement test first thing the next morning, somewhere in Princeton that Don and she had to leave early enough to locate. By now, it was common family knowledge that you didn't go with Mom when there was any doubt as to where something was. And scheduling the test there had been the only way Nancy could take it and still come East with us for graduation.

Scheduling came into play for Cathy too. She had seriously considered applying to work in the volunteer Vista program right after she'd graduated. I suggested that she might want to consider something that would bring in a paycheck instead so she could begin to pay off some of the loan debt she'd be faced with.

As a result, the offspring that had started out her first year as a math major and switched to art history had applied to and been one of a handful accepted in an Arthur Andersen program. This allowed her to study evenings for a master's degree in accounting at New York University and gain experience toward her CPA during the day working for the firm. The only problem was that the night before she'd even graduated, Cath had to be in New York City for her first class.

Somehow, Don got each daughter where she had to be, the weather cooperated, graduation was magnificent and we all rejoiced and relaxed. After the ceremony, even though no one could stay very long, we headed to Don's mother's home about halfway out on Long Island to visit and regroup.

Don, Jim and Cathy were the first to leave, their initial destination being LaGuardia Airport, to drop Jim off for a flight "home." From there, he'd take a bus to the base, pick up a key to the car we'd left parked for him at Base Operations and, hopefully, find his way to a house he'd not yet seen, and then begin his search for a summer job.

With all that we had to jam into the car, between a dorm roomful of Cathy's stuff as well as Jim's, we ended up pushing and shoving the doors closed with our feet before the three of them could take off from Ronkonkoma.

If having kids leave for college had evoked emotion, it was nothing compared to launching the first one out into the cold, cold world for life—especially, Don told me later, when he spied the yards-long origami chain of Japanese bubble gum wrappers from our Guam tour that Cathy had tucked in among the precious possessions he was helping her to load.

There was just no room for either Nancy or me to go along too. But, when Don finally got to the dilapidated NYU dorm on Fourteenth Street where he was to drop Cathy off there were enough tears shed and hugs shared between the two of them to make it a kind of surrogate farewell among all five of us.

Before I also left Ronkonkoma to go back, Nance and I planned to look at the East Coast colleges she was interested in. We were again borrowing Don's mother's car, this time to visit Yale and Harvard. But when Nettie Haw, a good friend of Don's family, got wind of our plan, she protested, "Oh no, you can't drive up there in that crazy Massachusetts traffic by yourselves. That's where I'm from. I'm coming with you."

It proved to be quite a trip. We soon discovered that the brakes were badly out of adjustment on the car and each time Nancy or I went to stop, the pedal would go down, down, and down some more, before engaging. The tension between Nancy and me seemed to increase in direct proportion to the brake's lack of it. It had to be unnerving for Nettie in the backseat, listening to us bicker about how to adjust stopping procedures for the brake's problems.

For the third time, an offspring's last-year-home scenario had begun to unfold and I had finally started to recognize a pattern. As seniors in high school, the kids seemed to go out of their way to be at least periodically difficult. I eventually came to see it as their way of preparing to break away. By the time their last year home was over, they couldn't wait to leave and it was easier for the rest of the family to let them go.

By the end of that trip, as we sat in the never-ending parking lot called the Long Island Expressway at rush hour, and Nancy and I got hotter and hotter, both under the collar and in the heat and humidity of an un-air-conditioned car, our third offspring's senior year had not yet begun and I still hadn't put two and two fully together. What we had done, together, was accomplish our mission. Nancy now knew she wanted to go to Yale.

Meanwhile, back on the West Coast, Jim had succeeded in finding his way to the house and started his job search. Because of Don's job, he was barred from working on base but was soon employed by day with a moving company, and by night restocking grocery shelves. When it got to the point that he was only getting a couple of hours sleep a night, Don put his foot down.

"Jim, pick one or the other. You can't do both and go without sleep like this."

Our son hauled furniture and boxes for the rest of the summer. It was his turn to be the "only child."

Although Nancy didn't return until the end of the summer from New England and Colorado, her letters reminded us she was dreading a return to the local high school. Don suggested she enroll in the community college at night as a supplement, but somehow I didn't think that would hack it. Over the summer, I had listened with interest to a mother who told me about Bellarmine Prep, a local co-ed Catholic high school. But, it had slipped my mind in the excitement of Nancy's coming home and Jim's heading back to St. Louis for his second year at Washington University.

When I remembered again, a few days after the term at Bellarmine had already begun but before the public school's had, it at least afforded Nancy and me the chance to have a look at the school in session when it was easier to get a feel for things. Despite coming in with a kind of devil's advocate frame of mind, we both very much liked what we saw and heard. Nevertheless, trying to do due diligence, we posed as many difficult questions of students, faculty and administration as we could think of.

With Jim still in college, and Cathy just having graduated, Nancy wanted very much to avoid having us take on still another tuition payment. And Father Weber, the president, understood the situation very well. He offered a small amount of scholarship aid to help out, with the understanding that once all our offspring had completed their educations, we would try to make some donations to help the school continue to do the same for others.

By the time we got home, Nancy had already decided. "You know, it's only another year. And then you'll be paying for my college, too, as well as Jim's. I'll just go back to Clover Park." The next day she did.

Even a stranger could have seen how unhappy she was when she walked into the house after school that afternoon.

"What's the matter, Nance? Do you think it might be a good idea to consider changing your mind?"

It took some cajoling before she finally spit out the words, "Well, maybe we could talk to Dad about it tonight."

It was what Don liked to call a no-brainer decision. The next day we withdrew Nancy from Clover Park to enroll in Bellarmine. Now all we had to do was figure out how she and I could work out sharing the VW to get her there and back, since there was no school or public transportation. It proved well worth the trouble.

I found it fascinating to go to Parent Association meetings and hear the faculty fretting that only 98 percent of the students were participating in extracurricular activities. And it didn't seem to matter whether a student was average, gifted or needed extra help. Each one got special attention. The school offered advanced placement college classes and Nancy's math teacher even designed a special advanced course for her.

The only fly in our idyllic ointment was the fact that Nance had been nominated for a National Merit Scholarship and now, being again in a brand new high school—her third—she was forced to seek recommendations from teachers who hardly knew her. It was particularly distressing when one of the nuns wrote that Nancy didn't really need any scholarship money because her father was an officer.

Back at home I, too, was once more "going to school" at almost daily meetings of various groups like Family Services, Red Cross and the Thrift Shop and involvement in the surrounding, very supportive civilian communities. Many evenings we also had to be away from home for events, and when we weren't, there was often something we ourselves hosted at home.

Beautiful as it was, where we were living on base was very isolated from the rest of the families' homes. In fact, our house was one of only three in the area. On top of that, Nancy's classmates regarded the base, with its gated entrance, as the end of the world, even though it was only about twenty minutes from the school. Nancy ended up home alone so much I felt terrible and frequently fretted out loud about it.

"Mom, I have plenty of work to do. It's just fine with me. Stop worrying," she'd reassure me.

Before long, she had become so involved with tennis, yearbook, newspaper and everything else at school that I suspected she was right—not that she had escaped the strain of being the new kid in the senior class. She did seem to work through it a lot faster at Bellarmine than she might have elsewhere.

When we'd first arrived at McChord, we were in the middle of the energy crunch of the Carter presidency and Don had been appointed Energy Czar. It was his job to conjure up ways to conserve. It also made him the grinch who had to announce the command policy of no outdoor holiday lights on base.

Increasing the insulation in base housing was one energy-saving idea he thought made eminently good sense. But the civil engineers came up with a time and cost estimate to do the job that negated the savings. Determined to prove they'd overestimated, Don decided to insulate the attic in our house himself, calculate the time and money involved and present a counter-case. Any evening he could, he'd head for the attic right after supper and had almost finished the job when Nancy came downstairs one night and tapped me gently on the shoulder as I was winding up the dishes.

"Mom, I think you'd better come upstairs. Dad's leg is hanging out of the ceiling in the little room next to your bedroom and there are mica pellets all over the shag carpet."

Fortunately, Don was OK. Of course, he was no neophyte at falling through attic floors. But the ceiling definitely needed repair and Don wasn't about to tell CE what had happened. He'd repair it himself. We weren't sure if we'd ever get all the junk out of the long fibers of the rug but we vacuumed and vacuumed until we'd gotten all we could.

After it got dark the next night, we sneaked out the back gate to a nearby Fred Meyer's store. The official back gate was already closed for the evening and only the occupants of the three houses in our area had keys to the small gate right behind our houses that we were now using.

Don bought the materials he'd need to patch the hole he had made but, unfortunately, the smallest wall board available was anything but small. The only thing for it was to mount and tie the massive piece of sheetrock down on top of the roof of the car, where it perched precariously at best. With Nancy and me reaching through the open car windows to hang onto our cargo for dear life, Don drove home.

For all his trouble, he had proven the net cost of insulating attics to be less than CE's estimates. He had also proven that we would never, ever allow him up into an attic again.

Before we knew it, Nancy's senior year was drawing to a close. As I pinned up the hem on a new dress for her and we talked about college, it suddenly dawned on me. For the first time in twenty-two years, come the following September, I'd be alone in the house when Don was away. Our nest was about to hold a big goose egg.

Almost as quickly, I realized I'd darn well better get used to the idea. I didn't want Nancy to feel as if there were subtle apron strings holding her back. And, thank God, Don and I would still have each other.

When women moaned and groaned about "losing" their children, it had always seemed to me a bit like saying to your spouse, "You're not enough anymore." I didn't want to deliver that message, however inadvertently. Life was about to change again and I was grateful to have the time to prepare myself for it. I was just going to have to adapt.

Chapter 21:

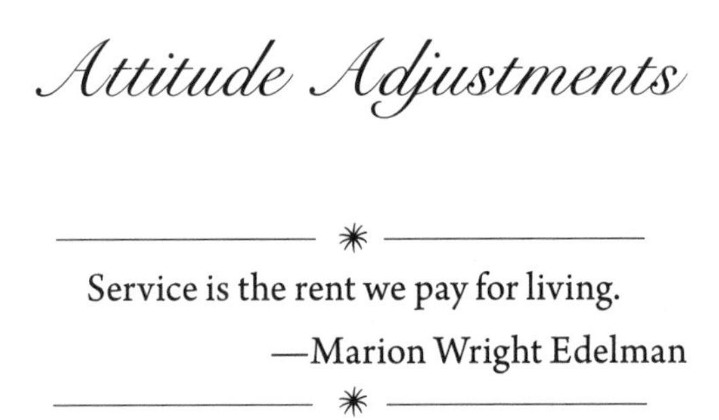

Attitude Adjustments

> Service is the rent we pay for living.
>
> —Marion Wright Edelman

Meanwhile, Don learned he would be taking over as Wing Commander in July. This meant responsibility not only for operating and maintaining fifty or sixty airplanes but for ensuring the safety and morale of four or five thousand airmen and their families as well. The family part entailed more responsibility for me too. At least it was coming at a time when taking on more wouldn't mean having to take time away from little ones at home.

One of the things I still found myself uneasy about doing was getting up to speak in front of a group. Even asking a question in a crowded room terrified me. It was obvious to others, too. When we'd left Illinois a good friend had confided to me that another had said I'd never be able to do some of the things at McChord that I'd be called upon for. I was just too shy and unassertive.

They'd neglected to factor in my stubbornness. Many with the same fears sidestepped the issue by having others deliver things like a "thought for the day" before a luncheon when it was their turn.

This was a time to share something uplifting that was neither overtly religious nor offensive to any group. I enjoyed writing my own script when I had to do it, and with Don's help got myself to where I could do a fairly good job of delivery.

But there were other things that bothered me even more than that. Don's job meant I had the responsibility for filling vacant volunteer chairmanships in things like the Thrift Shop and Red Cross as they occurred. Nancy and Cathy and I had already had many discussions on that very subject. At that time in the late '70s, there were fewer women in the military than there are today. Cathy and Nancy's take on the issue of volunteerism for the military family was that, with more and more women employed full-time, it was unfair to assume the military automatically got the services of two for the price of one from married couples. If volunteerism is good, they said, everyone should be involved, not just the wives. It was hard to argue otherwise.

My own philosophy evolved from the fact that when I was made to feel welcome to a new community it felt like being clasped to the bosom of a family. And family members do for one another. So for me, that had to be the motivation, not intimidation from a husband's boss's wife, not what a woman thought her efforts did or didn't do for a spouse's career, and certainly not a military member ordering a subordinate military member about what his spouse had to do.

Until I'd heard it discussed at a Red Cross ceremony I'd attended, I'd never known how peculiarly American volunteerism is. Even Alexis de Tocqueville had applauded it in *Democracy in America*, speaking of how Americans see a problem, and then seem to spontaneously come together to tackle solving it.

In addition, I soon learned at a community college luncheon celebrating women employed in federal government that experts now advised women seeking to return to paid employment to translate their life experiences into terms an employer understands. Volunteers had even "validated" their experiences to gain entrée into jobs.

In talking with one of the college administrators over lunch, I asked if they might be able to set up a course for volunteers on the base. To my mind, there were two problems that needed addressing: training for some of the situations volunteers face and respect for volunteer efforts that is at least the equivalent of that given to paid employees.

In response, the college put together a one-day case-study-type seminar on base that gave management training to every volunteer and potential volunteer interested in taking it. It also offered college credit to those who wished to go on and complete additional assignments.

More than anything else, it afforded recognition to an unsung, undervalued group of great human beings. It was geared to both those who wanted to get involved and those who were already contributing but wanted to fine-tune their participation. By the end of the day, people even came forward to volunteer for the positions they thought they'd do best. Afterwards, board meetings that had previously bogged down into three-hour "meetings of the bored" now zipped along smoothly.

I also heard about a group in town that was seeking volunteers for their program of tutoring people who had either not learned to read in school or needed English as a Second Language (ESL). I thought teaching ESL on base would be a great thing for the foreign-born wives who had married servicemen, and because others thought so too, we soon mounted our own program.

Serendipitous as all this was, there were speed bumps too. At a gathering one night I got into a conversation with a young woman whose husband was leaving the Air Force. She longed, as I had, for stability in life, especially in order to be able to pursue her own career goals, and had come up to me to ask, "When do you think you'll ever use your education?"

I'd never thought I'd stopped using it. But, much as I resented the implication that one didn't use one's education unless receiving money for it, I realized she didn't grasp the implied insult. I got off my own high horse long enough to do my best to answer, just as I had some years earlier when Cathy had come home from college for Christmas vacation and temporarily stopped me dead in my verbal tracks one evening when she came into the den in Illinois and asked me, "Mom, what do you think is the most important thing you can do with your life?"

"Well, I guess I'd have to say it would be to 'be there' for others." I half expected her to ask me next to evaluate how well I was doing at that but, mercifully, she didn't.

With or without all three kids at home, life continued to be filled with surprises and was anything but dull. Despite Sister's comments, Nancy had been chosen a National Merit Scholar and a Presidential Scholar as well. Once again we were invited to the ceremony in D.C., this time with Jimmy Carter presiding.

The summer after her graduation, Nancy worked in an office on nearby Fort Lewis, Cathy was still in New York and Jim labored at an Army fast food place. He was able to scrape up enough to buy a used car, and together he and Don worked on it nights and weekends, sanding, repainting and getting everything shipshape to take back to college in St. Louis with him.

If we thought we were both busy before, it was nothing compared to the pace of life now with Don's new job. It made things a lot easier that by fall we no longer had to worry about leaving anyone alone at home. In fact, although it took a while after both Nancy and Jim had gone off to college before we had a Saturday night that we didn't have to be someplace or have guests at home, when we finally did our newfound freedom left us amazed and giddy.

"Hey, we can do whatever we want. No one to worry about except you and me," Don said. We decided to head out for pizza, one of the best we'd ever tasted, topping it off with ice cream cones. It was like dating all over again.

We even planned to go off together on a trip to Travis Air Force Base, between San Francisco and Sacramento in California, for the retirement of Don's boss, Major General Tom Aldrich. We'd already bought the ticket for my trip down there when Don got the phone call that he'd be unable to leave the base to attend. The Aldriches insisted I come anyway and made arrangements for me to be picked up at the airport.

In a strange role reversal, the first since our marriage almost twenty-four years before, I was now the one away on a trip, with Don left behind. And I soon found out why he'd not been allowed to leave. The wing at home was in the midst of an Operational Readiness Inspection, and all night long planes from McChord landed and took off from the runway right next to where I was billeted at Travis. The whine of the engines made me lonelier than if I'd been back home alone. After all the years of feeling sorry for myself when I was left "home alone," I finally grasped, at gut level, that going away could be as hard on those who traveled as it was on those left behind.

All day long that weekend, people came up to me to ask how the inspection was going, but, of course, I didn't really know. I was just concerned because I couldn't be there to get meals for Don, do laundry and all the other things that would support him in the around-the-clock schedule I knew he was keeping.

But I was also very grateful that I could be there for the gathering of wives Ginny Aldrich had put together. It proved to be another mentoring experience I'd never forget. With so many of the wing commanders' wives in one spot, Ginny suggested we discuss any problems we had encountered and solutions we'd found. Often, what was an issue in one place had already been resolved in another, and without realizing it I came away with a template I would eventually put to use myself.

I also realized I'd done a complete about-face concerning where we might eventually want to hang our hearts. During our first few months of gray days and showers at McChord, Don had proclaimed, as we drove by rain-soaked golfers, "Why would anyone want to retire here?" I tended to agree.

Now, flying into California and driving through its browned hills, I was amazed to discover that nothing seemed green enough here. In fact, everything felt a bit puny in comparison to Washington's soaring peaks.

Don and I had both experienced the same sentiments as we'd flown back to pick up Nancy from college in Connecticut the previous spring, then on to Florida to celebrate my parents' fiftieth wedding anniversary. Until then we'd been sure we'd eventually settle in Florida. Now I could almost see the webs that had sprouted on feet that might well carry me back one day to the Evergreen State to stay.

Not that our wandering days were even near over. In fall of the year, the Air Force sent Don to a two-month advanced management course at the University of Pittsburgh. The university asked that spouses wait until the week before graduation to join them but treated us royally when we were finally allowed to be there, even setting up special classes for the entire group.

The class included civilian executives from all around the country and the world. Don and one other student were the only military. We became fast friends with classmates from Texas to Japan and Brazil.

Don came home just in time for the holidays that year and fellow Pittsburg student John Garrett, a geologist from Houston we'd invited up for a visit, hung on for dear life as we carted him around to a whirlwind of festivities, some we hosted and others just attended. But the most important thing of all was that Cathy, Jim and Nancy would soon be home with us too.

I loved stocking up on the ingredients to make their favorite recipes. And once it was time for them to leave again, I had to fight back the tears on my next big grocery shopping trip when the realization set in that it would be a long time before we were all together again.

This was also the year of a belated Christmas present, another promotion for Don. Again, we were told it wouldn't mean a move. But, of course, we soon got the word that it certainly did. We were headed back to the heartland.

CHAPTER 22:

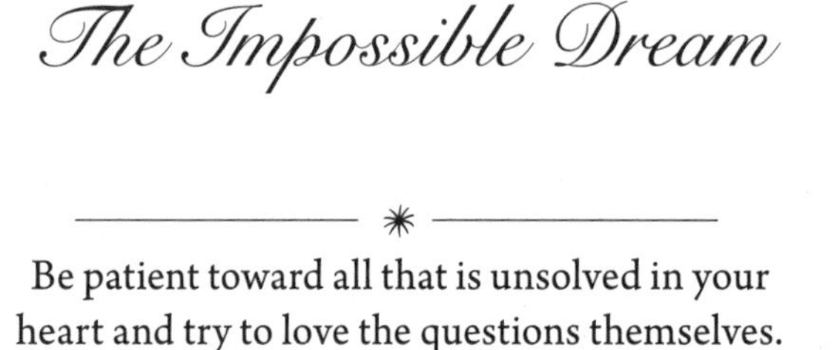

> Be patient toward all that is unsolved in your
> heart and try to love the questions themselves.
>
> —Rainer Maria Rilke

When friends from Southern Illinois told us about current snow accumulations already as high as a tabletop to the east of us, we cringed at the thought of mushing our way back to Scott Air Force Base through anything like that for our February move. But all went well weather-wise on our journey, and Don even found someone else being transferred there at the same time who needed transportation. He thought it would work well for both of us if we allowed him to take our Volkswagen. We'd have neither car nor offspring in tow.

It was, in fact, the first time since before Cathy was born twenty-three years earlier that just the two of us would be moving. Before we had even gotten out the gate, I knew one of us was very sick. Don was burning up with fever but, of course, insisted he was just fine and would do his share of the driving. I argued with him but, unsurprisingly, couldn't get him to budge. It wasn't until well after we had safely arrived that I succeeded in getting him to go to the doctor. He diagnosed double pneumonia and put Don on immediate bed rest.

"Home" this time around had stood empty and neglected for the previous nine months. Some of the walls had been painted after the last occupant moved out but most hadn't, and the house was a motley mix of two off-whites. The dishwasher was full of water and wouldn't drain. Neither would the bathroom tubs.

Outside, in the mile-high overgrown grass and weeds that covered the yard I uncovered other hidden treasures like sharp kitchen knives. And, although I didn't know it then, for the next three months I would spend hours trying to remove the multiple coats of liquid wax and dirt off the ancient asbestos tile flooring in the large kitchen.

Sick as he was, Don called the base commander right away to ask that something be done about the shape the house was in. After trying to convince us that it was normal to have a dishwasher full of standing water, tubs that don't drain and an unfinished paint job, the commander reluctantly agreed. But by then it had become a race against the clock to get everything done and the paint dry before the van arrived with our stuff.

It wasn't like we were moving into a cheap neighborhood. Our brick duplex looked out on the four-star Military Airlift Command's commander in chief's directly across the street. In fact, his wife was one of the first to welcome us, bringing over a bowl of steaming homemade chicken soup for Don when she heard about the pneumonia.

That was when I discovered that Don had told the young man driving our car to take his time, make a visit home en route, sightsee, whatever. There was no rush in getting the VW to us, he said.

Unfortunately, Don had neglected to tell me that too, completely overlooking the fact that I'd packed our vacuum cleaner in the car, along with basins, scrub brushes and every cleaning supply I'd need to get the house shipshape before our shipment arrived. This time I really needed them.

There was nothing for it but to beg, borrow and buy duplicates until the car and all the things in it finally showed up. And wait until Don got well to hang the drapes and pictures. Although I persisted in trying, I had about as much talent for installing things as I had sense of direction. It wasn't long before I found out that was the least of my worries.

Early one morning, elated to be finally nearing the finish line of a cleaning marathon after weeks of constant work, I fairly bounded down the three flights of stairs to empty a bucket of scrub water into the washtubs in the basement. But I came to a screeching halt when I saw the sewage that had backed up out of a drain in the concrete floor, right in front of the tubs and our washing machine and all over the old carpet we'd put down to make the cement easier on the feet. A call from our neighbor in the duplex next door soon told me we were not alone. They too had a cellar full.

"It's like this place has a little black cloud hanging over it," she said. Not exactly the thing a newcomer yearns to hear.

And there was more. "I told those workmen they'd better stop emptying the leftover plaster down the sinks when I saw them over there doing that when the house was vacant," she said. "Now we have this."

Whatever was causing it, I'd immediately called the civil engineers to let them know what was going on and ask how fast they could have someone over to fix it. They just told me, "We don't know. Everyone's plumbing is backing up today."

I doubted that but eventually followed up with a message for Don at the office to see if he could do any better. Since he never got the message, I never got an answer there either. But shortly before noon I did get a call that an old friend was visiting and Don was bringing him home for lunch.

At this point, I was ready to poison Don *and* the civil engineers who had just shown up, taken one look and said the problem was out of their jurisdiction. They were outside contractors now and base CE would first have to clear the main line. And, oh, by the way, that team was on its lunch break until about one or two p.m.

When Don walked in with guest in tow, I managed to have lunch ready and smile as I handed out no uncertain orders: "Absolutely no flushing or letting any water go down any drains."

It was late in the afternoon before the base people cleared the main line, and almost dinnertime before the contractor got back and opened the rest of it up. But the mess in the basement still remained to be cleaned and I was due to pick Jim up from college for his first weekend home since we'd come back to the Midwest. I called Don at the office to tell him he was going to have to pick Jim up instead. I just had to get busy taking up the piece of carpet we'd laid and swabbing everything else down with a Clorox solution.

"Gee hon, I'm sorry," he said. "I can't leave the base. There's an alert going on."

What next? I jumped in the car and made my way into St. Louis, so strung out from all that had gone on that I knew I'd be a worse "backseat" nitpicker than usual if I surrendered the wheel. I drove back as well, relating to Jim what the day had been like.

By the time we'd pulled into the base gate, a few blocks from where we lived, I'd pretty well calmed down. But that didn't last long when the security policeman on duty there stopped me.

"Ma'am, your car has been selected for a random drug search by the dogs."

"Fine," I said. But then he handed me my rights to look at before the search, and I realized I hadn't brought my reading glasses with me.

"I can't read this," I offered, by way of a quick explanation, never thinking that would result in the airman's beginning a funereal-paced recitation of the rights spelled out on the card he'd handed me, as if addressing an illiterate or someone unable to understand the language. And then it dawned on me. The guy thought I'd meant I couldn't read!

I tried again to explain that all this rights reading wasn't necessary. We'd just get out of the car and he could let the dogs search. At that point, I simply wanted to get out: out of the car, out of there—

out of Illinois.

When we finally walked in the door to the house, Don was already home and suggested we relieve some of the pressure by going out to eat. That was fine with me until we happened to run into the base commander, a kind of mayor responsible for all that goes on within a base or post. By the time I finished telling him about my day on Scott Air Force Base, I'd probably ruined his too.

Things calmed down a bit for the next month, and by the time Don was ready to leave for a week or two of school in D.C. we had actually achieved some semblance of order. The night before he was taking off, we had in fact come home from a fun evening at the Little Theater presentation the wives' club put on annually. Then we walked into the kitchen and discovered another sewage backup—this time in that sink. It was, of course, the same on the other side of the duplex.

All of this brought to mind some Thanksgiving stories I'd heard the last time we'd lived on base at Scott. After their big meal, people would run the garbage disposals in one duplex kitchen and the debris came spewing up in the other side's sink. Finding it there, the occupants ran their disposal, only to have it reemerge in their neighbor's kitchen. The origin of the problem was that no one had ever vented the kitchen sinks, either when they were first installed or since. Three years later, here we were—teeter-tottering on the same seesaw.

Since we'd just finishing re-laying the carpet remnant in the basement that we'd had cleaned from the first backup fiasco, I was less than thrilled to hear that the cleanout for both duplexes was on our side of the basement wall. I begged the civil engineers to find some other way to do it, and after much ado, they did. Finally, even the sewer began to behave and stopped barging in on us with unwelcome surprise visits.

Besides, I now had better things to do with my time than clean up over and over again. I had become very much involved with English as a Second Language, both as a teacher and the director of the program on base. We met weekly with our students, one on one, in a large room. Midway through the morning we broke for coffee or tea, cookies, and the chance for students to practice conversing in English.

I was fortunate to have Soon, a young Korean woman, who, while growing up, was so determined to learn English that she had borrowed her brother's English texts to begin teaching herself the language on her own. As I understood it, at the time it was only included in the boys' school curriculum. Soon's dedication was such that I felt certain whatever she wanted to do in life, she'd succeed.

In fact, although her husband was to be transferred, necessitating a family move soon after she'd given birth to their second child, she even managed to take her GED test. The family was in temporary quarters, about to leave the next day, when I got a frantic phone call from a woman trying to reach Soon because she'd come so very close to the passing grade.

Fortunately, the test person was able to reach Soon where I thought the family was staying to try to arrange an instant retest. I volunteered to drive her. Wracking my brain for a way to convey to Soon how certain I was that she could do it, I decided to tell her the story of *The Little Engine That Could* as we drove. Soon not only *could*—she did.

We were lucky enough to have come back to the St. Louis area just in time for Jim's graduation from Washington University. It didn't seem possible that we now had two college graduates, another halfway through, and the oldest soon sitting for her CPA exam.

While Nancy was home from Yale for the summer to work in St. Louis, studying muscle cells for a lab that was doing muscular dystrophy research, it wasn't long before she had a few unscientific words for Don and me. "You both talk constantly about how wonderful McChord and Washington State were. You've never done that before and I think you should stop. It's obnoxious."

Embarrassed to realize she was absolutely right, we worked hard to shut our mouths. But it was hard to cease the mental comparisons.

If I went out to weed the garden there in Southern Illinois, I had the choice of being eaten alive by mosquitoes in the morning or evening when it was coolest or being drenched with sweat midday from the heat and humidity. There were a lot of good things about living in the Midwest, but, generally, the weather was not one of them.

I was sitting backward out one of the upstairs windows early one lovely morning, though, trying to wash the top outside panes when Don's boss's wife came walking down the street.

"Hey, Joan," she hollered up. "Say, if you're crazy enough to hang out windows, I think you'd make a great chairperson for the upcoming luncheon that we're hosting in the fall for the wives' club."

I didn't quite get the connection but couldn't think of anything else to do but say, "Sure."

Shortly after that I got a call inviting me to a summer luncheon for our Ops group wives in the backyard of one of the off-base homes.

"We're having a woman who's an astrologist come to do the program. She's asked that we collect a few birth dates, places and times, and we thought since you're new here it would be fun to include yours."

I actually remembered the facts she wanted, gave them to her and forgot about it until the public reading of my horoscope—and all the others, too—to the gathered group.

The astrologist had just gotten to her recitation about my being "a perfectionist, hard on myself and others," when Ellen Reilly, the wife heading the decorating committee for the luncheon I was to chair, laughed and exclaimed at the top of her lungs, "Oh my God, and we have to work with **her**?" It was a strange way to begin what turned into an enduring friendship.

Early the next fall, our committee ended up creating a backdrop of the *Robert E. Lee*, a paddleboat anchored on the Mississippi River that had been converted into a fine restaurant. Maggie Hoybach, one of the wives who was a professional artist, had painted a striking waterfront scene, while others toted in bales of hay and other props to make it all look as if we had just plucked the boat from its moorage and plunked it on stage as the set for the singing group entertaining that day.

Even husbands got involved, fetching and carrying. I figured the best way to thank everyone would be to host a party for the entire committee and spouses. We had to be out of town when the invitations were due to be mailed so, for the first time in my life, Don's office sent them out for us.

Right after we got back, we heard the terrible news that Sue Calhoun, who had been with us in Washington, had lost her battle with cancer. The memorial service was the afternoon of the night of the party, just a few days after we'd come back from being on the road. For once, I would just have to be sure I had almost everything ready ahead of time.

I was confident enough of the progress I was making that, as Don went out the door to go back to the office after the service, I said, "Don't worry, hon. I'm doing just fine on time." I underestimated the subconscious toll the grief of the day had taken on me.

When he returned a little before six and went upstairs to get changed, I was still in the kitchen, in jeans, hair uncombed, but sure I had another half hour yet before party time. Then the doorbell rang. The first couple had just arrived.

"Gee," I said. "I think you're a little early," sure in my mind that the invitations had gone out for six-thirty, yet also half aware that other cars were coming down the street now, clearly headed for our place.

"No," the sweet young wife said, invitation right there in her hand as if she'd sensed she'd need proof, "it says 6 p.m."

I nearly died—but ushered her and her husband into the house, as well as all the others who were fast coming up our front steps, asked them to make themselves at home while I dashed upstairs to get changed and get Don to begin making drinks. Then the whole bunch pitched in with me to carry food to the table and laugh over "the perfectionist" who had just proven herself a colossal "goof-up." It was probably one of the best parties we've ever had. And everyone now knew how fallible I was, no matter what astrology readings said.

It didn't seem possible that we were already married twenty-five years that August, but the kids all came home and we celebrated as a family with a trip to the Lake of the Ozarks. Later in the fall we decided to celebrate such a special anniversary again by ourselves.

I was excited when Don outlined where he hoped to take me, Space Available, in Europe. We drove to New Jersey, and much to our amazement found there was room for us on a plane that was leaving that night.

"We'd better call the kids and let them know what we're doing," I said to Don, as he filled in the paperwork.

"Yeah, why don't you go ahead and do that," he answered, barely looking up.

I got right through to Cathy and Jim, but by the time I was about to dial Nancy in Connecticut, I realized I'd run out of change and Don was motioning to me to hurry up. We were about to board.

I couldn't go without calling our youngest too. With no change and no time, I decided to dial the operator and put through a fast call to Nancy's college room in the only possible way I could think of. I was relieved when one of her six roommates answered right away.

"Will you accept a collect call for Nancy Brown from Joan Brown?" the operator asked.

"Well... yes," the roommate who'd answered finally stammered, then shouted, "Nancy, your mom is on the phone—COLLECT!"

"You're calling me collect?" Nancy said as she came on, incredulous but laughing. I hurriedly explained why and scurried after Don so we wouldn't miss our flight. I'm sure it was one phone call and role reversal that everyone in the dorm heard about.

Don and I knew we would at least get to Germany, but it would be luck of the draw as to where we'd go after that. Our good fortune held, propelling us through brief but magnificent stops that allowed us to visit Naples, Capri, Rome and Aviano in Italy, then Athens, where we even took time to visit some of the Greek Islands.

In a few months it would be 1980, yet this was the first time Don and I had ever gotten this far away from the kids, and one night all my concerns seemed to come to a head in a dream. I was exhausted the next morning when the alarm went off but I certainly knew why. All night long, I had been "up," trying to pack three precious china teacups in metal cake pans to protect them as we traveled. But there was just no way to do it. The cake pans themselves would've broken rather than shielded the fragile pieces.

The analogy was hard to miss. Maybe I hadn't succeeded in letting go as well as I thought I had. Clearly, I still had much more work to do on a job I thought I'd already finished. I was so amazed at myself I even mentioned it over the phone to Nancy after we'd gotten back, this time in a non-collect call.

"You know, Mom, it really *is* impossible," she said. "Your three precious teacups are just going to have to take care of themselves from now on."

CHAPTER 23:

Our Lady of Perpetual Guilt

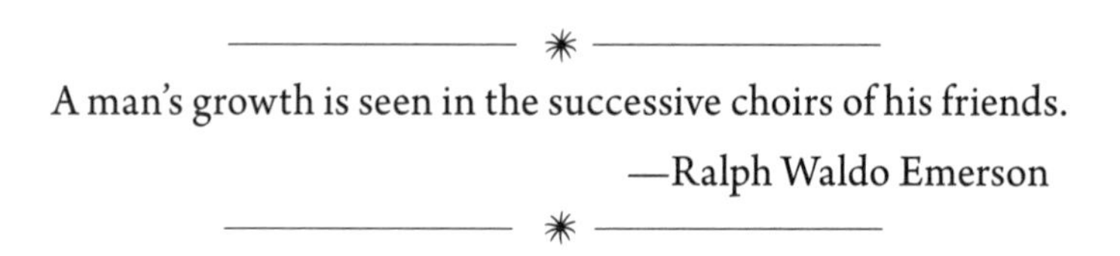

A man's growth is seen in the successive choirs of his friends.

—Ralph Waldo Emerson

Soon Don was changing jobs again, this time from military airlift Operations, the day-to-day running of transport airplanes all over the world, to Plans, looking out ahead to what airlift the country would need in the years to come. At least we weren't moving with this change in jobs, either cross-country or across the base.

I got a new "job" too, that of helping to produce a monthly magazine for the wives. Much as I'd loved the ESL group, this was even more up my alley.

But volunteers were needed elsewhere as well, and first thing every Monday morning, I headed over to the Thrift Shop with most of my neighbors. Together, we all did mark-downs. Much as I would've preferred to be teaching ESL, I found the camaraderie made it fun. It was also a worthy cause. Not only did the resale of household items raise money for the various charities the Thrift Shop supported, it was also a way for families to either get rid of or acquire things. Children grow and, heaven knows, we all needed to shed "pounds" as we moved.

In fact, I was so busy working outside the home—just not for a salary—that I still hadn't hemmed up our old drapes to fit the current windows. Embarrassed, I mentioned it one day to a new neighbor who'd been "in the moving business" even longer than I had and she said, "You hem them? Whatever for? I always just pin them. That way they're easier to redo each time."

The biggest frustration with all the volunteer activities that took me away from home was scheduling a delivery or a repair at the house.

"Do you work?" (translated as "for pay"), a voice on the phone would query when someone needed to come to the house. If I had had a "real" job, they'd have understood why I couldn't stay home half a day in the hopes that someone would arrive within the timeframe allotted. I finally decided the Red Cross, Family Services, Thrift Shop magazine and everything else were, in fact, work and routinely began to answer "Yes" without feeling the least bit guilty about "interpreting" the question.

It proved as effective as "We don't own the house" to the many who called proffering aluminum siding or some other goody while they were "in our neighborhood."

Don and I were busy day in and day out. In addition to hosting the old friends who came through for visits and stayed with us, our nighttimes were as full as the days, with rubber chicken dinners and all sorts of other functions to either host or attend. They could be fun, particularly because there was so much civic involvement and the chance to meet interesting people from all over the country—and the world.

It was on one of those evenings when, just before the traditional announced "potty" break after the meal and prior to the speeches or program, I was seized by a knife-like pain in my abdomen. It was so intense I mentioned it to a friend as I waited in the inevitable line in the ladies' room a few minutes later.

"Oh, that's probably that stomach flu that's going around, honey," she said. "I just got over it too."

Whatever it was, I thought the evening would never end. When the formal part of it finally did, I grabbed Don and told him I had to get out of there right away—before I upchucked in front of everybody.

Despite the fact that it was well after eleven, Don had a briefcase full of work he still had to do when we got home. He was intent on it in another room by the time I began throwing up in the bathroom. In between, I was holding the "barf bowl" we'd used for our young kids "just in case" I couldn't get there in time from the side of the bed where I knelt, doubled over and clutching my stomach to try to lessen the pain. Then Don came in and saw me.

"Come on, Jo. We're going to the hospital."

"I'm too sick to go anywhere. Just leave me alone and maybe it'll go away."

I was being as stubborn as my dad. When I was a senior in high school, the principal had called me out of class to tell me my father was in the hospital with peritonitis from a ruptured appendix. He'd done exactly what I was doing, absolutely refusing to see a doctor, until my mother called on my uncle to intervene and "make" him go.

My own unrelenting pain finally convinced me that maybe I shouldn't be that pig-headed. When I could fend Don off no more, I let him drive me, bowl in hand, to the emergency room, where they admitted me.

Tuesday night, Wednesday and Thursday went by in an agony of regurgitation, as I was wheeled through the corridors and on and off elevators for one test after another. They were feeding me intravenously and had inserted an awful tube into my nose, but no one could seem to figure out what in the world was wrong—until Friday morning when the doctor came in to tell me they'd finally found an obstruction in the small bowel. They were going to have to go in to do exploratory surgery.

Don and a chaplain friend, who brought Holy Communion, were there within minutes. As they wheeled me away, I couldn't help but wonder whether I was facing a malignancy.

I wasn't. But they told me later that what they did find was bizarre:

an intestinal blockage caused by adhesions from the hysterectomy I'd had seven-and-a-half years earlier. Had it taken another day to find it, it probably would've meant my losing a part of the intestine. Instead, they were able to cut away the adhesions and fix things. Other than the fact that abdominal surgery was about as much fun as the days of pain and that my lungs had also filled up with fluid, probably as a result of all that had gone on, I was at last on the mend.

The first few days I was in such a fog I got angry at Don for canceling our reservations for the Airlifters' Convention in Nashville.

"I would've been well enough to go," I protested. "I'll be coming home in a couple of days."

I was even more infuriated when he told me he'd called off the luncheon I was to have hosted the following week at the house. I was sure I'd have been well enough to do it. In my drugged stupor I'd been going over the shopping list for what I'd need to buy for it.

When I finally did get to go home after two weeks, my next-door neighbor Vivian and Nancy, the one who'd caught me window washing, came by with a schedule of who was bringing dinner meals over on which nights for the entire next two weeks.

"And there will be no arguments. It's all set," they said.

When I told my mother about it over the phone, she and my dad finally grasped the depth of the friendships I'd been blessed with. After all those years of wanting sisters and brothers, I had been granted my wish in a way I could never have foreseen when we first began our vagabond married life some twenty-five years earlier.

That didn't stop my folks from worrying so much about me in the aftermath that Don suggested I fly down to Florida while he was on another extended trip and I was well enough to go to let them see for themselves.

When Don had called them, my dad mentioned he had just given up smoking—again. It wasn't the first time and it hadn't taken much before he'd started in all over again after the previous attempt, despite the fact that he'd already had a lung collapse. We were both terrified he'd use what had happened to me as his excuse to begin again.

But this time he persevered, and I couldn't have been more delighted. While he was bringing the car to the curb at the airport I asked my mother, who was a bathroom smoker because my father disapproved of her doing what he did, "Did you quit too?"

She batted her big blue eyes innocently at me and said, "I never smoked," to which I just repeated, "*Mom* did *you* quit too?" Finally, she looked down sheepishly and whispered, "Yes."

It seemed that now Don was on the road more than ever. But I was long past being confined to the house day in and day out as I had been years before when I was solo, just trying to maintain our family stability and take care of the kids. Once I had realized how fast we became a part of a community no matter where we lived, I could handle it.

When I noticed *Norma Rae* playing at the base theater while Don and most of the neighbors' husbands were gone too, I called each of them and suggested we go together to see it one evening. Vivian was the only one who agreed, but insisted on doing the driving.

When we got out of the movie, she asked if I minded if she stopped at the Shoppette on the way home to get a Coke.

"I'm trying to cut down so I'm not keeping much in the house," she explained as she drove in through the exit.

"Should I say something to her?" I thought to myself, then decided there was no reason to be a sideseat driver. It was late and the store itself was already closed. She just wanted to get a Coke from the machine outside.

Right after she'd accomplished her mission, we headed back out toward the parking lot entrance, again contrary to the arrows.

With that, a military Security Police truck pulled across our path, red overhead lights flashing, and I thought, "Darn, I should've said something" while Vivian went on about how upset her husband would be if she got a ticket. She fished around in her purse for her license while we waited—and waited—and waited—for the cop who'd stopped us to approach the car.

Not a soul came near, though the red lights of the Security Police vehicle flashed all over in front of us. It was then that I thought I detected a voice in the darkness and suggested we open the windows to the bitter January late night cold.

"Get out of your vehicle. Put your hands up over your heads and face this way."

Scared to death, we both emerged, shaking, hands aloft. All the while the voice kept shouting, telling us to get them higher. I finally realized I must have been letting mine sink a bit because, after all, I wasn't driving. Why was I out here too?

The wind was blowing so fiercely my nose began to run. I could stand it no more when it got to the point at which any good mother, horrified at what was streaming down my face, would have come along with a tissue. Vivian swore I even began to ask the shadowy figure behind the bullhorn for permission to wipe it. But he only bellowed louder and Vivian hissed, "Sniff, Joan, sniff. He's going to shoot us!"

When the young cop screaming at us was finally satisfied we were cooperating, he let us know that an alarm had gone off on base. OK. It had nothing to do with entrances and exits, but what did it have to do with us?

He finally approached Vivian's car and told me to walk around to the driver's side. The fact that all the proper base stickers on Vivian's car said we belonged on the base didn't seem to matter. He wanted to see our IDs but didn't trust me not to shoot him while he was looking at Vivian's. We must have really looked dangerous because a second police vehicle had joined the first, cops crouched behind it as well.

By that time, Viv and I had each decided that if we were spread-eagled and patted down we were goners because we would probably sock this young man who riled us as much as any of the bad guys in *Norma Rae*.

Dangerous thoughts. Instead, he took one look at Vivian's identification and said, "You may go."

No "I'm sorry. There's been a mistake." No explanation of why we'd been stopped because of the alarm and made to get out of the car with our hands reaching for the heavens. Just "You may go."

Limp with fear and rage, we crept home along the dark roads. Neither one of us slept much. It wasn't just that it snowed later that night and plows worked noisily to clear the roads around our connected houses. Or that both our husbands were gone. It was that we'd never had to do anything like this before—and we still didn't know why we'd been stopped and treated that way. If the car had been full of all the wives that might have come along with us, one of whom was disabled, would we all have been made to stand out there in the night?

I don't remember exactly when we found out that they suspected us of trying to break into the closed Shoppette because that was where the duress alarm had come from. But for weeks afterward, every time some kind of alert took place anywhere on the base and cars were backed up at the gates, unable to enter or leave, a chorus of friends would intone that they wondered "what Vivian and Joan were up to now?" We had become unwitting partners in crime. And now I felt guilty about the indignation I still harbored within me about what had happened.

If there was one thing in life I excelled in it was guilt. As if to document the worries I'd had about ruining the kids' lives by imperfect parenting as they were growing up, one winter during our time in South Jersey, a blizzard had stranded a college classmate who was visiting us. Since we were unable to either leave or go anywhere, the classmate, by then a practicing psychologist, amused herself and us by having the two toddlers we had at the time draw pictures. The mommy in their artwork was consistently bigger—"clearly dominant in your family," she said.

I'd cringed when I'd heard those words—and for years afterward, certain she'd meant I was coming on too strong in their lives. It wasn't until, after eons of worry about it, that another friend heard the story, laughed and said, "Now tell me, Joan, who else would you expect to be supremely important in the life of children that young?"

In fact, I'd continued to find ways to keep my guiltiness quotient current. When I was still a neophyte on the staff of the wives'club magazine in Oklahoma, I'd been assigned the task of greeting and hosting one of the commanders' wives who was invited to a coffee we were having. I'd never met the woman before so I worried I wouldn't know whom to approach. But, I'd heard she was an alcoholic, whom her husband had someone drive around, lest she herself get behind the wheel. And, they said, she'd just had a facelift.

The minute she walked into the room, I knew this was *the one.* Simultaneously relieved and guilty, I actually went to confession the following Saturday to report my rash judgment.

The gals who worked the Thrift Shop with Vivian and me saw a connection between our "night of crime" and my delight in a Joan Rivers bit I'd heard late one night on the Johnny Carson Show.

Growing up as she did in a Jewish and Italian New York neighborhood, Rivers said the name of her alma mater was Our Lady of Perpetual Guilt. I could relate.

Don was away again the night Vivian and a bunch of the other neighborhood wives came by, a few weeks after our near arrest, to throw an impromptu surprise birthday gathering for me. Between sips of the wine they'd brought, I opened my presents: a water pistol marked "Bonnie," to arm me for those future encounters when "Clyde" was driving and a new T-shirt, with OUR LADY OF PERPETUAL GUILT stenciled over the heart.

I put it away in a special place to remind me of what I hoped I'd finally figured out. That might be my alma mater—but I didn't have to go back for reunions.

Chapter 24:

Where Comes the Bride

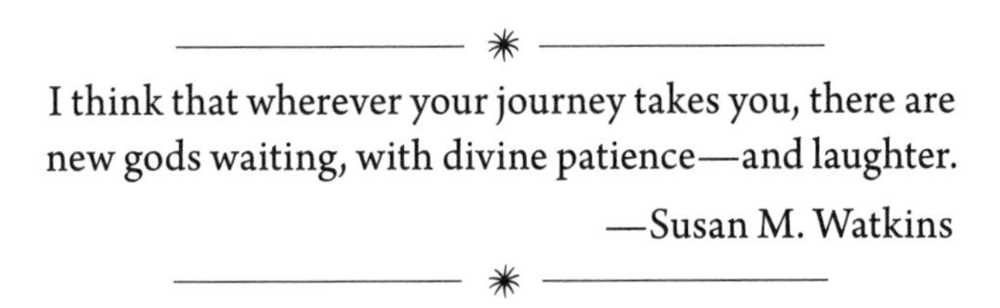

I think that wherever your journey takes you, there are new gods waiting, with divine patience—and laughter.

—Susan M. Watkins

Whether or not we physically change locations, life seems to have its own way of moving us on. Hard as that can sometimes be, it keeps things interesting.

Don's job as the "Planner" for military airlift soon began taking him to D.C. almost as often as he went to his office in Illinois. Most of the time it was to testify before Congress about budget needs and work to see that a new transport aircraft would be built to fill the gap in the nation's airlift capability in time to replace aging C-141 planes as they had to be retired from service. Without a replacement, we were looking at the old "for want of a nail" story. The various branches of the military couldn't go anywhere to do their jobs without adequate air transport.

On the home front, we were facing another rite of passage, the graduation of our youngest from college. Nance had decided to work for the next year while she made up her mind what she wanted to do about going to medical school. Although she'd majored in molecular biology and biochemistry and graduated Phi Beta Kappa, she'd been put off by the all-or-nothing attitude of some undergraduate premeds.

After she'd accepted a position with a Boston area firm that helped to clean up the environment from oil spills and other hazards, she couldn't seem to locate a single place in the Cambridge area on which she could afford the rent.

Just a few months earlier, Don and I had finally flown to Houston where John Garrett, Don's friend from Pittsburgh days, had long been begging him to come to give a speech. Little did we know that, in just a couple of months, he'd ask us to return there for Don to be best man at his wedding. When that call came from John, I knew there was no way Don would refuse but that didn't keep me from worrying about the expense of another airline trip for two. I was trying to manage guilt better these days, but I could still win a hand-wringing worry contest thumbs down.

Somehow, this time I found myself replacing the usual fretting with faith that there was some other good reason why we needed to make this trip. It was as if my grandmother had arrived to whisper into my ear, "You know, dear, everything always happens for the best."

Sure enough, her wisdom proved correct. Weeks later, during John's wedding reception, one of his sisters from California mentioned to me that her doctor daughter lived in Cambridge, Massachusetts, and was looking for roommates to help defray the expense of the apartment she had rented there. The two of us exchanged information and thought maybe it would prove to be a good arrangement for both daughters.

But whether they would even consent to check into it was anyone's guess, given the reluctance of newly independent young adults to consider parental suggestions. To our amazement they did, and Nancy was soon living with a large component of young women, sometimes numbering as many as seven, all of whom shared one bathroom.

We soon learned that one of Nancy's classmates from college was coming to Boston to visit as often as he could get away from his duties as a Marine at Camp Lejeune. He was the very young man of whom she'd said, "Don't go getting any ideas, Mom. He's just a friend—nothing serious," when she told her dad that Andy May had asked that Don commission him as a Marine lieutenant after their graduation.

It wasn't long after we'd heard about the frequent visits that we got a phone call from Nance telling us she'd taken the MCATs, applied for medical schools, been accepted at Harvard, and become engaged to Andy. They planned a January '83 wedding during her midyear break from med school, which was also the time he could get leave from the Marines. Since they'd decided D.C. would be the best central East Coast location for most family and friends to be able to get to the ceremony, cross-country planning went into full swing. I joined Don as a regular D. C. commuter. The big difference was I drove and Don flew.

Before that, Don and I decided to make a brief stop in Nashville to meet Andy's parents as we drove to visit my folks in Florida. Happily, we felt an immediate rapport and decided later that evening to call Nance to tell her how much we'd liked the Mays.

"I know," she answered.

"But how could you?"

"Well, Maria called Andy and reported how well everything went."

The groom's teenage sister had sat unobtrusively on the scene that afternoon, acting as her brother's mole.

When we settled on the Andrews Air Force Base Officers' Club in Maryland for both the ceremony and reception, we were lucky enough to find both available. And, despite her own family's upcoming move to Ohio, Mary Carol Muth, another Air Force wife, whose beautiful way with flower arrangements Nancy had seen and loved, agreed to take over that job.

Now the main stumbling blocks boiled down to finding fabric for the nontraditional wedding gown Nancy wanted—sans bridal veil—and dealing with the fact that our daughter wanted us *both* to walk her down the aisle.

"Nance, I can't do that. I'd die from nervousness. I don't feel as if I belong there. No one does that."

"You raised me too, didn't you? And it is so done—in Jewish weddings."

I very much wanted our girls to have what each of them envisioned—to plan their own weddings, rather than have it a parental affair. Don and I had been lucky enough to be able to do that and they deserved the joy of that freedom too. So if this is what Nancy wanted, this is what she'd get. With huge butterflies flitting around my stomach, I finally murmured, "OK."

The photographer was another issue. Don had seen one in action at some official Washington event and liked his style. But would it be subtle enough for Nance who didn't want anyone to even notice pictures were being taken? She had a look the family had dubbed ESAD, for the current phrase "Eat sh-- and die." It ended all discussion. If this guy could avoid that, we had it made.

For the reception music, Don learned that a part of the Air Force's Strolling Strings moonlighted in their off hours. And, in the chapel, a string quartet would play Bach's *Ode to Joy* rather than the traditional *Lohengrin* Wedding March for our grand entrance. That was a change I could enthusiastically embrace.

Once Father Flood had agreed to officiate, we met with the base chapel staff to finalize plans. Despite the fact that we were planning the marriage ceremony of a Catholic to a Jew, the chapel corpsman kept insisting on setting things up as if they were both Protestants.

By far the biggest hurdle, other than the geographic one, was the problem of finding someone in D.C. who would bake a carrot cake for the wedding. Eventually, even that problem was solved. And finally, Lynn and Charlie Ridgway, who'd been friends from

McChord days and were now stationed at Andrews, became kind of surrogate parents of the bride, advising us on local contacts and keeping an eye on things in general.

We were amazed to arrive and find January weather more like early fall than midwinter, and it proved to be a big blessing. After a series of incidents that included my flushing some blusher down the toilet, losing the key to our room and forgetting to put on any mascara or other eye makeup whatsoever, Don and I got into the car to drive Nancy across to the church, never even thinking about Cathy and Jim having to get there too. When they figured out their overwrought parents had left them behind, despite the fact they too were in the wedding party, they double-timed over on their own, in full wedding regalia. Thank goodness there was no snow on the ground.

It wasn't until late that night, when Nancy and Andy were ready to change into other clothes and leave the reception that we realized the base chapel was now locked up tight—with their car keys, along with the clothes they'd left in the church changing room, unreachable for the night. As a result, they spent their first married night in the room across from all of ours.

As it was, the newlyweds were going to spend the rest of their honeymoon in temporary quarters at Camp Lejeune before Nancy had to return to med school. When my uncle teased them about this, Nancy countered with the fact that at least they hadn't invited anyone else to come along. We'd long marveled at the fact that this same uncle had invited my mom and dad, their matron of honor, and best man to join them on his honeymoon so that, the morning after the wedding, the brothers could go hunting together in upstate New York. Miraculously, both marriages lasted.

But for these nuptials, it was just the families of the bride and groom that got together for breakfast the following morning before beginning the drive home. Shortly after we all went our separate ways, Andy's dad later told us he'd put his coat in the trunk and slammed it shut, along with the car keys he'd left in his coat pocket. There was nothing for it but to call in a locksmith.

There seemed to be no end to our joint key calamities that wedding weekend and the stories and laughter they spawned. Little did we know that in ten short months we'd face a real calamity and the stories we'd share would take on a far more solemn tone.

Chapter 25:

Mary Backstage, Noble Wife

Man can starve from a lack of self-realization
as much as . . . from a lack of bread.

—Richard Wright

Nancy was soon back in med school and Andy in North Carolina with the Marines. As they had put it at the wedding, "We're reversing the trend: we're getting married, but we're not going to live together."

Things took on a more serious note in May when Andy shipped out to Lebanon with his infantry battalion. I knew what Nancy was going through. Once he was involved in combat, there was hardly a waking hour that I didn't have every TV in our house tuned to the news so I wouldn't miss hearing any reports of what was happening over there as I went about putting away laundry, making beds or cooking. Watching and listening became a kind of prayer to please keep Andy safe.

Don had now changed jobs again, this time from Plans back to Operations and I was grateful not to have to think about moving on top of everything else. There was already enough excitement to go around.

Our own lives were hardly static. I went along whenever it made sense for Don to drive some place he had to be on business. The next to last weekend in October we returned from D.C. to find a very disappointed son already at our house. After years of working as a contract manager in industry, he'd decided to go into the Air Force. The only hurdle remaining between him and flight school had been the physical he'd just had that afternoon. It was then that he'd learned he had sufficient color blindness and astigmatism to keep him out of pilot training. The letdown he felt was almost palpable. But there wasn't a thing we could do to change things for him.

We weren't even able to stay home long enough to be much emotional support because we were also due over in St. Louis in just a couple of hours for the beginning of the annual Airlifters' convention. But then, Jim had to get on his way too. His winning bid on a newly established route between St. Louis and London had won him a plum of a trip to the British Isles and he was due to depart that weekend. We hoped that would help him move on.

Don's stay at the convention turned out to be remarkably short. When he left abruptly to return to the base, I had no idea what was going on except that I eventually learned the Crisis Action Team had been assembled and he was part of it. I only found out he was working the Grenada invasion and rescue when the story broke on the news. In the meantime, I was biding my time in St. Louis until Don surfaced just in time for Saturday night's dinner.

The television was blaring the next morning, as always, while Don shaved and I got dressed and packed to leave. But soon after I'd tuned in, I screamed for Don, bringing him running out of the bathroom. Almost in sync with the first pictures of the October 1983 bombing of the Marine barracks in Lebanon, our phone began to ring. It was the Ops Command Post, with Nancy on the phone asking to talk to her father.

"Dad, can you find out anything? Can you find out if Andy's OK?" Nancy's every question was echoed in our own minds. But when Don promised to try to get some answers for her, no one could have guessed that it would take almost all week before we knew any more than we did at that moment.

Monday, Tuesday and Wednesday went by and still no one, even Marine Corps Headquarters, could say who had survived and who had not. To make things even worse, Nancy's roommates seemed oblivious to her pain, keeping the apartment's one phone line tied up as if nothing had happened.

Their lack of empathy flabbergasted Cathy, who was visiting in Cambridge to watch the college women row the annual Head of the Charles races the weekend of the bombing. She and Nancy shared the additional bond of having gone out for women's crew at their respective schools.

As day after day dragged on with nary a clue, we kept vigil by both phone and television for even the suggestion of forthcoming news. We weren't the only ones. Despite being on his trip, Jim had of course heard the news and immediately called us from England, where he was visiting Father Flood, currently stationed there.

"What do you know? Is Andy OK?"

He was due to head up to Scotland but was as concerned as we were when he learned we couldn't find out a thing.

Finally, on Thursday, there was a phone number posted on the TV where relatives could call to get information. Since we had a portable phone that would allow us to continuously redial, I had earlier suggested Nance give me Andy's social security number so I could become her surrogate.

Over and over I redialed the toll-free number to an ever-present busy signal. It got to the point that I was emptying the dryer, folding the clothes and walking around the house putting them away, all with the phone tucked squarely to my ear.

I couldn't believe it when I suddenly seemed to be getting through and held my breath as I asked about First Lieutenant Andrew May.

"His Social Security number, please."

I read off what Nancy had given me.

"What have you been told, Mrs. May?"

Oh my God, they're trying to find out if I already know he's been killed I thought as I said, "Nothing."

"Well, we mustered all of the troops who survived and your husband was among them," she said.

Her explanation made sense of why it had taken so agonizingly long. All of the personnel records had been destroyed with the headquarters building and a painstaking headcount of the survivors took time.

Laughing and crying and thanking God all at the same time, I could hardly talk as I dialed Nancy to give her the great news. She immediately called Andy's mom and dad to share the relief and joy with his family. Nancy could finally drift off into a peace-filled sleep, one that was happily interrupted in the small hours of the morning by a call from Andy himself.

The only concern now was that the Marines slated to replace those in Lebanon had been diverted to Grenada. How long would that delay Andy's scheduled return? Despite the setback, by Christmas, our cup brimmed with things to be thankful for. Nancy and Andy joined Jim, Don and me at the house, followed shortly by newly engaged Cathy and Al. We could never have felt more blessed than we did to have everyone together at last, safe, sound and happy. Here we were with one couple about to celebrate a first anniversary and another making plans for their wedding. Once again a daughter wanted both Don and me to help walk her down the aisle. It was no longer a source of anxiety—but, as things turned out maybe I should have worried a little more about this walk and a little less about the last.

The months ahead found me becoming more and more familiar with Interstate 70 as I worked my way from Illinois to the East Coast, sometimes to see and plan with Cathy in New Jersey, sometimes to attend to wedding details for what was to be a late September wedding at Bolling Air Force Base in D.C. Again, the nation's capital seemed the best gathering place for friends and family concentrated mainly up and down the Eastern seaboard and west to Alabama.

But there wasn't even the suggestion of a letup on home front demands for either Don, who'd just been promoted again and seemed to take on more and more, or, for that matter, me. I was guilty of adding a few myself, like my decision to learn calligraphy so I could address the wedding invitations this time around. We'd paid someone who'd been highly recommended to do it the last time and been very much disappointed to find she hadn't really known calligraphy at all. I longed to have at least one day a week when the calendar wasn't chockablock with commitments of one kind or another.

I was hardly receptive to the message Don brought home one evening from some of the people who worked for him who had suggested the military and their spouses reverse responsibilities at our next dinner to welcome newcomers. I was to swap places with Don as host and the military members would decorate the tables. Nowhere near the talented speaker and ad libber Don was, I was engulfed in terror at the thought of getting up in front of a microphone at such a large gathering. I immediately declined.

But the guys with the bright idea weren't taking no for an answer. The next day Don brought home a script they'd written for me. Now they really had my attention. Did they think I was incapable of writing one myself? On the spot I reversed myself about hosting, determined to turn some tables of my own.

When we got there that night and saw the uninspired centerpieces the guys had ordered from a florist, it was easy to see how "hard" they had worked on their part. But who could blame them? Other than the camaraderie of the get-togethers at which decorations were fashioned, most of us wives had to admit there were a host of things we'd rather be doing than crafting arrangements. "We'll be all ready for basket weaving in the nursing home when it's time," was the theme song of many such work sessions.

What rankled most women even more was the official designation for the wives and children of military members as "dependents."

Somehow that one rolled off my back. What didn't was the fact that if, for some reason, a wife was introduced at a social gathering, she was inevitably dubbed "So and So's '*lovely*' wife." It was like being sloughed off as an ornamental appendage, Nora in Ibsen's *A Doll's House,* or the lead in the old radio soap opera *Mary Noble, Backstage Wife.* It was also one thing Don knew better than to do. He was the exception.

For this occasion, the task of announcing the names of all the newcomers we were welcoming fell to me. The first was an exchange officer from Great Britain. When I began by introducing "Brenda Adcock and her lovely husband, Wing Commander Sid," it brought down the house. There wasn't a woman in the room who didn't get the point. And those men who'd never before given it a thought had now had it 'splained to them. World peace was hardly at issue here, but domestic accord can be pretty significant too and, apparently, a lot of us felt strongly about it. I wasn't the only wife feeling the prick of that burr in my side-saddle. And now maybe a few macho partners got the point as well.

Chapter 26:

Another Blooming Move

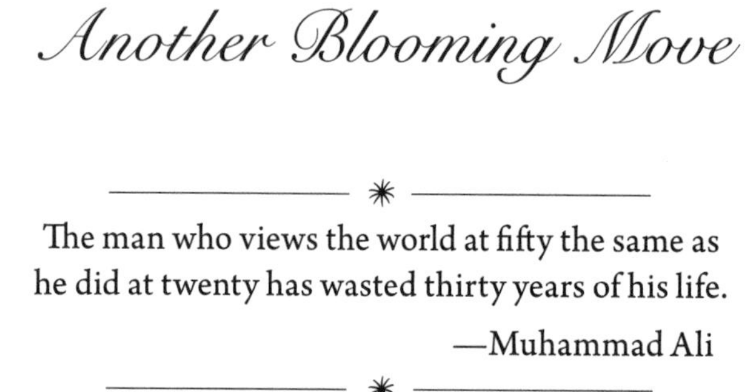

The man who views the world at fifty the same as
he did at twenty has wasted thirty years of his life.

—Muhammad Ali

Within a few months after Cathy and Al had announced their engagement, Don came home with the news that shortly after the wedding he'd be taking over Twenty-Second Air Force, responsible for military airlift in the Pacific half of the world. I couldn't have been more proud of him—or more grateful that we had at least been given a heads-up on a move that would take us from Illinois to northern California, just weeks after Cathy's wedding in D.C. But how in the world were we going to do it?

Nothing about the move would be officially announced for quite a while, so we couldn't even talk to anyone outside the family about our dilemma. It made the cross-stitched farewell gifts we had gotten together to sew for wives as they left the Plans group seem more apropos than ever. I too had received one when we'd gone back to Ops and it sat on our windowsill, reminding me daily to "Bloom where you are planted." Well, now that we were being transplanted again,

I was going to have to do a ton of weeding out in the old "garden" before they tore up my roots this time round.

After five-and-a-half years in one place, the longest we'd ever lived in the same house, I was amazed to find myself more than ready for a change of pace. Except for the cleaning out process. That was like imbibing the stuff you have to down for some onerous medical test.

Packrat that I am, I decided I'd better begin early to do something about all that I'd amassed in our semi-stationary "nest." It was going to take months, especially combined with everything else.

I wasn't the only one up to my eyeballs. As if Cathy didn't have enough responsibility in her position as comptroller-treasurer for a software company, she'd also decided to take on the task of making her own wedding gown and those of each of six bridesmaids. Whenever business or other travel took her through an area in which a bridesmaid lived, she arranged to meet them to do a fitting, even if it had to be on the fly in an airport restroom.

Then, lest guests go astray in D.C.'s traffic maelstrom, she'd made a dry run trip to D.C. to painstakingly scout out the route to the chapel, the reception and the hotel at which she'd negotiated a block of reasonably priced rooms. She wanted to be able to write foolproof directions for us to include with the wedding invitations. Cathy had driven with me enough to know some people might need that kind of help, especially in D.C.

Inspired by her organization and energy, I signed up for a calligraphy class that an artist friend was giving. I also decided to begin cleaning out our attic, now overflowing with all the boxes I'd saved for shipping gifts to our far-flung family. Surprisingly, I discovered there were lots of people eager to adopt some. But, the further I got into tossing the first of what ended up to be some 200 down from the attic, the more I knew I couldn't possibly line up that many takers.

When Don got his "I told you so" look as he counted the shower of cardboard teeming down from the attic, I reminded him some things are just in your genes. I'd heard one of my cousins had shipped empty boxes to Burma for exactly the same purpose. OK, so it hadn't been quite 200. But when you need to mail a present, you need the right size corrugated container. Even Erma Bombeck had written a column about her mother's knowing a good box when she saw one.

This was merely the tip of the cleaning-out iceberg, but there was no way to just sweep the calendar clean of everything else and stay home to shovel the place out. The one thing I vowed to start early enough to take my time and be extra careful with was addressing all those invitations with my newfound skill.

We also decided it would be best if, instead of us, Cathy were the one to receive the responses. That way we could avoid the problem of transshipping gifts from Illinois and California to Cathy in New Jersey or Al, who was already living in their new home in Cincinnati after International Paper relocated him from New York City to Ohio. There were moves galore to deal with.

Just like everyone else who has ever had a wedding in the family, we still didn't have a full head count even as late as a few days before the ceremony and were starting to sweat out how close we were going to be on the number of people the room would hold.

En route to D.C., we called Cathy to find out how the numbers were going and could tell right away from the tone of her voice just how concerned she was.

"Guess who you said could never make it all the way from Guam and who just called to say she's coming, Mom?"

Scheduled for a mainland conference about the same time as Cathy's wedding, Sister Mary Benedict had decided it wouldn't be that hard to include a stop in Washington. We were getting so close on the room capacity I didn't know what we would do if we went over. We certainly couldn't "uninvite" anyone.

Somehow it all worked out. And, true to form, despite her long airplane flight, Sister immediately pitched in to help Mary Carol Muth complete the mammoth task of arranging flowers and table centerpieces.

Cathy too was soon hard at work putting the finishing touches on a custom made fabric cover she'd designed to hide the part of a chest that held a Japanese doll collection in the room where the reception was to be held. Beautiful as it was, for this occasion, it seemed out of place in the room. After one final "fitting" of the cabinet, Cathy and Nancy set up a kind of sweat shop on the floor of Cathy's room, where they took turns sitting cross-legged, stitching away on the portable sewing machine Cathy had brought to finish the job.

When the big day finally arrived, we all gathered in the bride's room in the back of the chapel. As the bridesmaids began oohing and aahing over the exquisite gown Cathy had made, the loop for one of the hand-covered buttons that extended from the nape of her neck to her waist suddenly gave way. It was all I could do not to succumb to panic, but I dared not when I knew it would make us all too upset for anyone to even grasp a sewing needle. Despite shaking hands, we somehow got the errant loop stitched back into place in short order, finally all set to go.

But as we were getting into position in the chapel vestibule just before proceeding into the church, I stepped hard on Cathy's train. Had I torn anything? Oh God, please no. Rather than prayer, what slipped out of my mouth was "Oh sh--!"

Now I'd really "stepped" on it. Suppose someone in the church had heard me? Miraculously, at almost the same instant, the basso profundo voice of my Uncle John drowned me out as he turned around in his seat in the pews, glimpsed Cathy and exclaimed, "What a beautiful dress!"

So many other family members, from both sides, had managed to gather for the wedding that it turned out to be another sizeable family reunion as well. My Burma-box-shipping cousin Jean, God bless her, had gone to all the trouble of arranging to gather up and drive a group of our aging aunts and uncles down from New York. Andy summed it up as we all headed back to our rooms for the night: "This was so much fun. Let's do it again next year."

As we wended our way back to Illinois, the moving truck that would soon pull up in front of our house loomed larger and larger in my thoughts. Shifting into high transient gear, I finished sending the initial batch of changes of address to newspapers, magazines and companies. I knew though that some would inevitably have to go out two and three times before they "got" it.

In between, I took down drapes and curtains, unmade the beds we weren't using, washed, ironed, sorted, threw out and took stuff to the Thrift Shop. Less than two weeks later the packers descended, and once again all our worldly goods became little more than a houseful of floor-to-ceiling boxes.

I tried not to think too much about what condition it would all arrive in at the other end. You could be sure anything that was borderline junk would survive—and equally certain that it was your treasures that would be chipped, dented or broken. What showed up missing would likely be an irreplaceable part like something needed to put a piece of furniture back together. Why did it always seem to be the things you cherished that were damaged? Maybe it was the good Lord's way of teaching us detachment from material things so we could appreciate all that's really important in our lives.

On the night of the last farewell party, the packers were still at the house, long past time for us to go, when we discovered Don's electric razor was nowhere to be found, already buried deep within one of the cartons. Probably because I was ready to fall over with exhaustion, that somehow seemed the last straw and I began to cry so hard I didn't think I could stop long enough to get dressed to go anywhere, no less a party. From out of nowhere, Don produced a gold pendant he'd gotten me on one of his trips and planned to give me later on, took me in his arms and kissed me as he put it on my neck. He found an old-fashioned razor that was still unpacked to shave for the party and somehow I pulled myself together so we could rush out the door.

We'd planned our trip west to take us through Flagstaff, Arizona, where we hoped to spend part of the next day at the Grand Canyon. Don had seen it from the air, but despite all our travels neither one of us had ever actually been there.

When we awoke instead to a surprise mini-blizzard, we still kept hope alive that it would somehow stop in time for us to make the visit. But, instead of filling up with gas as we usually did before starting out for the day, Don decided we'd wait to do it someplace along the way where prices were a little cheaper. As we drove and drove and the snow came down harder and harder, I became more and more nervous. Prices hadn't come down a bit at the very few gas stations we'd passed and soon there weren't even any open to sell us gas at any price. I sat in the car conjuring up headlines: "Couple found dead in snowstorm as car runs out of fuel."

We'd gotten almost to the canyon by the time we finally spied both an open station and a sign that said, "Park closed due to weather." I was so overjoyed to see the gas gauge read more than empty, though, that I was content to just head out of the storm without any further delay.

Other than almost being sideswiped by a truck right after I took over the wheel once we'd outridden the snow, the rest of the trip proved uneventful. We arrived in California just in time to pick up the newlyweds, who, like Jim, had flown in the day before Don's change of command. Nancy and Andy would join us the next day.

Since we weren't yet moved into our new home, we decided we'd all have dinner that evening at the Nut Tree restaurant in nearby Vacaville, along with Howard, one of Jim's roommates from college days who now lived in San Francisco.

During the course of the evening we got into one discussion after another, hitting all the taboo subjects from religion to politics, with one family member often at loggerheads with another. Howard sat there politely taking it all in, sort of like Father Flood, who used to compare listening to us to watching a fast volley. As we were leaving the restaurant, exhausted from all the debates that had gone on, Howard said, "You know, I never realized before just how hard it must be to be a parent."

If I'd thought about it, I might have added, "Especially one in the middle of Move #19."

Chapter 27:

And Miles to Go Before We Sleep

What do we live for, if not to make life less difficult for each other.

—George Eliot

All too soon we were each back in our own little worlds, Nancy in Cambridge, where Andy, who was now out of the Marines, had joined her at Harvard; Al in Cincinnati with International Paper and Cathy commuting from there to continue working with InfoSci; Jim with McDonnell Douglas in St. Louis. Despite the fact we were still buried in moving boxes, Don I and were already immersed in work too.

It wasn't like there was anything "official" to mine, but it remained every bit as real. As we knelt at Mass that first Sunday in California and I watched family after family going up to Communion, I felt the magnitude of sharing some of the responsibility Don now shouldered for the well-being of so many other mothers, fathers and young people. They stretched out halfway around the world, from the Mississippi River to the east coast of Africa.

If I'd thought I had meetings to attend before, it was nothing compared to the daily schedule now. On top of that Don decided we needed to begin traveling to stateside bases right away. Once a year I was allowed to go with him, keeping a schedule almost as rigorous as his as I visited each of the social services—Red Cross, Thrift Shops, Family Services, Child Care centers, wives' groups—and anything else that locally pertained to morale and welfare. In the process, I learned about what worked and what needed help at each place and inevitably took away a list of questions that needed looking into to find answers.

Before I knew it, we'd been there well over a month and it was long past when I should have made plane reservations for the kids and us to be together at Christmastime. There wasn't a seat to be found on any airline and I didn't know where to turn.

Finally, I called an old friend whose husband had been long retired in the area to ask her if she knew anyone that could help. She suggested I call Morry Wasserman, also retired from the Air Force, who now owned a large travel agency in Vacaville with his wife Betty. Somehow he was able to call in all his chits and work the miracle we needed. Thanks to what proved to be the beginning of a very special friendship, we got to Cincinnati to be with the kids and have a great Christmas.

Just before the holidays we'd acquired another special friend. Don's secretary had come into his office one day to say, "Shirley Temple Black is on the phone for you."

"Sure, and I'm the president," Don answered, thinking she was pulling his leg.

"No, really," she insisted. "Pick up the phone."

The child star turned ambassador was about to turn over the reins of the Commonwealth Club to a new president and wanted to have an Air Force presence at the final luncheon at which she would preside.

"Could you and your wife join us for lunch—and maybe bring along the Air Force band? We usually have the Army, but I'm more of an Air Force person." That was the beginning of the wonderful experience of getting to know her and her husband Charles. They were quick to do things to help boost military morale, putting everyone at ease, despite the fact they were celebrities.

As the New Year began and we were preparing to take off again, this time to visit the overseas bases in Hawaii, Guam, the Philippines, Japan, Korea, Okinawa and Alaska, I couldn't help but wish that, like Don, I'd had some formal training in management and leadership. Why was it that no one realized volunteers needed just as much preparation for their jobs as those in paid positions? There was nothing for it except to incessantly pick Don's brain and read book after book to try to absorb as much as I possibly could on my own.

Not only was I dealing with bigger time changes on the overseas visits, jet lag or no jet lag our days began at six a.m. and ended at midnight. Visiting every group that impacted family welfare in each overseas environment proved to be even more of an education.

In the Philippines, one of the wives was a nurse who wanted me to see the conditions under which some of the airmen and their families were living. She and a few other women drove me out to see the garbage dump that neighbored some families' rentals. They explained there were those who sometimes had to go to the base in order to shower because they had no running water in the off-base places they lived in. There were so many work and living conditions that needed fixing right away. Over the years I'd heard Don beat the drum for what needed changing when he came back from visiting units. I knew I wasn't just along for the ride. I at least supplied another set of ears to pick up on what needed doing.

Often I found solutions at one base for some of the problems encountered at another. Some bases were agonizing over long commissary checkout lines that inevitably greeted shoppers around payday or if a new checker was being trained. When they tried another base's system, one line that fed into all the others, it sped things up considerably.

Elsewhere, Family Services eradicated a concern about possible liability over car seats they were lending out by adopting the form used elsewhere. The interchange of information proved invaluable.

But, between us, Don and I always flew home with a long list of things that needed more work to get fixed.

At the end of one long day I'd had to get up in the middle of the night to use the bathroom. For years, there had been complaints from crews billeted in the building we were staying in. And now there was graphic evidence in front of me. The toilet seat was alive with baby roaches racing around it. Complaints that had previously gone uncorrected were now so dramatically underlined they could no longer be ignored. I'm sure there were a lot of people who wished we'd never shown up, as well as those who maybe were glad we had.

For me, the hardest part of the whole thing was when I was expected to talk to a group of wives. The format I felt most comfortable in was that of a "fireside chat," where there was free give and take and not just one-sided speechifying. The only way I knew to do any of it was to tell the stories of our own mobile lives: the difference it had made to me when I was welcomed as a newcomer, dealing with the difficulties of moving children, and my own internal debate over the issues of volunteering. Through it all, I prayed a lot that I wouldn't muff everything up too badly.

As soon as we got home again from one of these trips, we checked in with my mom and dad, Don's mother, and each of our kids. It was during one of these phone calls that we got the wonderful news that Cathy was pregnant. The bad news was that the upcoming Christmas would be the first year we wouldn't all be together. It was the in-laws' turn to have Cathy and Al, Nancy and Andy with them. After we'd talked to Jim about it, we decided the three of us would celebrate together in San Diego. Then Don and I would fly to Cincinnati for a visit. This time I made sure to call Morry Wasserman early in the fall to set up our plane tickets. Maybe too early.

I had in fact bought our tickets so far ahead that, after we'd driven back from southern California to Alameda, where we stayed overnight to be in place for our plane to Ohio, it suddenly dawned on me on the way to the airport that we should've called the airline to check to make sure the time of the flight hadn't changed.

"Well, it's too late now," Don said as we sped across a bridge on our way to the airport for him to drop me off to go on to the gate while he parked the car in long-term parking.

I was sufficiently worried that, tickets in hand, I went up to a red-coated airline employee who seemed to be some sort of manager and asked him if we were still OK on time, since airlines sometimes changed schedules.

He took one look at the tickets and said, "Yes, ma'am, the time is still the same. But you're at the wrong airport. These tickets are for a plane leaving from Sacramento, not San Francisco."

Now what did we do? I'd completely forgotten that back in the fall, before we'd decided to drive to San Diego, I'd booked from Sacramento because that would be an easier airport to get in and out of from the base. There was no way we could now make the three-hour drive there in the little time remaining until takeoff. I must've gone white as a ghost because the red-coat reached out an arm to support me as he quickly added, "But it's OK. We can get you on this one. In fact, you'll be in first class from here to Dallas. You can board now."

The shock of my stupidity was bad enough. I wasn't about to get on without Don and he still wasn't back from parking the car. I stuttered out something about how I'd wait for my husband, not knowing he had encountered problems of his own.

At that point in the holiday season, there wasn't a parking place to be found in the long-term slots and he'd had to settle for short-term, then make a desperate call to a friend to please come move the car to someplace legal within the allowed time. It was too early in the day to have a drink, but by boarding time we both could have used one.

Unfortunately, living as the other half lives only lasted until Dallas. When a pregnant Cathy met us in Cincinnati and heard what had happened, she said, "I can't believe you could go to the wrong airport, Mom, and end up upgraded!"

A few months later, though, I almost missed getting there altogether for the birth of our first grandson. We were on our way to Las Vegas for the fortieth birthday celebration of the Air Force when it felt like I was coming down with a horrendous head cold. By the time we'd gotten to Edwards Air Force Base, where we were staying the night en route, I was burning up with fever and the local doctors said it looked to them very much like something akin to Legionnaire's Disease.

Sometime shortly before we'd left on the trip to Vegas, I'd been working at my desk at home when workmen had cleaned out the evaporative cooler on the roof of our quarters. As a result, birds' feathers, nesting materials and all kinds of debris had showered down around me from the vent above my head. Whatever I had, that experience certainly hadn't helped.

After a night of tossing and turning at Edwards, I woke up the next morning to the phone ringing and the happy news that Ryan had just been born. I could hardly wait to get back to Cincinnati to see and hold him. But first we had to turn around, get back home and hope I got well fast so I wouldn't infect our new grandson. Antibiotics did enough of the job that we were able to go. But whatever it was left me with a temporary asthma condition that I was thankful to see eventually clear up and not return.

We soon became as obnoxious as any other new grandparents, subjecting all our friends to baby pictures while Don expounded on the fact that being a grandparent was the best job he'd ever had.

Just a little over a month later the newborn Ryan joined the rest of the family gathered in Massachusetts for Nancy's and Andy's graduations, one from medical and the other from business school. Don and I were still so mobile that they'd decided to settle in Nashville, where Nancy began an internship in Internal Medicine at Vanderbilt and Andy went to work for a health maintenance organization. Jim was now a contract administrator with Emerson Electric in St. Louis.

But earthly euphoria can only last so long. It wasn't that our grandparent and other joys stopped or decreased. It was that the whole way of life it had taken me years to accept would soon be turned on its head.

Chapter 28:

Stop the World, We're Getting Back On

That's the way things come clear. All of a sudden.
And then you realize how obvious they've been all along.

—Madeleine L'Engle

During the time we were at Travis, I was delighted to see more and more evidence that the things volunteers were trying to accomplish were at last receiving recognition. Some training was even being provided. In fact, the powers that be now included spouses in some of the educational seminar type gatherings previously reserved only for military members.

Vern Orr, Secretary of the Air Force under Ronald Reagan, was one of those who helped turn things around. I thought what he had helped to do was so significant that when he retired I wrote a note to say thanks. My own thinking on the subject had included the realization that what we spouses contributed could make a difference—not to get our husbands promoted à la the old-school song and dance that we were given when Don first entered the service—

but to improve the quality of life for all of us. "Now we have a voice," about summed up how I now felt. "I'd hate to see them *stop* asking us to be involved."

It was during a three-day off-site seminar at Missouri's Lake of the Ozarks that Don and I, as part of a group of other husbands and wives, got to hear a lot of motivational speakers. But we had not even the slightest hint how soon we would ourselves need to use the information a psychologist imparted on how to deal with stress.

I guess maybe I should have had some sense of something coming. A guy who should've been a friend, but I knew in my gut wasn't, came up to me as we were gathering for dinner one of the three evenings and asked what I thought of Don's next assignment. I brushed what he said aside with an "I don't know what you're talking about" and halfway forgot about it until the following Monday morning when Don called me on the house phone from the lobby of the building we were staying in at Scott Air Force Base. Following the weekend retreat, he was there for a promotion board.

It was only seven in the morning and I'd just climbed back into bed, determined to catch a few more winks. I was almost half asleep when the call bolted me fully awake. Don had just been pulled aside in the lobby and told we were moving to Washington, D.C. At first I thought I'd misunderstood what he was saying until he said he was on his way back up to the room to talk to me about retiring instead.

The devil was in the details. He'd gotten this casual delivery of information from someone we'd just finished spending the weekend with. More significantly, the new job was one in which Don felt he could no longer contribute anything to the Air Force. After thirty-two years, it was time to leave, he told me. And now the shoe was on the other foot. I was the one who didn't want to "get out."

It wasn't as if I hadn't known we'd be turning over a new page in our life together in a few more years when Don retired. But this was three years early and he'd accomplished so much for the Air Force. How could they "let" him go short of that time?

Later that day, Cathy drove down from Ohio with Ryan to see

us while we were in Illinois, so she was the first of the family to hear the news. Having family with you at life's critical moments can put things in perspective and she certainly put a positive spin on the whole thing. As Don stretched out on the floor, bouncing our five-month-old grandson on his lap, he almost looked himself again.

The one thing he'd asked was that he be able to pick a retirement date that would allow our children to be there for it. This wasn't as simple as it sounded because all the kids and their spouses had to be able to arrange time off from work. And the powers that be had to agree. Eventually, it was decided that the ceremony would be the last week of February, which seemed to work for everyone.

But that was still months away and life and responsibilities still had to go on without our being able to utter a single word to anyone outside the family about the forthcoming retirement. Those were the orders that had come down from D.C.

As it turned out, Don was scheduled to fly to New Zealand to go on the mid-winter resupply of Antarctica and he decided it would be ideal if he took leave en route so we could have time to talk and think about the future together. He asked me to talk to Morry about booking a commercial ticket for me to meet him there.

I ended up in the "back of the bus," in a middle seat, on the seemingly endless flight, absolutely convinced that this was never going to work because weather would probably not allow Don to get in and out of McMurdo Station in Antarctica as scheduled. I was delighted to find myself absolutely wrong. Everything went like clockwork.

From Christ Church, we flew to Queenstown where we stayed in a secluded alpine lodge overlooking a lake. It was early spring down under so we were able to walk and talk among burgeoning blossoms about what should come next in our own newborn future. From there, we boarded a bus south to Milford Sound, lulled into at least temporary peace by the sheep-filled pastoral countryside en route and the magnificence of the Sound's fjords.

When we came back to California, it was back to work and pretend nothing had changed drastically in our lives. We had no idea where we would settle and only a vague idea what we would do.

Although I'd said, "Whatever you want, hon, is fine with me," and tried to mean it, I realized it was far from the truth. I was still a dog with a bone that I wasn't about to let loose. I felt strongly that there was no way Don should be leaving the Air Force yet.

Finally, after months of having to be quiet about it, the announcement was made that Don would retire. By then, we'd decided to seek out an apartment in one of the nearby towns until we knew where Don would be working. I was relieved to finally be able to go out and look for the next roof that would be over our heads, however temporarily. What took me by surprise was just *how* fast the word traveled once the announcement was made.

Even the paper boy who came to the door to collect for the month had overheard his military parents talking about it. "Why does your husband have to 'tire'?" he asked me as I handed him the money and a tip. "Mom and Dad said they wish he wouldn't tire."

I knew just how they all felt.

Inside, my heart was doing somersaults in time with the twitch of my eye that only happened when I was exhausted. Everything had happened so fast that nothing short of finding I was waking from a bad dream would set things right again.

Don talked to me till he was blue in the face, as did each of our kids, but that just made me angry with all of them for not understanding. They all thought the decision, however unexpected, was "for the best." Everyone but me. If the grandmother whose favorite expression that was had miraculously shown up, I guess I would have argued with her too.

"What is it you want, Joan, a personal guarantee from God?" Don asked me one day when my fear and worry had ignited a fight between us.

A week or two later, a fledgling chaplain newly arrived from New York delivered the sermon on Sunday. His speech pattern sounded reassuringly like "home" to me.

"When I was a boy," he said, "we lived in a row home on Long Island, and each house had a front stoop. To me, it looked very, very steep. Too steep to jump from, although I wanted to very much, and my father encouraged me, assuring me he would be right there to catch me.

"But there was no way I'd let go—in case he didn't. I was too afraid to trust him to not let me fall.

"The day I learned to have faith that my father would indeed be there with his arms securely around me, I was able to take that leap.

"Adult life can be like that too. Sometimes we have to remind ourselves that it's OK to jump off what looks like a precipice, because our Father has told us He'll be there to catch us."

It was as if he were talking to me alone. Here I was a grown woman every bit as frightened at the jump we were about to make back into the real world as he had described. Would Anyone be there to catch us?

Don looked at me as we filed out of church and laughed as he squeezed my hand. "I guess we can't ask for more specific advice than that. Even you have to believe now, Thomasina."

A few weeks later, hand in hand, we took that leap together.

Chapter 29:

Things That Go Bump in the Night

> Not just to love—but to *persist* in love... that's the only purpose grand enough for a human life.
>
> —Sue Monk Kidd

The idea of moving into an apartment made me uneasy. After years of detached or duplex living, I dreaded hearing every sound a neighbor might make—and having them do the same for us. That's how we came to pick a newly built complex that featured "luxury soundproofing."

Next we had to contend with deciding what to get rid of, what we would move to the apartment and what got put into storage until we knew where we were going to eventually make our permanent home. As always, we had to be careful that what was supposed to stay with the house didn't get packed and shipped. When we'd moved in, Velma Bennett had had to mail back the microwave probe that she found in a box with the rest of their shipped kitchen things. Broiler pans frequently got packed by mistake.

I'd tried signs and ropes and putting things in a special room or closet to segregate what didn't go. Nothing seemed to work. And it was impossible to be in different rooms with several movers at once. This time I decided to try one last thing: hunter-orange dots that we could change from day to day as a different group of movers showed up. If something had a dot on it that day, it got shipped. Otherwise, it didn't. It had only taken me nineteen moves to think of this. But giving our house the measles worked so well on our twentieth that I knew I would use it when we moved for what I hoped would be the very last time.

We were the first tenants to enjoy our Vacaville, California, apartment's 900 square feet of virginal—unstained and unmatted—carpeted space. Since we had no idea how long it would be before we decided where, why, or how we'd go next, the best of our furniture moved in with us—to guard it from the hazards of storage, as well as bolster our morale. Don called it the most expensive way to store and care for fifty-two houseplants that anyone could conceive of.

"You're exaggerating," I said—before I counted, then said no more.

The box buffet in the dining room was something else. The government would allow us one last move to a final retirement destination, after this one within the local area. But the prospect of exceeding the weight allowance and having to pay for every pound of overage sent chills down my spine. I had to finish culling and getting rid of what I hadn't yet had time to go through. We packed it all into a ten-foot wall of cartons, about sideboard high, and draped the whole thing with a sheet that I kept telling myself made it less noticeable.

It certainly "disappeared" for me the first two months as we hit the road to visit family and take one last trip before we settled down. Even my fear of inter-apartmental noises faded away as only the sounds of neighbor children awakening—or reluctant to hit the hay—found their way upstairs to us when we were home. Then, one day after we'd just gotten back from a trip, we were jolted by the living and dining room floor vibrating beneath our feet.

"My God, Don, we're having an earthquake," I shouted.

I figured it must have been a big one if we could feel tremors through a poured concrete building. When it stopped and I could see none of our neighbors running out of the buildings, I was relieved but confused about what had really happened.

Over the next week or so, the shaking went on every few days while its source remained a mystery. Then one afternoon as Don was working at the table, a new shaking took over both walls and floor of the dining room. This time there was no doubt what it was. Till recently, the apartment that backed on ours had stood empty—and silent. While we were away it had been rented. It was the beat from the new next-door tenants' tweeters and woofers blaring so loudly through the walls between us that we almost expected them to give way at any minute, like Jericho's.

It took no more than a quarter hour's communal percussion before the man renowned for never complaining about anything decided to walk over to talk to the manager. Together, they paid a visit to our new neighbor's teenage daughter, who had set up their stereo speakers squarely against the common wall between apartments. Our acoustical honeymoon was over. So much for luxury soundproofing.

For my part, I felt relieved to learn our new neighbor had readily apologized and quickly repositioned the speakers. Even better, her mother suggested we knock three times on the apartment wall if the volume ever offended us again so they could promptly turn it down. What she didn't mention was that, as a guard at the local prison that had recently housed Charles Manson, she would rarely be home to hear—or act upon—our knocks until the small hours of the morning.

"Oh, by the way, Jo," Don said as an afterthought, "I think I found the source of our 'earthquakes.' The neighbors work out with a set of barbells. I noticed them out on the balcony when I was over there."

There was a respite from noise for a little while, but on the days our single mom neighbor was away from home, our knocks went unanswered. And we weren't the only ones "knocking." A woman who lived downstairs complained to me that they'd had to pick discarded pork chop bones off the roof of their car where the same problem neighbors had tossed them from the balcony one partying weekend.

As the weeks went on, the volume on my anxiety about what we were going to do next was also mounting, so much so that I couldn't help but try my own version of knocking on walls for help.

"What's new?" I'd ask when I came back to the apartment from running errands. This phrase we'd always used after having been apart for a day or a week had now taken on new meaning. Don was no dummy. He knew I was really asking whether anyone had called offering a job. Though he was doing some consulting, what I longed for was closure—and at least an idea of when and where we'd make the final move to a home of our own. Day by day the 900 square feet seemed to shrink around us as we each struggled to close out the noise intruding upon our peace.

One day there was something new. Dutch Huyser, one of Don's former commanders, phoned to invite us to brunch in San Francisco the next Sunday. In a beautiful room overlooking the Bay, he laid it on the line about how patient we were going to have to be before an "afterlife" took hold.

"It'll take a good two or three months before anyone even realizes you're out there," he said.

But Don-the-optimist wasn't the one worried. And I wasn't sure I could take his being one whit less concerned than he already seemed to be.

"Just make sure you maintain a daily routine, getting up and going to bed at regular times, just like you were still working," was Dutch's parting advice.

It was not long after one of these regular getting up times, when I was brushing my teeth in the bathroom next to our bedroom, that I once again overheard rhythmic thumps coming from next door.

"Good grief, they must be jumping rope now," I said to Don, thinking of the barbells.

"They're not jumping rope, Joan," he said with a laugh, and I blushed with the realization of the true source of what I was hearing from the other side of the wall.

The one sound I longed to hear, that of the telephone ringing, happened all too seldom anymore. I suspected many were leery of calling because sometime, somewhere in the past they'd run into a new commander and wife who had been offended by someone maintaining ties with the old guard. It was one more reason I was anxious to decide what we were going to do and get where we were going so we could begin a new life minus the dregs of antediluvian concepts of protocol.

One vestige from the past that we were both having a hard time laying to rest was our propensity to be night owls. We might get up on time in the morning, but more and more we drifted into our old pattern of staying up too late.

Perhaps we would have been awakened anyway the night we were just climbing into bed about two in the morning when really loud non-jump-rope noises began bouncing off the wall right behind our heads.

Feeling like a voyeur, I lay in bed as guilty as if I stood outside our neighbor's bedroom window on tippy toe, peeking in. Don and I were surely talking loud enough to one another for them to hear us too. Any minute now they'd stop and move the bed away from the wall, I reasoned. But it didn't happen.

"What do we do now? Knock three times on the wall?" I stammered in the darkness as the minutes and thumping went on in the otherwise still of the night.

Don didn't answer. And then finally, as it stopped, he began applauding. Laughing, I joined in, clapping my hands together as loudly as I could. A stage whisper would have resounded through the silence that followed.

They seemed to have moved their jump rope after that.

CHAPTER 30:

The Joy of Jumping

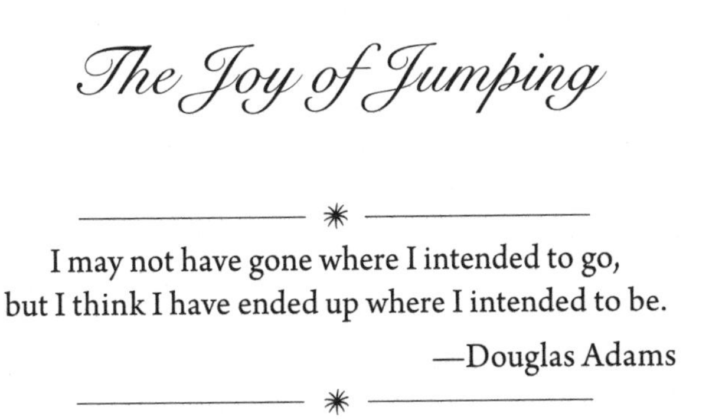

I may not have gone where I intended to go,
but I think I have ended up where I intended to be.

—Douglas Adams

Seven months dragged by before we finally edged closer to being able to decide where we were going with our lives—both literally and figuratively. When the day of decision finally arrived, it was swift and decisive.

"Pack your bag. I'll be there in an hour to throw some stuff together for myself and pick you up," Don said over the phone, sounding as chipper as could be. "We're going where we want to go."

For months, we'd each do-si-doed around where we really wanted to end up, neither wanting to push the other. Don had admitted he much preferred the idea of having his own business to a nine-to-five job. But he had nevertheless gone into one last interview in San Francisco with an open mind. When he found out accepting the position would've involved living and working in D.C., he called to tell me he'd turned it down and to get ready to drive up to the other Washington.

Somewhere during our three years in Washington State, we had each come to realize that this was what we wanted to come back to. There are countless other places of wonder and beauty in the country, but compared to Puget Sound the mountains elsewhere no longer seemed high enough, the hills green enough, the gardens lush enough.

We got into the car late Friday afternoon and by Saturday we were enjoying pizza with friends at the Tides Tavern in Gig Harbor, Washington. After church on Sunday we began the search for a house we could afford and negotiations for the one that seemed to have our name on it followed swiftly on Monday. By late afternoon Tuesday, we'd come to an agreement, signed a mortgage loan on Wednesday and, come Thursday, were already speeding back to our apartment to arrange to take our things out of storage. It helped to have had a friend who was a real estate agent keeping an eye out for what we wanted—just in case.

Don had decided it would be wise to leave a car in Washington so we didn't have to drive back up separately, one of us hauling a trailer full of plants, at the time of the move. What neither one of us had had any way of foreseeing though was that I would get so sick on our way back to California. The bus from the airport seemed to hit every bump in the road, compounding the terrible pain I was feeling in the nerve pathways along the right side of my back and waist.

It was almost a relief the next morning to find I'd broken out in shingles where it had hurt so much the night before. Time to again call up the deep-breathing exercises we'd learned in the weekend seminar the year before. That and some antiviral medicine the doctor prescribed to speed up recovery helped enough that by mid-October we were all set to face the movers one last time, finally on our way home.

Despite the fact that we'd let everyone concerned know our moving-in schedule, pallets of sod filled the driveway and soil was piled high in the street in front of our new house when we arrived, to the point that neither our car nor the moving van could even come close to parking nearby. The movers were not going to have an easy time of it. The contractor hadn't gotten the lawn in on schedule and now the route into both the front door and the garage resembled a dirt-filled obstacle course. But the sun shone brightly and it wasn't raining.

As Don started to help the lawn people clear at least a walking path before the moving van got there, a florist's truck pulled up and a cheerful young delivery man emerged to snake his way through soil and sod, a beautiful dieffenbachia in his arms. The card read, "Welcome back to God's country." I marveled that even a good friend could have timed its arrival that perfectly.

By the time the movers arrived, Don had swept a band of pathway and we were back into our old rhythm of checking off box numbers against the inventory and looking for, but not really wanting to see, any damages that might have occurred.

Inside, boxes began to climb as high as a clumsily built new set of walls and I wondered, as I always did, whether we'd find room for all the stuff that was inside them. The simple life I thought we were leading looked anything but when it was all stacked around us in endless cartons.

The refrigerator we'd ordered wasn't going to arrive for a couple of days and I wasn't sure what we'd do about eating in the meantime, but knew we'd manage somehow.

Although we'd spent the first nine years of Don's time in the service living in the communities surrounding the bases, I wondered what it would be like in a civilian neighborhood again, after spending the last fourteen on Air Force bases. I'd heard others talk about how long it had taken them to meet their neighbors off base, but I knew it didn't have to be that way and remembered all the good times on Mitchell Terrace in New Jersey.

As if to reassure us, other old civilian friends had already given us a Welcome Home party when we drove up to close on the house. And, we learned, there were a lot of people we still knew in the area, both retired military and civilian. Even after having been away almost nine years, it seemed as if we'd hardly skipped a beat.

But I really wasn't expecting lunch and dinner to be delivered when another friend drove up with enough food to get us through the first day. In California, we'd kept a picnic basket on our block and took turns welcoming each new neighbor with their first meal in their new home. I'd lost count of all the kindnesses we'd seen given and received over the past thirty-two years. Now we were reunited with part of that huge, sprawling "family" we'd acquired. "Friends of the road," as the African desert nomads put it, had become "friends of the heart."

Other friends also continued to keep in touch. We'd shared our adventures in apartment living with several in California and had a lot of good laughs over it. But we'd almost forgotten about all that when a housewarming gift arrived that took us back to those early morning bedroom invasions of privacy. When I slit the box and pulled aside the wrappings to see what they had sent, I started laughing as I pulled out a rope meant for children's games or exercise. The accompanying note read "Keep jumping!"

I certainly hadn't needed to worry about being the new kids on the block either. We'd found a new Mitchell Terrace. Months later, a neighbor from down the street, a new friend, came over with a picture he'd taken of the moving van, the boxes and the general havoc of our first day there. He'd entitled it "Lest You Forget." Mercifully, he waited to bring it until the rhododendrons, heather, and trees in the yard that we'd planted had started to look like they—and we—belonged and we could now laugh about moving pandemonium.

Lest we forget... I remembered all the times, growing up, when I'd come home to an empty house and envied those who had brothers and sisters. By college days, I'd had to struggle at first to learn to live with roommates, but then found it even harder to leave all that companionship and activity when it was time to go home for vacations.

Now vacations almost always seemed to include family, whether nuclear or extended. Even when we'd gone to church in Australia we'd run into someone we'd known from our time in Illinois. And who would have thought Sister Mary Benedict from Guam would come to D.C. to help put the finishing touches on the flowers at our daughter's wedding?

How long had it been since we'd first learned there was no longer any time in our lives to wait to reveal ourselves to others? It had become second nature to take the risk right away, before it was too late, and find that others did the same in response. Making friends wherever we found them had become a happy addiction. Somewhere along the way I had begun to become anchored within myself, rather than to others.

Our new challenge was to take the risk of putting down roots. The place to start seemed to be to continue getting rid of what we no longer needed. We sorted out the myriad drapery and curtain rods, sheers that I'd used to cover paint-spattered windows we got tired of scraping in government or rental housing, and drapes of every color, shape and fabric, accumulated from all the moves. The few that fit in with our new home we put to use. The rest went to Goodwill.

We had barely started the process when, just five days after we'd moved in, Don was offered and accepted a position with a company in Arizona, one which they agreed to let him handle on a part-time basis, commuting. His refusal to move, he said, proved I could now safely get rid of all the stereo boxes and packing I had always saved.

But a true-born packrat has to draw the line somewhere. Saving the boxes became my cheap form of insurance, sort of like hanging on to the last baby's crib till menopause.

Instead, we began the task of decorating a home we were finally going to stay in, not just "making do" or putting things together quickly so we could enjoy them before the next move.

When we had lived in Washington State before, Martha Strom, an interior designer, had given a course geared to the mobile family through the local vocational school and the wives' club. It had cost all of five dollars—the best five dollars I'd ever spent. Ever since, I'd been more comfortable taking down and setting up our homes, no matter how strangely the builders had configured them. I even felt I knew how high to hang the pictures, although Don thought he did too and we could never quite agree on it.

For the first twenty-six years I had conscientiously remade drapes and curtains to fit each new window in each new place. In fact, since Illinois, it had become almost a superstition that finishing the last seam on the last drape would get us orders to move.

As I stood on the ladder in the living room of our new house, hanging one of the blue drapes we'd had in a den eight years earlier, I marveled at how good it still looked and went to find a mate for the other window. Although I'd had to pin two drapes together to cover the wider window, it didn't look bad—from the inside of the house. Unfortunately, the second window needed a much narrower panel and there appeared to be nothing for it but to cut down the one we had.

The day Martha Strom, who was still in the area, came over to take a look at that and other projects we were working on, I asked what she thought. "Do you think I need to redo the drapes for both windows or do you think it's OK to leave one pinned as is?" Her answer wasn't Ecclesiastes, but it was more profound than it sounded. "I think," she said, "it's time to stop pinning the drapes." We were indeed entering a new season in our lives.

But that didn't mean that the answer to the old question, "Are we there yet?" was "Yes." The pilgrimage hadn't ended. I doubt it will in this life, where most of us remain a work-in-progress. Yet time also conveys the wisdom that, no matter how many places we've lived, we've always been "there."

Move is indeed a four-letter word. But then, so are *love* and *home,* which I'd finally come to know as a truly moveable feast.

Acknowledgments

I am deeply indebted to the many friends and colleagues who advised and supported me throughout the writing of this book: Alice Milam, Carol Hazelrigg, Natalie Humphrey, Suzie Schwartz, Kate Van Gelder, Maxine Donnelly, Mary Carol and Gene Muth, Ryan Peinhardt, editors Barbara Fandrich and Jennifer McCord, and the late Jack Cady. Thank you.

Loving and special thanks too to the saintly patience, prodding, and editing of my husband Don, daughters Cathy and Nancy, and son Jim, without which *Move—and Other Four-Letter Words* would still be in gestation.

QUESTIONS FOR READING GROUP DISCUSSIONS

1. Have you ever had to move? How did it affect you?

2. How have your moving experiences compared to the author's?

3. What are the advantages or disadvantages of reading about another person's successes and disasters in dealing with an experience? Is there anything to be gained by learning that we can be far less than perfect in how we handle life's tough experiences and still muddle through?

4. Some organizations, such as the military, larger corporations, and certain educational institutions, provide support for movers. Other moves are made without any such backing. Does that make a difference?

5. The author—and many other parents who relocate—put a significant emphasis on the quality of education for their children. Do you think education is a problem for mobile families? If so, what actions can parents take to minimize the problem?

6. Do you think a parent's approach toward relocating has much influence on his or her offspring's attitude? Does the effort to maintain a positive outlook when one is under pressure create an additional burden or help to alleviate the stress?

7. How do you think children who relocate are affected by the experience?

8. What are the ways the author found to reconnect in each new community? What have you found helpful?

9. How significant is moving as a stress on a marriage? How can it be alleviated?

10. Having to temporarily live apart from one's spouse is another situation discussed in *Move*. Have you had to deal with this? What was your reaction? Your spouse's? Did your reaction to reunion as a couple change with the length of the involuntary separation?

11. How does "emptying the nest" affect the author and her husband? Have you had that experience? If so, how did you react?

12. Have sudden and unexpected changes in your life, such as the author's husband's retirement, caused you anxiety? How have you dealt with that?

13. How does living in other parts of the country or the world affect one's views and interests?

14. How do you feel about sampling unfamiliar foods or cultures? Has it been a positive or negative experience for you?

15. Have changes in technology such as cell phones and email made a significant difference in the way relocations affect us? How or how not?

16. The author cites friends who become "family" as a major factor in enabling her to "blossom" despite being constantly transplanted. Have you had that experience? How has it helped?

ORDER FORM

Fax orders: 253-581-2149, using this form.

Telephone orders: Call toll free 1-800-398-7414 with credit card and mailing information.

Email orders: Orders@HearthlandPublishing.com.

Mail orders: Hearthland Publishing, 1425 Broadway #56, Seattle, WA 98122.

Please send ____ copies of MOVE—AND OTHER FOUR-LETTER WORDS @ $15.95 each to:

Name: ____

Address: ____

____

City: ____

Telephone: ____

Email address: _______________________________________

Sales Tax: Please add sales tax for books shipped to Washington State addresses.

Shipping and handling within U.S.: U.S. $3.00 for first book. Add $1.00 for each additional book.